ANGLICA GERMANICA SERIES 2

KAFKA'S NARRATORS

ANGLICA GERMANICA SERIES 2

Editors: LEONARD FORSTER, M. SWALES, AND
A. T. HATTO

Other books in the series

D. Prohaska: Raimund and Vienna: A Critical Study of Raimund's plays in their Viennese Setting

D. G. Mowatt: Friedrich von Hûsen: Introduction, Text, Commentary and Glossary

C. Lofmark: Rennewart in Wolfram's 'Willehalm': A Study of Wolfram von Eschenbach and his Sources

A. Stephens: Rainer Maria Rilke's 'Gedichte an die Nacht'

M. Garland: Hebbel's Prose Tragedies: An Investigation of the Aesthetic Aspects of Hebbel's Dramatic Language

H. W. Cohn: Else Lasker-Schüler: The Broken World

J. M. Ellis: Narration in the German Novelle: Theory and Interpretation

M. B. Benn: The Drama of Revolt: A Critical Study of Georg Büchner

J. Hibberd: Salomon Gessner: His Creative Achievement and Influence

P. Hutchinson: Literary Presentations of Divided Germany

I. R. Campbell: *Kudrun*: A Critical Appreciation

A. T. Hatto: Essays on Medieval German and other Poetry

F. P. Pickering: Essays on Medieval German Literature and Iconography

W. D. Robson-Scott: The Younger Goethe and the Visual Arts

KAFKA'S NARRATORS

A STUDY OF HIS STORIES AND SKETCHES

ROY PASCAL

CAMBRIDGE UNIVERSITY PRESS

CAMBRIDGE

LONDON   NEW YORK   NEW ROCHELLE
MELBOURNE   SYDNEY

Published by the Press Syndicate of the University of Cambridge
The Pitt Building, Trumpington Street, Cambridge CB2 IRP
32 East 57th Street, New York, NY 10022, USA
296 Beaconsfield Parade, Middle Park, Melbourne 3206, Australia

© Cambridge University Press 1982

First published 1982

Printed in Great Britain by Western Printing Services Ltd, Bristol

Library of Congress catalogue card number: 81–12202

British Library Cataloguing in Publication Data
Pascal, Roy
Kafka's narrators. – (Anglica Germanica.
Series 2)
1. Kafka, Franz – Criticism and interpretation
I. Title II. Series
833'.912 PT2621.A262/
ISBN 0 521 24365 3 hard covers
ISBN 0 521 28765 0 paperback

PREFATORY NOTE

When Roy Pascal died in August 1980, he had all but completed a book on Kafka's use of narrative voice, which broke new ground in the appreciation of that author's art. He intended adding an analysis of one or two more 'animal' tales to chapter 8 (notably 'The burrow') and writing a brief conclusion which would include suggestions of how the findings of his book applied to Kafka's novels as well as his shorter tales. The work can, however, stand without these additions, and is here presented in the form in which Roy Pascal left it. He called these, his last literary investigations, 'a genuine voyage of discovery' and felt, rightly, that he was bringing back from that voyage significant observations which would help others to a fuller and better reading experience. His book is published in the confident expectation that it will achieve its author's aim and will be received as a welcome addition to his many distinguished writings on the narrative art of European novelists and autobiographers.

CONTENTS

INTRODUCTION
NARRATOR AND STORY

By those whose horizons are limited, trifles are easily confused
with technicalities (Patrick Devlin, *The judge*, 1979, p. x).

The literary genre of story, that includes epic, novel, folk-tale,
short story, can be defined in relation to its content. In this
respect it is an account of an event or a series of events as it
involves one or several characters, so that the events are inter-
connected at least through their relationship to the characters.
These connexions will have temporal and spatial dimensions;
the impact of events on the characters will form psychological
links; and the coherence of the parts is consummated by the
ending, the outcome, that creates the meaning of the whole –
for the ending is a fulfilment of all that has gone before. The
characters order themselves too in a hierarchy of importance,
and it is the single 'hero' or the few central characters who
determine the scope of events and the character of the ending,
while minor characters are only accessories to the fate of these
main characters. This rough definition can be infinitely refined
and expanded.

But there is another element in the constitution of a story
that belongs to its essential structure. Before a story can come
into being it has to be told (or written) by a narrator to an
audience (or a readership). This is the narrative *situation*, and
this narrator–listener situation is as distinct a condition of the
genre of story as the actor–audience relationship is for the drama.

Much in the form of a story is determined by this narrator-
listener situation. For instance, it is this that insists on the use of
various means to win the keen attention of the listener or reader,
to promise and provide the thrill of intense imaginative experience, to stir interest when it flags. At all stages, a story must
awaken expectations, hold them in suspense, cheat them
temporarily, before it leads to some satisfactory conclusion.

This may apply to the simpler aspects of human existence and relationships and the more obvious external sorts of events, of success and failure. But it may also apply to some important spiritual message that has to become explicit, something about the world of social relations or morality, or of the soul. In modern times these large issues have tended to lead both authors and critics to neglect the apparently more primitive element of story and to acknowledge it, like E. M. Forster, only with irritation as a technical necessity that properly should belong only to trivial entertainment.[1] But however much one may disparage the thriller as a debased parody of the true novel, yet even major works of fiction cannot altogether rebel against the fundamental narrator–reader situation, and cannot repudiate the obligation to thrill with the mystery of an opening, with the undefined promise and puzzle of the situations and persons introduced, with the unfolding of anticipated and unanticipated connexions and meanings. If the object of the story is to create coherence, this achievement has significance and attraction only because it creates it out of the accidental and contingent, as Gallie has put it.[2]

Some of these consequences of the narrator–reader situation will concern us in the present study. But it is with another that I am centrally engaged. I have spoken of the 'narrator' and readers will perhaps have understood this term as referring to the author, the writer or tale-teller. But it is not intended to refer to the actual person who writes or tells a tale, but to a fictitious character he assumes as the story-teller, and notably to a non-personal, unidentifiable agent, one of the great inventions of the human imagination. From the earliest beginnings of tale-telling, in ancient myth, in folk-tale and fable, in anecdote, a mediator was placed between the person telling his tale and his audience. The teller disguised himself, transparently, behind a greater authority, an authority far transcending any mere human, who would be able to tell of the most diverse characters and activities, of the secret thoughts of individuals and the secret conferences of persons, would move unrestrictedly in time and space, yes, would be able to report the quarrels and purposes and decisions of the gods themselves and of all the mischievous spirits that hold limited sway in folk-tales. No wonder the epic poets invoke the supernatural aid of the Muse; no wonder the bard or village tale-teller adopts a special impersonal tone and uses ritualistic formulae. It is perhaps misleading to use the term 'narrator' for this impersonal agent, this 'spirit of the story'; the term suggests a personal character such as later and more sophisticated cultures invented. But it would be wearisome to use a vaguer term.

When epic and romance came to be replaced by the modern forms of story and novel, that is, when the mythical, legendary and heroic themes with their idealised poetic figures and scenes gave way to what Hegel described as the prosaic world of the private citizen with his concrete activities and circumstances, this impersonal narrator was still retained. Indeed, in the great novel that ushered in the slow collapse of the heroic romance, Cervantes' *Don Quixote*, one can detect the puzzled speculations this all-knowing narrator was causing. For his own novel Cervantes pushed the problem a little further out of view by sometimes pretending that his account was a translation of an Arabic original, thus substituting the question 'is it a true copy?' for the more important question 'what assures us that it is a true history of a real man?' Or, at the beginning of part 2, he proves the falsity of a spurious part 2 (that had been published) by demonstrating that Don Quixote never went to Salamanca, as the false author claimed, and had not gone there in order to prove the latter wrong. Or Cervantes pokes fun at the rationalistic explanation of the mystery by professing to admire the faithful scribes who attend the heroes of romance through all their vicissitudes in order busily to record all their deeds, thoughts, and utterances; he allows Don Quixote himself to think the mysterious historian of his exploits must be a 'sage enchanter'.[3] Similar speculations and jokes occur in the novels of Fielding and Sterne, Diderot and Wieland, and clearly arise from problems caused by this type of narrator as a result of the growing demand for truth in stories whose credibility must depend, as all practical men agree, in some degree on the identity of the witness.

In spite of such doubts, the impersonal narrator was not abandoned, nor has it ever lost its value. Many of the great nineteenth-century novels are composed in this form – Jane Austen's novels, Goethe's *The elective affinities*, Dickens's *Our mutual friend* and part of *Bleak House*, George Eliot's *Middlemarch*, many of Balzac's novels, Flaubert's *Madame Bovary*, Tolstoy's *War and peace* and *Anna Karenina*, Dostoevsky's *The idiot*, Thomas Mann's *Buddenbrooks*, etc. etc. The fiction of the impersonal narrator offered an incomparable instrument for describing an infinite variety of settings and moods, for penetrating characters and milieux, for composing a dramatic structure with varied phases and shades, for creating and controlling exciting actions and thrilling tensions, as well as providing the practical and psychological grounds for the connexions of people and events and for a comprehensive ending. And all this without the reader having to worry about the credibility, the testimonials of this reporter, since from the beginning he was not a person, not subject to our frailties, and accepted as an absolute and objective authority for the purpose of this story.

There is a significant change in the functioning of this impersonal narrator that corresponds with the evolution of the novel. While the narrator of epic and romance could freely transfer himself to many different characters, the novel narrator often tends to align himself much more closely to a particular person or group, to impose on himself a particular angle of vision, in place of his earlier unrestricted freedom. This is very evident in Henry James and he was the first to make this a theoretical requirement of story-telling; but it is clear in many earlier nineteenth-century novels too. That is, the narrator may inform us of everything going on in a particular character's mind and convey the latter's view of other people and the environment, but other people remain relatively obscure and inscrutable, out of focus as it were. In this respect the impersonal narrator seems to submit to something akin to the normal limitation of humans, and we must believe this tendency, so marked already in Jane Austen, was the more or less conscious outcome of the constant striving for verisimilitude, for authenticity, that marks the history of the novel. At the same time, however, it was a rich source of story in the formal sense, since by distributing clarity and obscurity according to the consciousness of the central characters and the movement of the story, it not only provided for variety and suspense but also created the concentration and organisation necessary for a compelling, spellbinding narrative.

Very early in the history of the novel another way was found to adapt the mode of narration to the secular, prosaic, more everyday world of the novel. This was the invention of the personal narrator and of the story that is told by a person about his own experiences. Several of the novels of the Hellenistic age, such as *The golden ass* of Apuleius, are told in this autobiographical form as, in post-Renaissance Europe, is Defoe's *Robinson Crusoe*. Though the Hellenistic novels still indulge in flights of fancy and romance, the fundamental achievement of this form is to construct an imaginative world that in essence corresponds to that of the actual world of man, with its specific activities, characters, and problems, especially in the sense that the narrator is, like each of us in his own life, the focus of experience and central actor and concern, whose motives and purposes provide the framework of the story. While we know him as we know ourselves, from within, we depend as far as the rest of the world is concerned on the sort of information we can glean about our fellow human beings in ordinary life. If through this form the reader loses that access to universal and authoritative information that the impersonal narrator could provide, and perhaps too the astonishing thrills and suspense that such a narrator can devise; yet the mode of experience is much more lifelike and hence intense and vivid, and the spell such a personal narrator weaves can be more unbroken and penetrating.

Other varieties of the personal narrator established themselves in the eighteenth century, notably in the form of the epistolary novel, in which the story is borne on the exchange of letters between a number of correspondents – as in Richardson's novels, in Rousseau's *La nouvelle Héloïse*, and Goethe's *The sorrows of young Werther*. Later generations found the gain in authenticity arising from the apparent elimination of a narrator was largely cancelled by the abnormal self-explanation required of the letter-writers, and this type has not become a great tradition. On the other hand, the use of a personal narrator who is not the central character but a minor participant and bystander has become a favourite medium of the modern novel, offering great variety of writing allied with the authenticity of a natural human perspective, with its uncertainties, its insight, and its limitations. To this type belong many classical novels, *Wuthering Heights* with its several narrators, those of Conrad that the character 'Marlow' tells, Thomas Mann's *Dr Faustus*, and a host of others. Sometimes they merge into the autobiographical form, sometimes into the impersonal form (like *Madame Bovary* and Dostoevsky's *The brothers Karamazov*, which both start with a personal narrator but later abandon this limited standpoint). These various types – the novel with the impersonal narrator and those with varieties of personal narrator – form the main categories of the novel defined in Percy Lubbock's *The craft of fiction* of 1921 and more recently in F. K. Stanzel's able analysis.[4]

The narrative with the impersonal, undefined narrator seems to differ radically from the other forms since it presupposes the possibility of privileged insight into a whole number of characters and situations, while the personal narrator presents the world from a real-life situation, in which everyone knows only one person, himself, from the inside. *War and peace* is a striking example of the first type, *David Copperfield* of what we may call the autobiographical type. The implications of these forms are not at all self-evident, particularly in relation to the presentation of the inner self. For though the autobiographical type might be thought to offer the greatest room for self-exploration in depth, in fact, since the explorer is that same self who is the object of these introspective investigations, he may thereby seem obsessedly, pathologically engrossed in himself without intending this.[5] Paradoxically it is the impersonal narrator who, able to range freely in the psychic depths of his characters, can create the fullest image of an inner life, which must include not only the images and thoughts by which the character expresses his consciousness of other people and his world but also those perceptions, sentiments, gestures, actions, that vast area of mental and practical activity in which the character engages at lower levels of consciousness. It is for this reason that, as I indicated in my study of free indirect speech, *The dual voice*, the evolution of this form of reported speech as a narrative instrument came about essentially within the tradition of the impersonal narrator, who was able over stretches of text that gave the character's thoughts, speech, impressions, vision etc. to unearth his most secret movements in the idiom he used or would have used had he been conscious of them.[6] All the main forms of novel have uncovered extraordinary literary potentialities and shown themselves remarkably adaptable to new purposes, not least because, as Lubbock pointed out, they rarely exist in a state of absolute formal purity but allow intrusions from the other forms where this seems of advantage. The novel is altogether a rather lax form, largely I believe because it is consumed in private over many hours and days with many interruptions from other activities, so that it requires not only consistency but also change, relief, liveliness in order to re-engage and maintain the reader's attention. This leisurely reception that it enjoys also invites the reader to enjoy disruptive interpolations into the narrative providing these come from an original mind.

From its beginnings it was understood that the novel required a central character (a 'hero' or 'heroine') or a central group of characters, the essential precondition for winning the imaginative attention of listeners or readers. The great achievement of the 'classical' novel of the nineteenth century was to supplement this unity of interest with a unity of experience, realised through the imaginative identification of the reader with the feeling, thought, the point of view, of the chief character – a general process we can follow, for instance, in the case of Charles Dickens in the development from *Pickwick papers* through *David Copperfield* to *Bleak House* or *Great expectations*. This unity of experience still permitted numerous interruptions, and in the English and German novel the old intrusive author, that is, the author in his or her own person, still could intervene in the novel's events to assert an 'outside' comment, in Trollope, George Eliot or Hardy, and in Wilhelm Raabe or Theodor Fontane. Indeed the simplest objective of this new development was the removal of this intrusive author from the pages of the novel so that its events should unfold entirely within and through the experience of the fictional characters.

Of course, the elimination of the intrusive author was only a symptom of a deeper intention. With Flaubert, the most devoted champion of the new novel, the fictional narrator himself, the impersonal narrator, or what we should better call the narrative function, was as far as possible to become invisible, only evident as the arranger of the story and the instrument for the presentation of the thoughts and feelings of the fictional characters. The strange power of Dostoevsky's novels was largely due to what Michael Bachtin has called his 'polyphonic' form (in place of the traditional 'monological'), through which the truth and judgment of the narrator is often subordinate in authority and significance to the insight and truth of the characters.[7] Henry James was the first of this type of writer to formulate theoretically the new principle of 'point-of-view' composition. In all these writers we find a profusion of free indirect speech used in the communication of the characters' thoughts and sensations, a typical substitution of the characters' own experience for the narrator's comment on it. These innovations affected all the forms of the novel, those with personal narrators as well as those with the impersonal, though they were most clearly to be felt in the latter. The general objective might be summed up under three heads: first, the objective was to give an account of human relationships in terms of the fictional characters involved, without introducing an external view or judgment; second, to concentrate on the mode of experience of the characters and to transmit to the reader their vision and values, motivations and responses – these two objectives derive from an urge towards greater truth, greater authenticity, in the representation of human life; and third, to present persons and events in an artistic shape, that is, in a form where all events and elements are organically related and can be absorbed as parts of a whole.

This endeavour began to engage the attention of theorists of the novel in the decades round the turn of the century and produced the first systematic examination of narrative structure in 1921: Lubbock's *The craft of fiction*. But as often occurs, Lubbock's definition of point-of-view story and of what is now called narrative perspective, like the excellent structural and stylistic studies of other critics, was worked out at a time when novelists on all sides were expressing unease about the classical form of the novel including its latest developments.[8] The role of this impersonal narrator, the 'thread of the story', the accepted patterns of cause and effect, and the function of an ending, were variously challenged through the new-modern novel of Joyce, Proust, Virginia Woolf, Robert Musil and many other writers of fiction. It took some time before this modern movement found an adequate formulation and there is no single model that can do justice to its variety. But perhaps the most comprehensive statement of the modernist situation, and certainly that most relevant to Kafka, the subject of this study, is Sartre's *Qu'est-ce que la littérature?*, which was not published in book form until 1948 although many of Sartre's criticisms of the traditional novel found expression in his novel *La nausée* of 1938.[9]

Sartre powerfully argues that the classical novel distorts the nature of human experience through its very form, by which he means both the story-structure and the narrative perspective.

He delivers a central attack on the impersonal narrator since the role of this agent, with his knowledge of the inner thoughts and being of various characters, his ability to follow numerous destinies and link them in a story with a beginning, middle and end, his capacity to establish an end that somehow fulfils these lives and turns accident into destiny, this role totally misrepresents the nature of human existence, in which we can never know with certainty the motives and reactions of our fellows and in which it is impossible to find a completed and meaningful plan. This so-called omniscient narrator is, Sartre says, a religious relic, a piece of obscurantism, encouraging us to evade the truth of life. But Sartre also finds a fundamental deceit in the functioning of the various forms of personal narrators, even if their scope is more true to life than that of the impersonal narrator. For all novels, he argues, presuppose their ending, they are all, explicitly or implicitly, built upon this ending, for it is only the outcome that decides what in the past is relevant and significant and thus permits us to construct a plot or development; and yet it is an essential condition of life that we never know the outcome of experiences while we are engaged in them. Sartre thus destroys the foundation on which all stories are built. In *La nausée* he gave a model of how a novel might be made without superhuman insight and without the assurance deriving from retrospective knowledge and understanding. It is made up of diary extracts, written by a young man of whom we know nothing but what engages his interest, confined almost entirely to events of the day, presenting the people he sees or meets in all the opacity that surrounds casual acquaintance and in all the unforeseeableness that even closer acquaintance brings, with no story-line, and an ending that resolves no problems and forms no conclusion except that it confirms the narrator's alienated and incoherent existence. The diary form allows Sartre to avoid in general using the preterite tense, the 'past historic', and the novel is carried out in a mixture of other tenses, the present, the imperfect and the composite past; in his treatise Sartre condemns the preterite as the instrument of a deluding sense of a completed, structured sequence of events.[10]

The question that arises from Sartre's criticism of the traditional form of the novel, of story altogether, is formidable. He seems to be destroying the very foundations of story-making, and we ask 'How can a novel be possible?'. Theodor Adorno, whose criticism of the classical novel is close to Sartre's, defined the modern position in exactly such terms: 'It is no longer possible to tell a story, while the form of the novel requires a story.'[11] A malicious opponent might observe with some pleasure that in his novel series *Les chemins de la liberté* Sartre fell back on a fairly conventional narrative form. But, despite Sartre's inconsequence, and despite the faults and extravagance in his treatise (which have been admirably delineated and discussed by Frank Kermode in *The sense of an ending*),[12] his criticisms of traditional novel structure correspond to many of the experimental and innovatory novel forms that occur sporadically in the modernist literature of Europe and America. Whatever faults one may find in Sartre's theory – and especially in his misunderstanding of the function of structural narrative fictions – it focuses attention on essential structural features of story-making in general and the modern novel in particular.

It is in this context that I approach Kafka in this present study. Though Kafka is acknowledged to be outside the usual literary groupings and in many ways is evidently a story-teller of a peculiar, almost unique character, there have been several attempts to associate his work with this or that tendency or group, with the surrealists, the expressionists, the Freudian tendency and so on. None of these attempts is successful and all are based on just one element in his writing. The most valuable of these attempts limits itself to the character of his narrative structure and style and is itself based on the best analysis of Kafka's narrative form that we have, Hartmut Binder's *Motiv und Gestaltung bei Franz Kafka*.[13] It is one of Binder's chief conclusions that Kafka's stories are borne on the two pillars of Flaubert's narrative, the impersonal narrator who describes events from outside and the characters themselves whose experience of these events is given, through various devices, in their own terms (these form the two strands which provided me with the title for my study of free indirect speech, *The dual voice*). But while this conclusion is true and important, it neither takes into account other features of Kafka's stories nor does it allow for a development within Kafka's work (which Binder in fact explicitly denies). While I shall in several places need to refer to Binder's excellent work, I believe it is a mistake to associate Kafka so definitely with Flaubert and to ignore the unease over the Flaubertian form that was already stirring before Kafka's death in 1924. It will be my object to show more particularly his relationship with the modernist movement and the formal innovations I mentioned in relation to Sartre.

Not that I have undertaken this study simply in order to demonstrate that Kafka belongs to the modern tendency. Rather, I have tried to use the insights provided by the modern movement in order to clarify the formal structures Kafka invented and the inherent intention within these narrative forms. I hope thereby to contribute to a more accurate and sure reading of these difficult texts and hence to a clearer understanding of them, although an essentially formal analysis cannot hope to solve all problems of meaning and interpretation. With such an author it would be folly to expect to reach definitive and unchallengeable interpretations of even the 'simplest' fables and stories, since Kafka insists on remaining an elusive, teasing, secretive author. But a scrupulous analysis of the type envisaged may perhaps be successful in ruling out certain readings and types of interpretation that clog the reader's path, and it may even point in the direction in which Kafka's meaning lies.

1 · THE KAFKA STORY: STRUCTURE AND MEANING

If Kafka's style of narrative is instantly recognisable, his type of story is very difficult to define. One can perhaps detect a model behind each of the novels and some of the stories, but the variation from the model is always so profound as even to suggest parody – one thinks of the relationship of *America* to Dickens's *David Copperfield* (that Kafka discusses in his diary)[1] or of 'In der Strafkolonie' ('In the penal colony') to Octave Mirabeau's *Le jardin des supplices* (*The torture garden*). The variation between Kafka's stories themselves is also great, so great that serious misunderstandings arise from expecting from one what one got from another.

Since all Kafka's imaginative work takes a more-or-less narrative form, this elusiveness and instability of his story-types might seem strange; a writer who seems naturally to imagine in the form of fictional narrative would find earlier and fall more easily, one would think, into a form that suits his purposes, even though his basic form undergoes modifications as he proceeds. This is the case with the great novelists, those we think of as the born story-tellers. But Kafka never reached such naturalness and ease and seems to the end to have been struggling to find a suitable form.

Apart from his stories, Kafka's persistent literary activity was his diary and the fragmentary thoughts he jotted down from time to time. In both of these forms he often drops into narrative too, finding in an imaginary scene or situation the expression of some experience or thought for which an abstract formulation did not suffice. Perhaps this profound need of his spirit explains to some extent the instability of his story-forms. For just as, in his exploration of himself and his search for philosophical formulations (religious or ethical), he needed to have recourse to imagined situations, bits of narrative, so also his stories were born out of the same need and were closely bound both to a personal search for clarification and to a desire for some sort of philosophical understanding. His stories are indeed unusually closely related to his own individual situation and at the same time pregnant with some symbolical or at times allegorical meaning. This fact gives the peculiarity of his narrative forms an especial significance since they are not the contrivances of an abstract and polemical concept of story, nor intended to shock or amaze, but arise out of Kafka's need to embody and transmit his sense of living.

But what do we mean when we speak about Kafka's 'stories'? In 1919 Kafka published a collection of pieces entitled *Ein Landarzt* (*A country doctor*), giving it the subtitle 'Kleine Erzählungen'. Yet of the fourteen pieces that make up the volume very few are what normally would be called a story. 'Ein Bericht für eine Akademie' ('A report for an academy') could be called a story (an ape's life-story), and perhaps the surrealistic 'A country doctor' and 'Ein Brudermord ('Fratricide'), though both these are strange fragments seemingly torn out of some context. Two of Kafka's famous parables are included, 'Vor dem Gesetz' ('Before the law') and 'Eine kaiserliche Botschaft' ('The emperor's message'), each abstracted from its original context in *Der Prozess* (*The trial*) and 'Beim Bau der Chinesischen Mauer' ('Building the Chinese wall'). Most of the others present particular situations like 'Auf der Galerie' ('In the gallery'), a mysterious image like 'Die Sorge des Hausvaters' ('The worry of a caretaker'), or a gnomic fragment like 'Das nächste Dorf' ('The next village'), in which we can detect scarcely any event, any 'story' or 'character'. Clearly Kafka called these pieces 'stories' only for want of any more adequate term; and I think a scrupulous editor like Paul Raabe, who also uses this term both for the pieces in *A country doctor* and for the other pieces he includes in his excellent edition, does so partly out of embarrassment, partly out of respect for Kafka's usage.[2]

In this volume of Kafka's *Sämtliche Erzählungen*, Raabe also includes the early collection that Kafka published in 1913 under the title *Betrachtung (Observation)*. So far as I can see Kafka himself does not refer to these pieces as stories; in letters to his friends Brod and Felice Bauer he calls them *Stückchen* and to his publisher Rowohlt *kleine Prosa*. All the pieces are short, and most fix fleeting moments in a daily experience that has no marked direction. A number of them have a narrative form, a reference to a specific situation, a walk or an excursion, a meeting with an acquaintance or a stranger, a dialogue, but all are fragmentary, indeed intended to be fragmentary and to mirror a fragmentary existence. The separate pieces belong to the several years preceding publication and many of them were taken by Kafka from their original context in his unfinished *Beschreibung eines Kampfes (Description of a struggle)*. In his notes Raabe speaks of the collection as 'stories and texts'.[3] But, though they do reveal a characteristic tendency to adopt a narrative form, I do not think any of these texts can fully justify the description 'story'. As a collection they deny any coherence except the constant incoherence of the writer's experience and mind; and each 'text' is itself fragmentary, lacking a development and an ending, proposing a problem, a thought, not rounding off a graspable event. The person who appears, frequently as the narrator in the first person, speaks of his meetings, his observation, his thoughts and fancies, but seems incapable of finding an objective event which might act as what T. S. Eliot called an 'objective correlative', an artistic counterpart and symbolic revelation of his experience. All is fluid, fleeting, incoherent, unfinished. As such this work has its own interest and value, its biographical significance too, but does not belong to the body of Kafka's achievement in the genre of story except as a preparatory stage.

What we shall be concerned with in this study are the stories that have taken on an independent existence, that are complete in themselves. This means that they are detached both from their personal source and also have escaped the depersonalisation of the all-too-general reflection. They are extensive enough to provide for the engagement and self-definition of characters, and their parts must be coherent; that is, the ending must be such as to establish the coherence of the parts. It may be thought that some of Kafka's recognised 'stories' and even the three novels scarcely fulfil these conditions, and certainly there are borderline cases among the works discussed in this study. But on the whole there would be little disagreement over what works deserve to belong to this category, from 'Das Urteil' ('The judgment') and 'Die Verwandlung' ('The metamorphosis') onwards to the latest, the animal-stories 'Forschungen eines Hundes' ('Investigations of a dog') and 'Der Bau' ('The burrow'). As we shall see, the terms of this definition are highly ambiguous, especially 'coherence' and 'ending'; it is well to remember the theme of dissociation and incoherence in the early collection *Observation*, since one might define Kafka's narrative career as a search for a completed form that would not overcome this consciousness of incoherence but embody it – a seemingly impossible undertaking, squaring the circle.[4]

When stories fulfil these conditions we feel that they have 'meaning'. But this term too is ambiguous and especially for Kafka requires a more exact definition. The word functions on two levels which he himself distinguishes in the brief piece entitled 'The worry of a caretaker'. Here the caretaker describes a strange object called Odradek, star-shaped, wrapped in tattered thread, the purpose of which cannot be guessed yet which seems to be a whole: 'The whole appears meaningless, admittedly, but in its own fashion completed.'[5] He is using the term 'meaningless' here to interpret his inability to find any function for the strange object, or any functional reason for its various parts; while the 'completedness', the self-sufficiency of its appearance, on the other hand suggests that in some obscure way it is coherent. When we read Kafka's stories we have similarly two types of meaning to wrestle with. There is the meaning that derives from recognising the formal self-sufficiency of the story, the relationships of the various parts, the functioning of each part in relationship with the others and the endings; and the other meaning may arise, does arise, when we ask, what does it all mean? what is it all about? Both questions are in Kafka's works insistent and difficult.

In the case of the conventional story, the formal unity is not hard to grasp. The beginning raises certain questions like: who is this character? what is he doing? and certain expectations about him and the function or outcome of what happens. When the course of the story fulfils or corrects these expectations, explains the obscurities, establishes a readily recognisable series of causes and effects according to a psychology and a society to which we have grown accustomed, we can find in the ending, whether tragic or happy, all the 'meaning' we may require. But this sort of meaning, at its simplest in adventure stories or love stories, seems to be lacking in a Kafka story. The relation of motivation and action, of event and psychological reaction, of cause and effect whether material or psychological, is often very baffling – so baffling that the early reviewers of such a story as 'The judgment' thought the work fantastic and eccentric. A shadow even lies over the truth of events, for the reader cannot be quite sure at times whether what is described is intended to be a reality or a hallucination. The endings often seem arbitrary and may, at first reading, seem merely to add a further puzzle to what has preceded them. It is easier for a later generation, for we no longer expect the same sort of coherence as was normal in Kafka's day, but there are still many problems. Unless however we can find that the parts hang together, that the ending illuminates the rest of the story and turns what seemed accidental and irrelevant into something significant and organic, we can never say that the story has meaning, even if we can find no other definition of its meaning than a feeling that it belongs together, that it satisfies the reader.

The second sense of the word 'meaning' is one we normally associate with an object or work of art that we think of as symbolic. That is, we ask not only whether a structure hangs together, but also what function it is meant to serve. We do not necessarily ask this question of a story; its form may explain itself. But this question is insistent in a Kafka story, not least because its formal coherence remains so teasingly elusive and intangible. Also, there are many signs within Kafka's works that indicate we are invited to look for some meaning of this type. His liking for the fable and parable, literary genres that postulate a meaning of this type that the 'story' is written to illustrate, is clear evidence, even if the lessons or 'morals' that are to be drawn from these fables are anything but simple. The stories themselves do not have so simple a structure, and usually the search for a meaning arises because of the impossibility of understanding the narrative structure without invoking some other dimension. So in the end we find a close relationship between the formal structure and the symbolic meaning, each sustaining the other.

This is why Kafka interpretation is so dangerous a business. Most new studies ask the reader to abandon presuppositions and stick to the Kafka text; but soon they abandon their own intention. And this is unavoidable, since the texts offer obscurities (usually in the form of dislocations) which we can make sense of only by some hypothesis of the meaning. And this practice does not impose a distortion on the text if we remain ready to revise the hypothesis whenever the text should demand it. But such mobility does not come easy to most readers or critics, and the pandemonium of critical interpretations with which we are confronted suggests that most critics would prefer a fragmentary certainty to a more comprehensive hesitancy. Yet even if one suspects that many of the Kafka stories are not amenable to a precise and definable meaning and that there will ever be variant and contradictory interpretations, there have been textual studies that have shown the peculiar structure of Kafka's narratives and have thus provided a surer foothold for the understanding. I refer primarily to the work of Friedrich Beissner and Heinz Politzer. In the essays *Der Erzähler Franz Kafka* (1952) and *Kafka der Dichter* (1958) Beissner showed that the impersonal narrator of the novels and some of the short stories (e.g. 'The judgment') is not an objective authority, as in the classical novel, but confined to the viewpoint of the main character, so that the reader never escapes out of the restless subjective consciousness of the character into the calm of sure knowledge and objective judgment. Though many subsequent stylistic studies have shown that Beissner's thesis requires some adjustment, it is a necessary prerequisite for the understanding of Kafka's work.[6] To Politzer we owe the formula 'open parable' to describe the character of Kafka's stories, that is, a frank acknowledgment that in his work we are presented not just with a self-sufficient story but also with a meaning of some kind, analogous to that of a parable; and at the same time a meaning that eludes precise definition and may, indeed, assert a puzzle, not clarification. Since the novel itself, and literary criticism, had for so long sought to free the concept of story from the old didactic purpose, it was a great liberation when Politzer made it possible for us to treat Kafka without embarrassment within the old tradition of fable and parable.[7]

When I began to busy myself again with Kafka, I did not at first have the present systematic investigation in mind. I had recently completed my study of free indirect speech as a narrative form and in my book *The dual voice* had come to the conclusion that the development of this type of reported speech, known in Germany as *erlebte Rede*, was bound up with the development of the resources of the impersonal narrator in what can be considered the classical novel of the nineteenth century. I also observed that the problematic fate of free indirect speech in the twentieth-century novel was closely bound up with the crumbling of the classical categories of narrator, as defined by Lubbock and Stanzel and challenged by Sartre. Some reviewers of my book regretted that I limited my scope to the nineteenth-century novel, and I have from time to time since then examined modern novels with this problem in mind, though I have not got much further in general than to identify texts in which the classical syntactical forms do not apply.

Kafka's narratives provided examples of such texts and for a time I thought of examining his style as representative of a general modern stylistic feeling. But what I found drew my interest more deeply towards his work in itself, rather than as an example of a general trend, and I rapidly became immersed in the questions of Kafka interpretation. For I found that not only is his narrative method very subtle, intricate, and puzzling, but also it is diverse, and I came to believe that, in the great mass of contrary interpretations, some faults were due to a failure to understand the narrative perspective he chooses, some to a tendency to judge a work by implicit reference to an inapposite model, and some to an assumption that his stories conform to one model when in fact Kafka is continuously inventing or adopting modifications.[8] In many ways the problems of the Kafka story are the problems of the modern novel: the peculiarity of his impersonal narrator, his unease over the composition of a story, the difficulty he had over his endings, his growing preference in his later works for an identified personal narrator and even for the present tense in place of the preterite. But his work is at the same time so unique that it seemed an injustice to consider his work simply as an example of a general trend, and this all the more so since the peculiarities of his narrative forms and their modifications arise not out of a theory of story nor out of a theoretical interest in experiment but out of the requirements of his themes, his need to transmit the sense of his experience. So my work came to concentrate on Kafka's works, on the narrative structure in the first place, but also on the secret of the structure, that is, the secret of its coherence, which meant that where necessary I had to speak of interpretation. Though I have conducted, and ask for, a close study of Kafka's text, I hope it will be evident that I do so not out of grammatical enthusiasm but out of a search for meaning.

When I set out, I intended to include a chapter or chapters on Kafka's novels. But I have come to the conclusion that these large and intricate works cannot be adequately discussed in so small a space, especially since the vast quantity of critical studies on them requires careful attention too. So I have, somewhat reluctantly, decided to limit my own study to the shorter stories and to content myself with occasional brief references to the novels.

2 · THE IMPERSONAL NARRATOR OF THE EARLY TALES

'The judgment' ('Das Urteil')

I start with the narratives told by an impersonal narrator – often ill-named the omniscient narrator – since Kafka employs this agency for his earliest short stories 'The judgment', 'The metamorphosis' (both written in 1912), and 'In the penal colony' (1914), and for the three novels.

The narrative perspective in the first two is not so consistent as later stories and more difficult to sum up. It is clear that it has much similarity to that of the novels since the objective voice that tells the story normally chooses the chief character's angle of vision and, while communicating to us the latter's thoughts, wishes, feelings, and intentions, can in the main describe the other characters and the physical settings only in so far as the chief character knows them. Most readers feel the last sentence of 'The judgment', referring to the stream of traffic crossing the bridge as Georg falls into the river, and the last pages of 'The metamorphosis', describing the recovery of the Samsa family after the death of Gregor, as a dislocation of style, since elsewhere throughout both stories we are so tightly held within the orbit of the chief character. But this feeling is not fully justified, and the objective narrator, the objective viewpoint immanent in these endings, appears at many moments of the story. If I now proceed to disentangle the stylistic evidence for the narrator's objective viewpoint, as distinct from that of the character, I do this only in order to assess the effect upon the meaning of the story that this double perspective produces. It is best to examine the two stories separately, though they show very much the same features.

The first paragraph of 'The judgment', in which Georg Bendemann and his home are described from outside, might seem to be a conventional introduction to the story. It creates a mood of uneventful idyllic innocence on a Sunday morning in spring, a row of inconspicuous houses, a lovely outlook, and a young man putting his letter into an envelope 'with playful slowness'. With the second paragraph we enter into the troubles and questions of the story and at the same time into the perspective of Georg, for it is through his thoughts that we are introduced to the friend in St Petersburg and then, in a long passage of free indirect speech, to his internal debate about what he should tell the friend. So the narratorial opening is not without thematic function, even if it is only a means to make the coming gloom more striking by contrast. But there are also narratorial intrusions later. As Georg goes to see his father about the letter, we are told about their habits since the mother died (p. 26).[1] This also must be narratorial, and the brief description of their daily routine, a close association at work and home lacking all intimacy, is more than a sort of stage direction, for it creates in us a feeling of inert cohabitation that bears an objective judgment on them both. It is consonant with this that the description of Georg's final flight to the river also is an objective, not subjective account, even more emphatically so through the two striking similes – Georg hurtles 'as over a tilting surface' and he clutches the railing of the bridge 'as a hungry man clutches at food' (p. 32).

There is the same double perspective in the presentation of the characters. We see and hear them only in so far as they appear to Georg, we know their thoughts only as their behaviour and speech indicates them to Georg, through our repeated identification with his angle of vision. But here too the narrator may add something, an observation from outside the character. Thus we are twice told that Georg forgets a resolution 'for he constantly forgot everything', once with a simile: 'forgot it, like pulling a short thread through the eye of a needle' (pp. 31, 30).

Usually the two perspectives are not clearly separate but more subtly interwoven; in many cases we are not able to be sure in what perspective a particular statement stands. The reason for this is the extensive use of free indirect speech and, more particularly, the modern form that Kafka's free indirect speech takes.[2]

The thoughts, inner reactions of most characters are given directly, as they themselves express them in speech, and indirectly as inferences from their behaviour. The narrator has immediate access only to Georg's thoughts, and only in his case can he use introductory verbs like 'he thought, imagined' etc. followed by reported speech. If the thought or intention of the other characters is detected, it is legitimised as an inference from their expressions and behaviour. Free indirect speech is therefore almost completely reserved for the main character, and for him it is indeed abundantly used.

Just as Kafka follows an old convention in the reproduction of thoughts by putting them in direct speech enclosed in inverted commas, as if they were spoken, so he also often uses the conventional indices that betray free indirect speech and leave no doubt in the reader's mind as to the source of the statements concerned. Thus he can open a passage with exclamatory questions that transfer the reader to the consciousness of the character (pp. 23–4). Or statements can be accompanied by an explicit 'he thought', 'he believed', 'he remembered', 'he felt' (*er dachte, er glaubte, er erinnerte sich, er fühlte*), which clearly define from whose mind they emanate. Sometimes we may be misled on first reading, though closer attention reveals the subjective nature of a statement. For instance: Georg, undressing his sick father, 'reproached himself with having neglected his father. It would certainly have been his duty to keep an eye on his father's change of underwear' (p. 29). We might first read the last sentence as the comment of the narrator, but realise that it is one of the 'reproaches' that Georg makes himself. Similarly later in that paragraph: 'Doch jetzt entschloss er sich kurz mit aller Bestimmtheit, den Vater in seinen künftigen Haushalt mitzunehmen. Es schien ja fast, wenn man genauer zusah, dass die Pflege dort. . .zu spät kommen könnte.' ('Yet now he swiftly decided with all certainty of purpose to take his father in to his future household. Admittedly it seemed, if one looked more closely, that the care he intended there might come too late.') The *schien* must mean that it seems *to Georg (ihm schien)*, the *ja* indicates his argument with himself, and *mit aller Bestimmtheit* is not the statement of the narrator, but indicates what Georg himself thought about his resolve. Verbs and particles that indicate an inner debate – like *sollen, dürfen, vielleicht, ja, doch, sicherlich* – frequently betray the subjective character of the statements concerned and their presence can justify us in taking associated neighbouring sentences as Georg's thoughts in spite of their having a normal objective–narratorial form. This is the case with the paragraph on p. 24 that follows a series of exclamatory questions and concludes with a repeated *vielleicht* ('perhaps') and similar words – *wahrscheinlich, jedenfalls, zweifellos* ('probably', 'in any event', 'doubtless'), all of which tell us of Georg's thoughts and persuade us to read the earlier part of this paragraph in the same way. Thus, too, in the following paragraph, it is not the narrator who thinks that the figures of the friend's business in St Petersburg are *verschwindend* ('dwindling') compared with the size of Georg's own turnover, but Georg, and we properly understand that word as a slightly arrogant, impatient expression of his feelings with regard to this friend.

In all these respects Kafka's use of free indirect speech is essentially the same as that which we meet in nineteenth-century novels and rests likewise on a clear distinction of an objective narrator from the subjective character. It shares some of the uncertainties that dog this form, especially those arising from the fact that its syntax is identical with that of a narratorial report, its tenses are normally the same and the characters referred to in the third person, while it lacks the verb and conjunction ('he said, thought that') that identify normal reported speech. Thus Georg may, in the thoughts ascribed to him, seem to think of himself not only as 'he' but even as 'Georg', not as an infantile self-address but simply as a stylistic device, needed because 'he' might apply to someone else. Thus, 'quite contrary to Georg's intention' (p. 25) is not a narratorial intrusion but Georg's own thought. At the same time it is a marked feature of free indirect speech that it can alternate very freely, from sentence to sentence, with objective narrative, so that we cannot always be sure which is intended. On p. 24 we read a reference to the death of Georg's mother, and the addition of 'which had occurred some two years previously' must be a bit of information the narrator conveys to his reader rather than a thought in Georg's head; while on p. 25 the explanation that his fiancée was 'from a well-to-do family', that at first sight seems also to be a narratorial explanation for our benefit, turns out to be the phrase that Georg has used in his letter to his friend, so we recognise that here his thought is quoting the smug phrase intended to excite his friend's envy or silence his disapproval.

But this paragraph shows problems of perspective that are not traditional, and needs closer examination. After the first sentence that tells us that Georg had hitherto not been able to bring himself to write to his friend about his betrothal, it continues:

Oft sprach er mit seiner Braut über diesen Freund und das besondere Korrespondenzverhältnis, in welchem er zu ihm stand. 'Da wird er gar nicht zu unserer Hochzeit kommen', sagte sie, 'und ich habe doch das Recht, alle deine Freunde kennen zu lernen.' 'Ich will ihn nicht stören', antwortete Georg, 'verstehe mich recht, er würde wahrscheinlich kommen, wenigstens glaube ich es, aber er würde sich gezwungen und geschädigt fühlen, vielleicht mich beneiden und sicher unzufrieden und unfähig, diese Unzufriedenheit jemals zu beseitigen, allein wieder zurückfahren. Allein – weisst du, was das ist?' 'Ja, kann er denn von unserer Heirat nicht auch auf andere Weise erfahren?' 'Das kann ich allerdings nicht verhindern, aber es ist bei seiner Lebensweise unwahrscheinlich.' 'Wenn du solche Freunde hast, Georg, hättest du dich überhaupt nicht verloben sollen.' 'Ja, das ist unser beider Schuld; aber ich wollte es auch jetzt nicht anders haben.' Und wenn sie dann, rasch atmend unter seinen Küssen, noch vorbrachte: 'Eigentlich kränkt es mich doch', hielt er es wirklich für unverfänglich, dem Freund alles zu schreiben. 'So bin ich und so hat er mich hinzunehmen', sagte er sich.

(He often spoke to his fiancée about this friend and the special relationship that he had with him because of their correspondence. 'So there is

25

no question of his coming to our wedding', she said, 'but after all I have the right to get to know all your friends.' 'I don't wish to upset him', Georg replied, 'don't misunderstand, he would probably come, at least I think so, but he would feel awkward and inferior, perhaps even envious of me: certainly he would be discontented and have no way of shedding his discontent, and then he would have to go back on his own. Do you know what that means – to be on one's own?' 'Yes, but could he not learn of our marriage in some other way?' 'I cannot prevent that, but, given his way of life, it is unlikely.' 'If you have such friends, Georg, you ought not to have got engaged at all.' 'Yes, that's a guilt we both share, but I wouldn't have it any other way now.' And when she, breathing faster under his kisses, still managed to interject 'but even so it does actually offend me', he thought that there could be no real harm in writing everything to his friend. 'That's the way I am and he'll have to accept me on those terms', he said to himself.)

The passage is stylistically surprising. It represents Georg's memory of several discussions with his fiancée that have led to his finally telling his friend about the betrothal. But these 'frequent' discussions are boiled down to one, and this is given in direct speech, i.e. a form that belongs to an objective narrator. It has been taken as a single conclusive conversation, but this is a mistake.[3] The memory of the character reduces the conversations to their salient points and the narrator reproduces these in the form that best communicates the experience involved, for this purpose subjecting his separate identity to that of the character. The passage lays bare the transition from the traditional narrative situation of the nineteenth-century novel to that of the modern novel. The narrator relinquishes his separate view or identity in the interest of expressing the experience of the character, but does not thereby disappear. He re-asserts himself in his function as the arranger, the composer of the story whose presence, as we have just seen, can be detected even in those passages where he seems only to be the instrument of the character. This double function of the Kafka narrator, that of giving the experience of the character and that of narrating events, has been accurately and extensively analysed by Hartmut Binder in relation to 'The judgment' and other tales.[4]

26

What help towards the understanding of Kafka's story does this more precise recognition of the narrative perspective give? We cannot expect that it alone will cleanse the Augean stable of conflicting interpretations; but it may to some extent explain why there is such diversity in these and even rebuff some, especially those which result from the imposition of a pre-conceived stereotype upon a narrative structure that is the reverse of typical – I think of interpretations that see the tale as a religious or a sexual allegory. The clearest gains from our analysis can be summed up as follows:

1. Since Beissner first defined the narrator of Kafka's novels as 'dwelling in the soul of the character' even saying of that of 'The judgment' that he has 'completely transformed himself into the lonely Georg',[5] critics have been able to grasp the subjective quality of this impersonal narrator and have been chiefly concerned to define more precisely the relationship between narrator and character. Thus Ellis, one of the most observant of readers, properly insists that though the narrator of 'The judgment' usually adopts the standpoint of the main character, his identity is not absorbed into that of Georg. But Ellis, no more than Sokel, comments on the significance of the occasional, truly objective intrusions of the impersonal narrator, if indeed he notices them. For instance, like Sokel he interprets the first paragraph of the story as a communication of Georg's thoughts as he sits in his comfortable study.[6] Ellis makes indeed the valuable observation that the description of the setting is not the harmless bit of realism it has usually been assumed to be but betrays a strange confusion of mind, since the row of houses is said to be differentiated 'almost only' in height and colour, whereas such a difference would mean a marked variety. As a consequence Ellis must explain this oddity, like the 'playful deliberateness' of Georg's gesture, as a sign of Georg's mis-relationship with reality. These and other difficulties fade if we recognise that the spatial and psychological focus of this first paragraph lies outside Georg's consciousness, that this paragraph

is a comment from outside the events to be related and indeed, with its confusion and oddities of expression, is an amusingly misleading parody of a conventional story. In general, the mistake that even good critics make is not to recognise the mobility of Kafka's narratorial standpoint, which among other things allows for the frequent intrusion of humour.

2. Ellis's grasp of the prevailing subjectivity of the narrative provides the insight for the best analysis of Georg's character that exists, for he sees that ostensibly narratorial statements about his generosity, friendliness, love, consideration for his friend and his father are only Georg's own self-justifications and his means to disguise his real envy and furtive hatred of these two and to depreciate, triumph over, his rivals. But again Ellis does not differentiate clearly enough. The subjectivity of the statements does not mean that everything is false, only that every statement is suspect. Thus, we can well accept the deep falsehood in Georg's professed kindness and generosity, but we have no reason to doubt his claim that the friend's business is not doing so well as his own, or that the father is ill and incapable of leading the business. Ellis considers that Georg is a failure and a parasite on his father, the stay-at-home son of the parable of the Prodigal Son, while the Petersburg friend is the favoured prodigal. But the only basis for this interpretation is the claim of the father in his violent battle with Georg, and Ellis seems indeed to accept as true everything the father throws at the son. Quite apart from the fact that there is no external, objective corroboration of the father's charges (that he is in league with the Petersburg friend, that he has Georg's customers 'in his pocket', that Georg is thoroughly incompetent in business etc.), there is such spiteful malevolence in his behaviour that we have no right to believe either the truth of his accusations or the justice of his sentence. It is strange that the acumen that detects the inner falsity of Georg should not recognise that of the father.[7] But, it may be argued, the abject failure of Georg in their contest and his consent to the death-sentence

28

prove the truth of the father's assertions. I would suggest that Georg's ludicrous evasiveness in the argument and his acceptance of the sentence are due, not to the truth or falsehood of arguments, but to the terrible conflicts of love and hate, in both father and son, that is nakedly revealed through the father's reckless malevolence, the culmination of which is the father's collapse and the son's suicide. Such an interpretation is consistent with what the narrative perspective permits.

3. It is the absence of an authoritative voice in 'The judgment' (as in many other Kafka stories and in all the novels), both in respect to facts and to judgments and meaning, that has provoked so great a variety of interpretations. The puzzle of the meaning and even connexion of events invites a search for symbolic and allegorical structures, and since there is little authoritative control in the text, these are often based on very frail and arbitrary associations. Ellis's discussion of them, though sympathetic, shows how slight and contradictory is the 'network of Christian imagery', into which the figure of Georg as a sacrificial Christ can be fitted only on the philological principle of *lucus a non lucendo*.[8] But there is a more general and serious error that Kafka's narrative structure invites.

Its source is not simply in the narrative perspective, for it arises also from the opacity of meaning. Most readers, like most critics, approach Kafka with the expectations that traditional works of fiction arouse, in which apparent incongruities of behaviour and puzzling contingencies are ultimately cleared up in an ending that brings understanding and order (often in a moral as well as logical sense) into the events and relationships recounted. It cannot be too emphatically asserted that in the case of Kafka's stories such expectations are totally misleading. A glance at his fables or parables like 'Kleine Fabel' ('Little fable'), 'Vor dem Gesetz' ('Before the law') and 'Heimkehr' ('Homecoming'), can warn us, for these, inviting us by their form to expect an unambiguous moral, in fact present us with an abstract model of reality that baffles our efforts to find in it a lesson. The stories, more realistic in their form and seeming in their structure more like normal relationships and situations, also seem to promise a meaning, but as they proceed our hopes are deceived and ultimately we are left before a baffling and painful puzzle.

It is painful merely to accept this fact; even more, the influence of traditional narrative literature leads us to believe there must be a meaning, and even a palatable meaning. Even Ellis, whom I quote because of the intelligence of his examination of 'The judgment' succumbs to this habit and provides a moral explanation of the catastrophe in terms of guilt and punishment. Georg's self-centredness and destructive hostility to others, Ellis believes, has woven him into a cocoon of falsity, of unreality, that is broken apart by his father; the sentence of death pronounced by the latter expresses symbolically the meaning of the story.[9] This analysis of Georg's character seems to me, as I have already said, to be true; but are we satisfied with his punishment? Do we feel this to be a moral tale? Politzer was surely right when he wrote that there is no guilt in Georg's life that would justify a sentence of such severity, but when he calls this misrelationship 'a technical flaw' he also, it seems to me, is judging the story by a wrong stereotype.[10] All such critical judgments supply that objective observer, that trustworthy narrator, that is not there in this and other stories of Kafka. But his absence is not a mere technicality, nor a mere attempt to bring immediacy into the narration; it means that an objective and authoritative moral understanding of the events is not accessible as well. There is guilt in the world, in Georg, there is consciousness of guilt, there is punishment, but though we can experience and recognise suffering and the evasive tricks men devise to deaden their consciousness of pain and guilt, yet we cannot understand why men should suffer so, nor can we see a necessary relationship between guilt and punishment. The story does not demonstrate a moral, it sets before us a moral riddle; and the title. The judgment, that is appropriate for the father and the son, to the reader must seem deeply ironic.

4. Ellis rightly says that the terms 'nightmarish' or 'dream-like' so frequently used in respect to Kafka's stories do not by themselves 'carry understanding further'.[11] His own explanation of the irruption of grotesque elements as products of the unreality that Georg's self-centredness requires goes some way towards the understanding of this nightmarish quality. But here again, I believe, the lack of an intrusive narrator and objective perspective plays a large part. For, immersed in the subjective perspective of Georg, the reader lacks any objective reference, any norm against which he can judge the reality of the forms that emerge. Except at odd moments, when another perspective may be suggested or when a touch of humour intervenes, the reader is held spellbound, lacking those pauses for reflexion which the more traditional narrative forms, even those with a first-person narrator, provide. This spell extends to areas of Kafka's narrative that in themselves contain no fantastic or grotesque elements, like for instance the opening passages of 'The judgment' that describe Georg's thoughts about his friend; it is the fact that we are so deeply immersed in his consciousness that makes the fantastic elements in his great contest with his father so readily assimilable. It is real nightmare country, swarming with potent significances which we feel, though we lack the keys for their interpretation.

For all this, however, we are not utterly lost; indeed if we were, the spell would be broken, for spells must have a binding quality. At moments, as we have observed, a narrator is evident, not as an interpreter or judge but as a guide who spins the thread of the story. The opening belongs to a mind that knows the outcome, that carries on the story by unobtrusive means, sets the changing scenes, describes its close. The structure of a story is that aspect of which the reader is, as a rule, least conscious and perhaps especially so with Kafka, where the narrator who guides the story's destinies refuses to appear as an authority over against the characters. Yet this itself perhaps greatly contributes to the spellbinding character of the text since it is carried so swiftly from the opening to the dénouement and has so self-confident a structure, even though we are rarely aware of the agency that brings this about.

'The metamorphosis' ('Die Verwandlung')

For his second story, 'The metamorphosis', Kafka adopted the same non-personal narrator, and its first sentence proclaims the subordination of the narrator to the chief character. 'When Gregor Samsa awoke one morning out of restless dreams he found himself in his bed transformed into a monstrous bug.' From this moment the narrator identifies himself almost completely with Gregor, sees and hears through his eyes and ears, and accepts the truth of his metamorphosis as the victim himself must. Except in the coda of the last few pages, describing the revival of the family after the death of Gregor, almost everything we know is passed on to us via the consciousness of Gregor. To his thoughts we have direct access, the others we know as Gregor sees them through the open door and overhears their conversation. His thoughts and impressions are sometimes reported by the narrator much like his spoken words, in inverted commas introduced by such verbs as 'thought'. But they also invade many passages which, while seeming to express a narrator's view, betray the personal source by a characteristic word here or there. For instance, in the first paragraph, the last sentence might be read as a narrator's comment: 'His many – in relationship to his bulk pitifully thin – legs waved helplessly before his eyes.' But the preceding sentences have described what Gregor could see of his body when he raised his head, and we are meant to feel the 'pitifully' is *his* thought as much as the 'waved' applies to *his* vision.

The text continues:

'What has happened to me?' he thought. It was no dream. His room, a proper human room – albeit a little too small – lay calmly between its four familiar walls. Above the table on which a collection of materials had been spread out – Samsa was a commercial traveller – hung the picture which he had recently cut out of an illustrated magazine and mounted in a pretty gilt frame.

The first sentence in inverted commas seems to distinguish Gregor's thoughts from the 'facts' the narrator lists. But this distinction does not hold. 'It was no dream' is evidently a conclusion of Gregor's, not the narrator's, since the normal appearance of his room proves it. Not merely 'calmly' has meaning only if thought by Gregor, also the odd phrase, 'a human room – albeit a little too small', critical and reassuring together, has meaning only if it is a rumination of Gregor's, showing the mean, carping spirit in his smugness. Other items in the room, his samples and the picture, are mentioned as his eyes travel to them, and again the expression 'pretty gilt frame' with its smugness has meaning only if it belongs to him and not the narrator. But, on the other hand, the parenthesis 'Samsa was a commercial traveller' is an explanatory communication from narrator to reader.

This narratorial passage is followed by Gregor's resentful reflexions on his unsatisfactory profession and his superiors, given in direct speech; a long passage of free indirect speech, peppered with exclamatory questions and characteristic phrases (as when the porter is called 'the boss's minion, a creature with no backbone or mind of his own', p. 58); narratorial descriptions of his behaviour as he tries to get out of bed, listens to what his family is doing or saying when the chief clerk (*Prokurist*) arrives etc.; and reproductions of the discussions Gregor hears, and takes part in, given in direct speech. None of these methods provides problems of interpretation except the narratorial descriptive form, which consistently betrays that ambiguity we have already observed in the opening two paragraphs. That is: while the narrator's standpoint is determined by the consciousness and concern of the character Gregor and he usually is concerned only to make Gregor's feelings and intentions evident, he also sometimes demonstrates a more independent purpose and indeed offers the reader the chance of becoming the objective observer he emphatically does become in

33

the final pages, after Gregor's death. It is this narratorial stance that requires a closer examination, the object of which can be formulated thus: why, if the supreme function of the narrator is to communicate to the reader the chief character's view and judgment and his world, without the corrective of an authoritative evaluation, does this narrator still retain some independence of function? This independence appears in several forms.

The chief form is as a technical aid to the narrative. This we have already seen when the parenthesis 'Samsa was a commercial traveller' enables us to understand why Gregor's eye lights on certain objects in his room. There are many such bits of helpful information that the narrator smuggles in, as if, when we are looking at a detective film, a neighbour who has already seen it whispers to us what we should look out for. In this way we are told that the Samsa's maid keeps to the kitchen and locks the door (p. 79), we receive a precise description of the elaborate meal that Gregor's sister puts out for him (p. 72), and brief character-sketches of the new charwoman and the trio of lodgers (pp. 88–9). It is true that often there are suggestions that these facts are present to Gregor's consciousness, as when the information that all three lodgers have beards is, as it were, validated by the statement 'as Gregor once noticed through the crack of the door' (p. 89) but it is clear that our information often comes from some other source than Gregor. I do not think these occasional bits of supplementary information weaken in any way the intensity of the narrative, since they do not offer an alternative view or evaluation.

It is different with one such addition. The scene when Gregor intrudes into the family room, in which his sister is playing to the lodgers, is in all essentials described from his point of view, perhaps with a few enlargements to compensate for the limitations imposed on his vision. But as he creeps into the full sight of the lodgers and the family and creates panic among them, we are told of the filthy state he is in, with 'threads, hair, remains of food' clinging to his back (p. 91). For a moment we see him as the others see him, in a state he is unconscious of

34

(normally he is only too aware of his disgusting appearance). This constitutes a change of perspective that is different from the others mentioned, since it means a switch from the main character's consciousness to that of other characters, and though it is only a momentary effect, I find it disconcerting. That we feel it as a dislocation must be due to the depth of our normal absorption in the perspective of the chief character. For, from the first sentence, it is Gregor himself who sees himself changed into a loathsome bug, while the others (including the narrator) only confirm what he feels and asserts. It is only under this condition that the story – fairy-tale or parable – is presented to us.[12]

There are also other ways in which the narrator's hand is evident, especially when the story is temporarily released from the account of concrete events as they occur in Gregor's presence. Occasionally the narrator summarises a process, telling us for instance 'In this way Gregor was given his food every day' (p. 73) or 'Gregor spent the days and nights with almost no sleep' (p. 87). The long account of his labours for his family and his hopes to retrieve his father's business failure and provide for the education of his sister is expressly stated to represent the 'utterly useless thoughts' running through his head while he listens to the family discussion, but the succinct narratorial account here again puts the reader at a distance from the situation, frees him from the immediacy of the tale, gives him the relief of an intellectual grasp of the situation (p. 75). The most striking passage of this kind is the opening of the third section of the story (p. 85). Here the narrator sums up the change in the father's attitude to Gregor during the month that followed his father's furious attack on him. Now, we are told, the father seemed to have decided to treat him as a member of the family, not an enemy; and we understand that Gregor gathers this from various bits of evidence available through the open sitting-room door. We can even hear a typical bit of complex free indirect speech in the last words of this paragraph, that 'family duty commanded that one swallowed one's disgust and suffered, accepted and suffered', for it is Gregor's thought quoting unmistakeably the overheard words of his father. Here again, though we cannot speak of a different perspectival angle in these words, since their source is as ever the character Gregor Samsa, there is the difference of distance, a distance in this case peculiar to story-making, a long temporal focus replacing the near focus and thus inducing a relaxation of the almost unbearable tension of the story. For this tension arises not simply from the horror of the events but above all from our inescapable immersion in them through the nature of the narrative perspective.[13]

Such pauses in the movement of a narrative are very common in traditional novels and function as a temporary relaxation of tension – Cervantes makes fun of them when he closes a chapter at the moment when Don Quixote's sword is about to cleave his antagonist's head (book 1, chapter 8). They belong naturally to a type of narrative structure in which the intrusive authoritative narrator has many such tricks at his disposal. But, while in 'The metamorphosis' such changes in the temporal or spatial perspective are few and slight, they achieve a relaxation of a different type, one that affects not the tension of a dramatic event but the whole oppressive spell the reader submits to as a result of the narrative perspective. These slight pauses are indeed anticipations of the change that occurs after Gregor's death, when the family revives, decently rejoicing in its liberation from the son who, while he was their chief support, had because of this drained them of responsibility and confidence. The reader too, now freed from the mediation of Gregor, has direct access to their thoughts and feelings, even to those of the charwoman. So that this coda seems in fact to be outside the magic circle of the story. Kafka twice expressed his distaste for this 'unreadable ending', but gave no hint of the grounds for his dissatisfaction.[14]

Different readers will feel these variations in the narrative perspective with different intensity. But all would agree that, if there is any inconsistency in the structure, it impairs hardly at all the power of the work. If we have in part answered the questions posed above, we have still to face the most important, underlying question: why does Kafka employ in these tales an impersonal narrator, if his essential function is only to communicate the chief character's view? Why should he not have written a first-person story and avoided the lapses that have been pointed out? The question has relevance in regard to other Kafka stories too, and in particular to the novels.

In the first place, the use of such a narrator is a great technical convenience, since it makes it possible to establish a physical scene or sum up a long process with greater clarity and economy than if the author is closely bound to the consciousness of the character. Though the narrator stands beside the character and remains true to his perspective, he can select and order the objects or events in the character's experience in order to make the appropriate impact on the reader. Every character, like every living person, registers his outer and inner experience with differing grades of awareness, and at any particular moment will not always be able to distinguish the significant from the trivial; the narrator can so differentiate and by various means can subtly make the reader aware of a line of significance within a chaos of contingency – as for instance he does at the opening of the story, when Gregor responds to his appalling transformation with the apparently ludicrously irrelevant and trivial resentment directed at his employers.

Of course, in stories of the type of 'The judgment' and 'The metamorphosis', in which the chief character dies, an external narrator is particularly useful, not simply because the character cannot describe his own death and its results, but also because it is hard to find for a dead man the perspective in which he would see his past life. There are in fact stories written in the first person in which this person dies, but the endings always seem awkward and contrived. We shall find that in his later stories Kafka repeatedly prefers a first-person narrative, but for stories which describe a continuing situation which lacks a conclusive ending.

The interpretative function of the objective impersonal narrator in both these early Kafka stories is, above all, the provision of a guarantee for the events recounted, a guarantee of a special kind. The objective voice seems to confirm the character's situation through an impersonal affirmation and a slightly different focus, slightly further away from things than the character himself. We can detect its general effect in that startling first sentence of 'The metamorphosis': 'When Gregor Samsa awoke one morning out of restless dreams he found himself in his bed transformed into a monstrous bug.' Though we later discover that this statement corresponds to Gregor's own conviction, it is in its form deliberately and emphatically an objective narratorial assertion and this fact should not be wiped out of the reader's consciousness. We hear in it the objective voice of fiction, the invitation to enter the world of imagination and to suspend disbelief. Because of the authoritative nature of this narratorial voice, that makes itself heard from time to time later in the story, we are warned against taking the story as the mere account of a character's hallucination or as a study in psychopathology. But what guarantee does this voice give? This calm constatation of a fantastic monstrosity is clearly not intended to persuade us that it and the following events belong to the normal order of reality, however realistic, psychologically and physically, their description may be. How then do we read it? I believe as a folk-tale or parable in which, if we are presented with unrealistic fantasies, we know that we are not thereby invited to take them as real in an ordinary sense but urged to look into them for some meaning, some illumination on life that they will provide through their impact upon the circumstances into which they burst. The guarantee of the impersonal narrator is a guarantee of meaning; he asks us to accept the presupposition of Gregor's metamorphosis in order (as we find out) to enquire into the relations of son and father, son and family, and especially the power-rivalries involved – in the same way as in Kafka's novels, *The trial* and *The castle*, we are not to question the reality and authority of the law courts or the castle but to experience the meaning they have for the characters who seek admittance. This is a typical feature of Kafka's story-telling that, as was pointed out in my first chapter, forces the reader to look beyond the surface network of the story for another, symbolic meaning.

But if we now consider together these various items that the impersonal narrator contributes to 'The metamorphosis', we find this contribution is of greater significance than we earlier suspected. For, taken together, they establish the structure of a story – not only are the scenes filled out by pieces of narratorial information, but the narrator opens and closes the story, sets the scenes, establishes them as phases of a story for which he also determines the movement in time, allowing us sometimes to be absorbed in the moment, sometimes from a longer focus to view the passage of days. In 'The metamorphosis', as could be observed in 'The judgment', the narrator's adoption of the main character's perspective makes the reader experience the events as if they were present, especially in the sense that they have the incoherence of the present and do not point to an outcome. But this presentness of experience is conveyed through the past tense, the narrative preterite, with which both stories open and continue. And, from the beginning of each story, this past tense proclaims that we are to read events that make up a completed whole, that is told, as it were, in retrospect. Because of this, the story can be articulated in its structure, have its phases that lead to its outcome. Thus a double process takes place in the reader. On the one hand he is immersed in the experience of the main character, cut off from an alternative source and alternative evaluations; but on the other hand he is directed by the structure of the story, which is cunningly devised both to provide an intense participation in the character's experience but also to establish it as forming a whole with a peculiar coherence. In this way the Kafka narrator provides therefore not only for experience but also for understanding; for understanding is the *raison d'être* of story-telling, even if the understanding implied is not what we usually expect by the term. In chapter 1 I have suggested the relevance of that strange abstract form that Kafka called Odradek: 'The whole seems meaningless, it is true, but is in its peculiar way complete.'[15] The 'meaning' Kafka refers to here is not any allegorical message, but more simply the use or function of the various parts of the figure, their relationship to one another, their coherence. It is the same with these stories. The reader is at first troubled to grasp the psychological coherence of the various parts, the connexion of event and mental response, of purpose and behaviour, of words and thoughts. But the story structure, its completedness, forces us to seek this coherence, to discover relationships between thoughts and situations, the coherence of this apparent incoherence, to accept in fact a coherence that is startlingly different from that which the conventional story has lived by.

HUMOUR

There is a good deal of humour in these early stories as in the novels and later stories, but it is often ambiguous and can be overlooked. The reader's uncertainty in this respect is due, I believe, to the nature of humour, since in many of its forms it arises when the author gives us the possibility of viewing a person or situation from a new angle – Dentan in his intelligent discussion of the nature of humour defines it as 'a provisional appeasement of suffering' through a change of attitude by which one detaches oneself temporarily from pain and takes pleasure in contemplating it from a distance.[16] This alteration of viewpoint may apply to narrator or to character, but in either case Kafka's stories do not seem to offer easy chances of humour, since the narrator's attitude to his story rarely separates itself from that of the main character, who is himself obsessionally bound to his suffering. Yet there is much humour, even if it is humour of a curious and rather black type.

Much of it arises from parody of conventional attitudes, fleeting references that are difficult to identify. In 'The judgment' the first paragraph with the description of the young man in his pleasant surroundings and relaxed mood is seen on reflexion to be a parody of the conventional magazine story of the nineteenth century, that is humorous only since it raises expectations that are totally dashed by the Kafka story. This is one of the few passages that signals a narratorial standpoint and its irony is directed perhaps as much against the conventional 'sovereign' narrator as the conventional story. Commonly the humour arises from a contradiction in a character's speech or behaviour. In the conversation between Georg and his fiancée Frieda, part of which is quoted above, there are several odd, slightly illogical conclusions drawn by Frieda that I think must have brought a smile to the author's face as he wrote them. When Georg describes the muddy relationship with his Petersburg friend, she logically comments that since he does not know of the betrothal, he will not be able to come to the wedding, but adds complainingly 'after all I have the right to get to know all your friends', though this right is not in question. Later, again with curious logic, she says 'If you have such friends, Georg, you ought not to have got engaged at all.' One smiles, thinking she means 'Now you have got engaged you will have to give up such friends.' But then we appreciate that her remark was not illogical but only a logical short cut, since she instinctively senses some deep inadequacy in Georg. It is serious humour, then; and a similar sort of serious humour appears in the remarks of Georg to his father, or his thoughts about him – a humour of which he is not conscious and does not intend. We, on the other hand, see that his rather ostentatious concern for his father, his wish to shelter and care for him, betrays his wish to demonstrate his power over his father and reduce him to nothing. Even quite trivial and irrelevant observations betray this secret wish. After Georg has undressed his father and carried him to bed, when his decision to take his sick father into his new household proves his noble conscientiousness, he is betrayed by the thought that it will not be for long: 'Admittedly it seemed, if one looked more closely, that the care he there intended for his father might come too late' – the pedantic qualifications of the thought make it comic. More strikingly humorous is the transformation of the sick father to a grotesque ogre, as he rebels against this humiliating care and turns the tables on his son, standing up in his bed and viciously attacking him with a reckless battery of accusations. Georg can counter this monstrous spiteful attack only with absurd and irrelevant thoughts that betray his impotence – for instance, when the father boasts about his strength and his alliance with Georg's Petersburg friend and the customers whom he has 'here in my pocket', Georg's riposte is comically absurd: ' "He's got pockets even in his nightshirt" said Georg to himself, thinking with this observation he could put him beyond the bounds of the whole world.'

Many readers will not wish to recognise these particular examples as humorous and may indeed find no humour in this lacerating story. It is true that they do not provide that 'provisional appeasement of suffering' that Dentan sees as the function of humour. For though they show mental and physical behaviour that in normal circumstances we consider humorous, in this tale they rarely evoke a smile. The relationships from which these oddities of thought and behaviour spring are too tense, too sinister, and the psychological causes too inaccessible and uncontrollable; one does not smile at the writhings of a cut worm or the crazy bounds of a wounded hare. It is a desperate conflict of life and death, and the squirming and postures of the chief figures are not funny but agonising. And yet it is necessary to register the incongruencies that I have called, for lack of a better term, humorous since they do indicate moments when we, the readers, are removed a little distance from the characters and see what is comic in this human tragedy. This feeling that the human predicament, however tormenting, may have a comic aspect is often present in Kafka's work, itself arising perhaps from a deep ironic pessimism about human hopes and aspirations.

We find the same types of humour in 'The metamorphosis', more prominently indeed, yet ultimately with the same ambiguity of effect, so that we are not certain whether there is true humour present and whether what has the appearance of humour does not simply intensify the horror. This applies most evidently to the central situation of this story, that creates what Dentan calls the basic condition of Kafka's humour: the placing of the character in a new situation that he vainly tries to cope with in terms of his usual habits and way of thinking.[17]

'The metamorphosis' begins with this new situation. After the shock of finding himself transformed into a monstrous bug, Gregor Samsa's first extended thoughts are bitter and spiteful reflexions on his exhausting and arid job, that develop into querulous resentment against other commercial travellers and his boss and the hope, characteristic of the underdog, of one day getting his own back and freeing himself. Readers are often puzzled that Gregor should have these thoughts, so irrelevant to his transformation, but of course that is the point: he tries to evade the new reality by continuing to dwell on what we assume is a normal grievance. It is a comic response recalling many in normal life, and it is several times repeated, as when Gregor shouts through the door that he is getting up and will go to work, or when he pursues the chief clerk out on to the landing, or when he makes that disastrous incursion into the sitting-room where the lodgers are listening to his sister's playing. This basic incongruity between Gregor's thoughts and behaviour and the new reality that has been thrust upon him is similar to that affecting Blumfeld in Kafka's story 'Blumfeld, ein älterer Junggeselle' ('Blumfeld, an elderly bachelor') when his arid routine is broken by the two bouncing balls. But Blumfeld's thoughts and actions are *comically* inadequate to the new situation; their effect is *humorous* since the visitors who dance attendance on him are harmless and charming, and Blumfeld's behaviour only shows the smug indestructibility of his warped mind and life. What I have called the 'comic' situation in 'The metamorphosis' hardly strikes us as comic and cannot evoke the relief of laughter, and the reason is clear: the cause of Gregor's transformation is sinister, its effect is his annihilation. The members of his family can cope with this change in their different ways, both sister and father profiting from the responsibilities thrust on them through the incapacity of their breadwinner and tyrant. They are not comic, even if in the father's behaviour we detect the triumph of the displaced tyrant rejoicing over the collapse of the usurper and justifying to himself his loathing of his rival. All these elements might be humorously treated in a less dire situation but not here, where we are so firmly held in one perspective. And the incongruity of Gregor's behaviour and thought, which is overcome only when he succumbs and dies, is never truly comic but only serves to make the story unvaryingly grotesque, horrible, even nauseating, since he remains incapable of the tragic dignity that only a self-distancing from the immediacy of suffering can provide.

Where every reader detects humour is in the minor characters, not members of the family – the chief clerk, the charwoman, the three lodgers. All have grotesque features but are free from sinister influences and hidden implications. The clerk is a representative of that absorption of a person in a function that appears so often in Kafka; since his whole being is identical with his job, his incapacity to cope with the fact of Gregor's transformation is complete and farcical. But he appears only for a moment. The charwoman and the lodgers, on the other hand, are more extensively handled and are present at the end of the story. They might almost be felt to be an unwarrantable intrusion into the story, an erratic element.

These figures come from popular farce. The charwoman is completely unaffected by the atmosphere of the home, and is the only character impervious to the horror of shame over Gregor's transformation. Raucous, always slamming doors, she does not suffer from sensitive nerves, and even talks to Gregor familiarly, as one might to a pet animal – 'come over here, you old dung beetle', etc. When he creeps out of his corner she threatens him with a raised chair and would have no compunction in crushing him. It is she who finds his corpse and comes with the good news to the family, shouting out to them 'it has

44

croaked' and calling them to come and look. Their feeling cannot respond to her cheerfulness until the father introduces a divine sanction with 'now we can give our thanks to God', and their restoration becomes complete only after the charwoman has disposed of the corpse. It could be said that the charwoman plays a part in freeing the family from the incubus, but it is difficult to believe she was essential to the story. One welcomes the breath of fresh air she brings, the slightly grotesque unconcern, for she is a great relief in that strained tension. But she is really an erratic block in the sense that she exists almost entirely outside the consciousness of Gregor, so that the humour of her character does not emanate in any way from him. With her we feel from the beginning an authorial note, a comment on the story from outside the magic circle in which it essentially moves.

This is the same with the three lodgers. They belong to a type of humour common in the popular tradition, that recurs several times in Kafka's work, when two or more people act as if they were one; it is like that of the comic figure of the automaton, since in both types the humour arises from the contrast between apparent individuality and actual automatism. The three lodgers in 'The metamorphosis' not only act as one, without any differentiation at all – no such differentiation as between the three combmakers in Gottfried Keller's *The three just combmakers*. But also, the character of their spokesman is reduced to an abstraction, the colourless clerk with his devotion to order, propriety, and routine for whom the discovery of the uncanny housemate, Gregor, only serves to promote his self-importance as he vents his righteous indignation and grasps the double opportunity of giving notice and saving on his rent. That the other two merely multiply his attitude increases the comic element, just as the fact that three of them share a small room and have the same normal habits makes each more comic. After Gregor's death they give Gregor's father the opportunity to recapture his old energy and authority when he turns the tables on them and gives them notice. But their positive function in the story is minimal and far outweighed by the sheer relief their grotesque intrusion creates, not for the family but for the reader. Again, as with the charwoman, though Kafka half-heartedly suggests that they are being seen through Gregor's eyes – that all the lodgers have beards is observed by Gregor when the door is left ajar – in fact they exist independently of him and the humour of their role takes us outside Gregor's world.

The humour that arises from the description of the char-woman and the lodgers seems essentially different from that encountered elsewhere in 'The metamorphosis'. It does not arise from a hidden reference to some sinister power or some patho-logical compulsion; their behaviour is not incongruous in the way that Gregor Samsa's (or Georg Bendemann's) is. If there is a satirical intention, it is drowned in the clowning and in any case largely irrelevant to Gregor's situation and catastrophe. This humour seems to me to belong to a separate type that one might call the type of playfulness. Dentan recognises the presence of this 'intention ludique' in many of Kafka's stories, but tries to subsume it as part of an all-embracing form of humour that I have mentioned. But it seems separate, and it is significant that in 'The metamorphosis' it alters the narrative perspective and breaks through the baneful spell that otherwise grips us. For this 'playful' humour engenders an unembarrassed laugh, amuses us without awakening sinister forebodings or unease. It arises from the observation of human peculiarities or eccentricities which do not need to arouse our concern; the fact that they are grotesquely magnified makes it possible for us simply to enjoy the play of fancy, the fun of exaggeration, with-out being invited to think of serious implications. It is near to the fun of the circus, of clowning, and I believe that Kafka often found in this type of humour a solace, a relief from the intense oppressions that so often are his theme. But its signifi-cance is negative, since these figures belong to a world in which Gregor's fate does not count.

46

THE FATHER–SON CONFLICT IN KAFKA'S STORIES
AND CONTEMPORARY GERMAN LITERATURE

The narratorial stance and narrative structure form only one (double) element of many that make up a story, all of which require the attention of the critic. While it is peculiarly true in Kafka's case that analysis of the narrative perspective is remarkably illuminating, with him too one must examine other aspects – the literary sources, the personal experiences and thoughts expressed in his diaries and letters, the social and intellectual environment and so on. The importance and relevance of these other aspects vary very greatly from story to story, as will be seen, and often they do not need exposition. In respect to these early stories, 'The judgment' and 'The metamorphosis', both of which centre in a son–father or son family conflict, there is an unusual approach that yields insight. In Kafka's early years there was an abundance of literary works that are built on this theme of family conflict, and it is helpful to compare his image with that of his contemporaries. In my book *From naturalism to expressionism* I gave a few pages to this theme in which I referred to Kafka's stories among many other literary works; it now seems to me that I did not at that time appreciate the originality of his interpretation.[18]

Wedekind's play *Awakening of spring* (1891) provides a model for a whole generation. Parents and schoolteachers combine to form a ruthless authority whose object is to force children into subjection to the social norm, that means the adoption of a middle-class career and observance of middle-class values particularly in relation to sex. Both the natural affection and the fears of children are worked on in order to win their compliance, so that any involuntary or voluntary failure to conform (e.g. at lessons or in the troubles of puberty) is accompanied by torments of conscience which may lead the young to suicide. The absolute authority of father or schoolmaster often, though not necessarily, turns them into monstrous figures who torment the young lives. The reader's sympathy is won for the young people whose happiness and perhaps life are crushed by the all-powerful elders, and for the successful rebel who challenges them and asserts his independence. The battle is for self-fulfilment as opposed to conformity to shallow and hypocritical 'bourgeois' social values (above all practical success and public esteem). Among the many variations is that in the Expressionist plays of Sorge (*The beggar*, 1912) and Hasenclever (*The son*, 1914) in which the son's revolt becomes a symbol of an idealistic social revolution and is crowned by the murder of the father.

The liberation of sexuality from the stigma of evil and shame plays a large part in this rebellion of youth, and in some works this extends to homosexuality and the incestuous love of brother and sister. But in this period Freudian concepts are not greatly evident, especially in that the mother rarely figures as the focus of the father–son rivalry. Hofmannsthal applied the Freudian model in his play *Oedipus and the Sphinx* (1906), but by adopting the mythical setting he removes the guilt of Oedipus from the ethical and social environment which gave the problem of sexuality its specific importance to that generation.

How do these two stories of Kafka fit into this literary trend? The most striking feature about them, in this context, is the absence of rebellion, either wished for or intended by the young men, and the absence of any symbolical reference to social revolution. Can one even speak of a 'father–son conflict'? The 'heroes', Georg and Gregor, are their father's heirs as the breadwinners of the family. During the lifetime of Georg's mother, we are told, his father had insisted on having his own way in the family business, but since her death Georg had enjoyed a free hand and had greatly increased the workforce and output. His father has not made difficulties over his marriage plans. When Georg goes to speak with him about the letter to his Petersburg friend, he sees how frail his father is and resolves to devote loving care to him after his marriage. During the sudden quarrel that then breaks out over this friend in St Petersburg and that leads the father to bitter and crude taunts over his love-affair which has 'profaned the memory of his mother', Georg succumbs without a struggle and hurries away to execute the death-sentence pronounced by his father, protesting his love for his parents with his last breath. Similarly, in 'The metamorphosis', Gregor's father is old and weak and, after the failure of his business five years ago, has yielded the place of breadwinner to his son, taking on the habits of an ailing dependant. Differently from Georg, Gregor expresses much irritation and vexation with his post in his firm and is jealous of colleagues with easier jobs, but even his father bears witness to his devotion to his work and he readily undertakes the responsibility towards his family, including the plans for his sister's education. Both 'heroes' seem in fact to be on the way to taking over the powers and position of their fathers, and in Gregor's case this natural process is interrupted only by his strange metamorphosis into a bug. So, neither is a rebel, a champion of freedom, and the fathers, if once they were tyrants, have at the opening of the stories ceded their dominance and become powerless.

But of course this easy and harmonious process and situation are an illusion and deceit. The violent outburst of the father in *The judgment* betrays tensions that have always been there. What truth there is in his reckless charges against his son is often unclear: there is no proof at all of his alliance with the Petersburg friend or of the decline of his son's business, only the word of an outraged, resentful and impotent old man. His crude attack on his son's fiancée is obviously malicious. But what strikes us as true is his bitter resentment against the son's ostentatiously loving care, as he bears the old man to bed, 'getting him down' as the father cries. And this seems true to us since we know Georg's thoughts as he undresses his father, lovingly deciding to take him into his own household and at the same time registering the treacherous thought that his father will not live long. The quarrel is ostensibly about the friend in St Petersburg and many critics have felt bound to attribute some great significance to this absentee whom we know only through the contrary opinions of father and son, neither of whom is a reliable witness. I would suggest that while the absentee has a psychological importance earlier in the story, since Georg's attitude towards him tells us a lot about his inner insecurity, his chief function in the quarrel is his irrelevance. Quite apart from the father's unconvincing assertions of his secret alliance with this friend, which suggest some unacknow-ledged cause, the passion of his explosion against his son that leads to the death-sentence he utters (and to his collapse as Georg rushes from the room) must be due to a deep-seated, long-smouldering resentment, which takes advantage of this slight, harmless pretext to burst into flame. We get the first clear suggestion of this cause when we read that father and son, though living in the same house and working in the same business, have fallen into an empty routine of co-habitation and are strangers to one another. The odd responses of the father to the son's first statements are mysterious, suggest hidden thoughts, and the son's demonstrative care for the feeble old man begins to rouse our suspicions. Then the real outbreak that occurs blurts out the deepest cause, the loss of authority that the father attributes to the son's lust for power. As he sees the son's confusion and uncertainty, the father piles on humiliations and contrasts the son's foolish egoism with his own love for him. Wavering between the wish that his father will fall and die and an irresistible veneration for him, Georg is finally reduced to helpless obedience.

Why should Georg be so reduced? Again we must look, I believe, for some inner cause since none of the reckless claims and charges the father makes carries much weight. We have seen in the account of Georg's relations with his friend that he tends to avoid awkward and difficult questions, to put off unpleasant problems, even when it is so slight a matter as informing the friend of his engagement or telling him of his success in business. When he thinks of his success in the business he is aware that his father has ceded the priority to him but does not worry about the profound dislocation this must have meant. So he comes to his father's room – the first time in many months that he has entered it – thinking his father will be grateful for his visit and appreciative of his trust and love. As his father's suspicions become evident he intensifies the display of 'love', but these only provoke the father's outburst. Why he should be overwhelmed by the father's attack is not simply the result of its ferocity. It shows the falsity underlying their professed relationship, since its malice is evident; but still worse, it forces into the open the conflict in his own feeling, since he now begins to hate this father whom he always professes to love and to hope that he will 'fall and be shattered'. The whole hypocrisy in the family relationships lies bare, and Georg succumbs to the shock, proving his love by carrying out the death-sentence, yet by that act confirming the hatred his father's passion and behaviour express. Yet in neither case is it a simple hypocrisy, hatred hidden under a cloak of love. For not only do both feel love for the other, we too have no right to say they do not. The terrible thing is that they both love and hate, and it is the realisation of the existence of these two irreconcilable passions that strikes Georg with paralysis.

The situation in 'The metamorphosis' is fundamentally similar, and most strikingly illustrated by the behaviour of the father and sister. At the opening the father, as seen through the eyes of Gregor, seems content with his reduced situation, spending his days in an idleness that reduces him still further, and always like mother and sister fixing his care and hope on Gregor, their only support. But once Gregor's metamorphosis has occurred the father shows more and more clearly his loathing and hatred of this vermin. He drives him, 'hissing like a savage' and giving him a strong push, back into his room, on the first occasion when Gregor ventures out, and the latter flees in fear of 'a mortal blow'. The father will never go into Gregor's room and when the sister wants to move furniture from it she does not 'dare' to ask her father to help. When Gregor, this time by accident, leaves his room again, the father arrives to find him in the family sitting-room and cries out 'Ah!' in a tone of rage. Gregor knows that he believes in using 'the greatest severity' towards him and runs round the room, pursued by the threatening father, who at last drives him back into his own room with a hail of apples, one of which gets impaled on Gregor's back. These undisguised expressions of his resentful anger over Gregor's metamorphosis into a bug are accompanied by a transformation of the father. On the first day the father already shows initiative, reckoning up the family's assets and showing that they must all find jobs. And when the terrible battle occurs, the father has just returned from his new job as a commissionaire and Gregor is astonished to see him in a splendid uniform, erect, with life and fire in his eyes, full of energy (it is at this point in the narrative that we are told of his earlier decrepitude). Henceforth the father insists on wearing his uniform even at home and refuses to go to bed early so that he proudly demonstrates his rejuvenation and at the same time, complaining of the great sacrifices he is making for the sake of the family, can demand the loving fuss and care of the women – an echo of Gregor's own complaints about the demands his job as breadwinner had made on him.

While Gregor's mother, already feeble and asthmatic, is plunged into helpless, bewildered suffering by his metamorphosis, his sister undergoes a change similar to the father's. Gregor, on becoming the breadwinner, had secretly planned to send his sister to the music academy; that he keeps this plan a secret tells us that like his father he enjoys his power. The impact of his 'illness' transforms the young girl into a woman. She immediately insists on taking charge of the bug's meals, enters his room freely, makes plans for his comfort; she has suddenly become necessary in the household as it is only through her that the parents receive news of Gregor's behaviour. She now takes part in the family discussions and prepares herself to take a job. However, the novelty of her responsibility for Gregor wears off and she soon begins to lose interest in him, showing her disgust and impatience at his behaviour. Weary too with her stenographic work, she shares in the despondency that falls over the whole family after the scene of the apple-throwing and that is summed up in the father's conclusion that all they can do is to suffer.

When Gregor's final venture into the sitting-room results in the indignant departure of the three lodgers, matters come to a head and it is the sister who now takes the lead and expresses the opinion that this bug cannot be given the name of her brother and must be got rid of. The father agrees but his enquiry: 'But what ought we to do?' only provokes her to a hysterical reiteration that things cannot go on like this. Gregor has been present at this discussion and he draws the right conclusion; the next morning he is found dead. Now the father recovers all his lost confidence and authority. He finds the words and gesture that bring release: 'Now we can give our thanks to God' and crossing himself, so that the ghastly experience is somehow fitted into the old assumptions. A few minutes later, when the lodgers are clamouring for their breakfast, he appears in his full 'livery', wife and daughter each on an arm, and with imperative dignity orders the lodgers to leave his house for ever. He tells wife and daughter to dismiss thoughts of the past, promises to dismiss the charwoman who has reminded them too painfully of the corpse she has got rid of for them, and takes them out on a country excursion. As they cheerfully consider a happier future the parents suddenly realise that their daughter has grown into a blooming girl who will soon be needing a husband.

If one compares these two stories with contemporary works on similar themes, the absence of a struggle for freedom and self-fulfilment is perhaps the most striking feature. In both we are concerned only with the family and its survival and are not asked, not allowed to consider any alternative objectives. The family appears in both as an economic unit, dependent on the father's earnings and business. It is bound together through this fact, but also as a social unit, since the chief object of the father, the breadwinner, is to provide for the family, and that means primarily for the well-being and success of the children. All members feel love for the others, the children give respect as well as love to the father just as he governs as well as shelters them. The mother has an important practical role, as cook and housekeeper, and provides a sentimental element to the family solidarity, but has no independent part to play.

The replacement of the aging breadwinner by the son belongs naturally to this concept of the family and seems in both these Kafka families to have taken place without dislocations, until the events described in the stories. That is, both sons have taken over authority in the conviction that this is their duty, with pride in their success (mixed in Gregor Samsa's case with some irritation at the discomforts his work and absence from home cause him), and with the naive belief that the father gladly acquiesces in this transfer of responsibility to his son. The events of both stories reveal to the son the falsity of this belief which is shattered both by the ferocious hostility of the father and by at least some recognition of the admixture of an enjoyment of power in the son's love for the family and his father in particular. Neither of the sons can resolve the conflict within himself between love for the father, veneration even, and rivalry and both fall victim to this conflict. From the rather meagre information we are given about the period before Gregor Samsa's metamorphosis we can believe that this change into a loathsome vermin occurs after his parents had failed to show 'any particular warmth' over his breadwinning success (p. 75), i.e. as an instinctive recognition of the baleful conflict behind the façade of love. Kafka's heroes collapse because they can see no means of resolving this conflict which itself destroys the whole sustaining image of the family.

In comparison with other contemporary discussions of the family problem, Kafka's seems to lack any aggressive hope and challenge or the fierce energy of accusation; his heroes despair and acquiesce. But also he escapes the delusions and romantic gestures common at that time. He does not attribute the problem to accidental personal faults but to the family in itself. Nor does he have recourse to a solution outside the family, the antibourgeois victory of the rebel who leaves the family to become a non-implicated observer or artist etc. Kafka cannot so dismiss the family. For his characters, for the heroes through whose eyes we see and experience the events of these stories, the family is the world, and we might say it is in a sense a symbol of the world; the problems it engenders cannot be solved from outside nor ignored. This is the peculiar incorruptibility of Kafka's vision.

THE FUNCTION OF KAFKA'S NARRATOR

In this comparison of Kafka's two early stories with contemporary works, some of them plays, I have not tried to compare the narrative style as this would have entailed too large an excursus. But we cannot evade the question of the style and in particular the question, what contribution does the narrative stance and structure make to the meaning of 'The judgment' and 'The metamorphosis'? I will try to answer this question within the wider framework of the modern novel.

The general trend in the modern novel to integrate the fictitious narrator into the imaginative structure, to reduce the identity and function of this once near-omniscient and obtrusive authority to that of privileged insight and imaginative empathy, takes different forms in the work of James Joyce, Virginia Woolf, William Faulkner, Alfred Döblin, Jean-Paul Sartre and others. In these early stories of Kafka we can recognise this trend, though in a highly characteristic, peculiar form. In fact Kafka's form emerges so naturally out of the imagined situation and seems to be so lacking in theoretical intention that for a long time he was looked on as an odd-man-out, and I believe that the first imaginative writer to recognise the representative and theoretical significance of his narrative perspective was Sartre in *Qu'est-ce que la littérature* and, after Sartre, Robbe-Grillet.

In these two stories the narrator has been divested of most of his traditional powers: he is not an independent authority, can offer no significant objective information and no independent explanations, whether material or psychological, cannot present scenes or events from an angle of vision substantially different from that of the chief character, and cannot provide the reader with authoritative moral judgments or norms. He offers no grounds for an explicit interpretation. One is tempted to say that all this narrator – or rather this narrative function, since the narrating medium has no personal identity – can do is to immerse us in the experience of the chief character, and this certainly seems to be the most marked aspect of our reading experience. Characteristically it means immersion in the present situation of the character, in the stream of events and thoughts along which we are borne in their ambiguity and uncertainty of direction and meaning, without foreknowledge or presentiment of the outcome, the future. The past of the characters we know essentially only through the thoughts and memories of the chief characters which give anything but an unbiased, undistorted, authoritative view. Thus, when the ending comes, it has not the traditional enlightening, fulfilling function of an ending, for it does not resolve puzzles and problems, it does not relieve the distress of the story, but seems only a reaffirmation of the arbitrary doom that has weighed on the character from the first. We are tempted to feel the title 'The judgment' to be a supreme irony, for is this sentence that Georg accepts and executes a judgment in *our* eyes? The narrator does not let us know whether he acknowledges it as such, and I believe critics are on the wrong tack when they seek some moral or other formula that would demonstrate the justice of this sentence and thus assuage its harshness – as they also are when they propose moral justifications of Gregor Samsa's fate.

This narrator is a wonderfully apt instrument for these stories, as he is for the novels. In both these early stories the chief character is hemmed in and crippled, spiritually distorted by his relationship with family and father. His fitful activity only spins him more inextricably in a web of love and hate, dependence and power, selflessness and egoism; half paralysed, he is unable to break out into independence and capable only of suffering; his tormented thoughts only intensify his suffering and impotence. That there is here no independent narratorial voice, viewpoint, judgment, is of profound significance, since we are faced with a fateful situation which defies any objective judgment, blame, or apportionment of responsibility. The fact that this narrator is absorbed in the hero is what creates that intense enclosedness of Kafka's stories. There is no escape from the spell they weave, scarcely an opportunity for reflexion, contemplation, for a relaxation of tension, until the spell is broken by the death of the narrator's chief medium, the chief character. And at that point the reader looks back in almost uncomprehending horror, cut off from this strange experience as the awakened sleeper is cut off from his nightmare.

But, if this is the dominant experience of the reader, that he feels most consciously and keenly, it is not the whole truth and needs qualifications here and there. In these stories we are not imprisoned in the unrelaxing obsession and suffering of the chief character as we are for instance in Dostoevsky's *Notes from the underground,* in which the only medium is the character himself. I have pointed out the many ways in which an independent narrator does appear, not as a person or judge but as an agent in the story-telling. Some of these interventions, as when the narrator inserts some necessary bit of information, are of little significance. But some, though scarcely registered by the reader, are a powerful subliminal influence: those in which a black humour asserts the independent comment of the narrator and especially those through which the narrator sets a new scene, condenses the flow of time, creates phases of the story – for instance the three sections of 'The metamorphosis' and the variations of temporal and physical focus within them. Not only the endings of the stories betray this independent agency, but also the structure of incident, including the striking opening of each story. None of these interventions offers an 'explanation' or interpretation of what is occurring. Their significance is that through their form they create meaning in the sense that they create a story-whole in which each part and item has a place, a function. The narrator, however much he identifies himself with the chief character, always also is carrying out this constructive task, placing his hero in a narrative whole. This is nowhere more clearly evident than in the endings, not only since the independent narrator most clearly emerges at this moment, but most significantly since the ending is recognised to be the goal to which the whole of each story is directed and which determines the relationship of the incidents: a goal that is implied by the preterite tense itself, the instrument of retrospective narrative. Television daily gives us clues to the profound significance of the compositional function of endings: the experience of a football match as it takes place is astonishingly different from viewing it after the result is known. Of course, the relationship of the characters in a story to the ending is infinitely more complex and variable than that of players in a competitive game, but in the final analysis it is the ending that holds all together. In the case of the Kafka stories, the sort of coherence and 'meaning' that we discover is so puzzlingly unconventional that we should be lost if the story structure and ending did not imperatively require us to seek them.

So there are two contrary impulses in the narratorial stance of these stories – one, the immersion in the present situation of the character, that seems to preclude a knowledge of an outcome, and the other, the subtle assertion of a completed action seen in retrospect. Together they create the story structure even though at times, especially in the endings, the replacement of the first by the second can cause the reader unease. I believe Kafka's own unease over the ending of 'The metamorphosis' (as of 'In the penal colony') must have been due, at least in part, to this contradiction of form, since we find that he creates in 'In the penal colony' a different type of ending, one that is inconclusive, open, and in the novels could not bring himself to complete and round off the experience he was communicating. And perhaps this contradiction in narratorial stance is an important element in Kafka's later adoption of a personal narrator writing in the present tense about a non-completed situation and continuing problem. This is a development I hope to investigate – though of course I am not suggesting that Kafka's development arises from a technical problem. I see it as a struggle to find a medium for his vision or message, a struggle that involved the discovery of an appropriate narrative form.

3 · OFFICER VERSUS TRAVELLER: 'IN THE PENAL COLONY'

('In der Strafkolonie')

Kafka's first two published tales offer only a slight invitation to readers who would find in them a religious message such as Max Brod believed to be the main intention of Kafka's work. There is punishment and suffering in them, and what might be called sin, but the suffering is not commensurate with the human frailties displayed nor is there any suggestion of expiation or mercy. Many critics who recognise the significance of the religious issue in the novels and other later works also recognise that 'The judgment' and 'The metamorphosis' belong to a period in Kafka's life that preceded his preoccupation with the religious meaning of sin and suffering, and this view is borne out by the testimony of his diaries.

'In the penal colony' however was written in October 1914, two years after the appearance of the earlier stories, and while Kafka was engaged on *The trial* in which the religious imprint, though difficult to decipher, is unmistakable. In the new story there are scarcely any directly and unambiguously religious terms, yet no reader can fail to observe religious analogies, suggestions, implications.[1] How to elucidate and interpret them is a different matter and here again we can make serious errors if we fail to take into account not just words and images that occur, but also what position they have in the narrative: if we fail to ask the very simple question, who is it that utters or imagines these words and thoughts? For this reason, though not for this reason alone, therefore, we must start our enquiry with an examination of the narrator, who here once again is that disembodied spirit, the impersonal narrator, whose functions we have investigated in the earlier stories.

NARRATOR AND MAIN CHARACTER

Very unusually for Kafka, there are in 'In the penal colony' two main characters, the officer in charge of the execution and the traveller who is visiting the colony. Most critics and readers will see its theme as a sort of contest between these two, though the outcome is unclear and disputable. It is clear that the officer sacrifices himself to his faith and his machine, when he finds they find no favour in the eyes of the traveller. It is clear too that the traveller, though momentarily succumbing to the fascination of the officer's devotion, turns away in horror from the injustice and cruelty of the system embodied in the torture machine, though his panic flight from the colony makes us dubious about the superiority of his humanitarian principles to the inhuman but selfless devotion of the officer. Most readers will sympathise with Gray's and Thieberger's condemnation of the 'pusillanimity' of the traveller, who not only displays a wavering sympathy for the officer but also can oppose to his impassioned conviction only a cowardly evasion. Both these critics draw a parallel between the officer and the tortured tragic heroes of other Kafka stories – with Georg Bendemann, Gregor Samsa, and Josef K. (of *The trial*) – and with some logic they consider that, like these other works, 'In the penal colony' would have most appropriately ended with the death of the protagonist, the officer.[2]

Not everyone would agree with this view or consider the officer to be the protagonist. Many would claim that, in the contest between the savage authoritarianism of the officer and the somewhat pallid liberal humanitarianism of the traveller, our sympathies, like the narrator's, tend towards the latter. But I think in nearly all discussions of the story this argument between the two is seen as one between two contrasting ideologies, similar to that gigantic battle waged in Thomas Mann's *Der Zauberberg* (*The magic mountain*) between Naphta and Settembrini. But this comparison would limp, not because the ideological attitudes are incomparable, but because the form

61

of the contest, the argument, is so. It is to this conditioning factor, and specifically to the *Erzählhaltung*, the narrative perspective, that we must pay close attention, if we are to be able to assess the weight of the arguments the contestants adduce.

The narrative perspective is not always consistent. Kafka found the impulse for his story in a novel by Octave Mirabeau, *The torture garden* (1899), from which he took the general situation, the visit of a Western traveller to a penal colony in China, and many items including a 'torturer' devoted heart and soul to his task, the description of torture instruments and a visit to the 'tea house', the functions of all of which are transformed in Kafka's work. The French novel is narrated in the first person by the visitor and it may be that the slight variations in the perspective of 'In the penal colony' are due to the transposition to a non-personal narrator, even though this new narrator aligns himself with the original. These variations can therefore be seen as momentary lapses from Kafka's main narrative stance; they will be examined in due course.

The first paragraph of the story opens with descriptions that seem to suggest an independent and objective narrator, not omniscient but competent to describe the scene and the characters, equally detached from both officer and traveller as they approach the place of execution. The officer 'surveyed with an almost admiring glance the machine which he after all knew so well'; the traveller 'seemed to have accepted the commandant's invitation only out of politeness'; 'the interest in this execution was probably not very great in the colony either'; 'incidentally, the condemned man displayed such doglike devotion that it seemed as though one could let him run free on the slopes and would only need to whistle when the execution was about to start for him to come' (p. 100).[3] All the tentative speculative suggestions imply a narrator whose knowledge of both men (and of course the victim) is limited, and I think might suggest an actual person, who is present at the scene. The last rather heartless speculation about the 'doglike devotion' of the victim might even suggest something about the narrator's character.

The second paragraph continues in this vein. While the traveller's lack of interest in the machine is mentioned, the busy preparations of the officer and the speculations as to why they are not left to a technician seem to belong to the narrator. He reports the irrelevant comment of the traveller on the unsuitability of his uniform, and when the officer insists on talking about the machine it is apparently the narrator who comments: 'he was trying to take precautions against every eventuality'.

In the next paragraph a change occurs. The traveller is persuaded to sit down beside the pit of the machine. 'He now sat on the edge of the pit into which he cast a fleeting glance', and the following brief description, though exactly similar in form to preceding narratorial statements, is clearly a statement of what the traveller observes as he glances over the pit. The officer then begins on his lengthy and enthusiastic description of the machine, to be interrupted from time to time by the traveller's brief comments or the behaviour of the guard with the condemned man (both of whom are soldiers). But we discover that a fundamental change has occurred. Not only in that the essential confrontation of 'In the penal colony' now begins, the officer's demonstration and defence of the penal procedure and his machine to the stranger, whose support he wishes to win, but also in that the narrator has taken up his stance. From this point he describes all the events as they impinge on the traveller's consciousness, interprets the intentions or motives of officer and soldiers as they are accessible to the traveller's intelligence and not otherwise, and on the other hand tells us directly much of what is going on in the mind of the traveller. The objective balance between the two characters is abandoned, and the story is told as the traveller sees and understands it, while the officer becomes the rather opaque object of his observation and speculation. That is, we, the readers, though distanced from the traveller through the mediation of the narrator, also repeatedly identify with him and share his dilemma, while the officer remains for us, as for narrator and traveller, an alien.

The alignment of narrator and character is not quite absolute. There are traces here and there of the independent narrator we have met in the first paragraph. Further, there is a limitation highly characteristic of Kafka, since much of what is in the traveller's mind remains unrevealed, notably of course his thoughts after the death of the officer and his motives for hurrying away from the colony. The function of these variations is not always understandable, though those of the first two paragraphs seem most likely to be due to waverings on the author's part before he discovered the narrative his story demanded. Richard Sheppard makes a comparable and justifiable assumption when he sees the style of *The trial* as an approximation to that of *The castle*.

The basic features of the narrative structure reached in the third paragraph and thereafter maintained are: the officer's dress, gestures, and actions are vividly and concretely described, while the traveller's are indicated, if at all, far more sparsely and less precisely. The officer's extensive speeches are given in elaborate detail, his descriptions of the legal procedure and the machine, his complaints, his self-justifications; the questions and replies of the traveller are brief and muffled. The place of the officer's arguments is taken, in the traveller's case, by observations by the narrator, many of them in the form of reported speech that transmits the thoughts of the character. This distribution of information corresponds to that given in a first-person narrative, in spite of the fact that the actual medium of the narrative is the impersonal narrator. The dominance of the traveller's viewpoint is reached in this third paragraph and is made explicit in such statements as 'the more admirable did the officer seem to him', which concentrate our attention on the traveller's responses; so much so that when we meet phrases that syntactically might be either narratorial or subjective, we read them as referring to the character's thought: 'He [the traveller] had not listened with complete attention, the sun was too fiercely caught in the shadowless valley, it was difficult to collect one's thoughts.' If we are told by the narrator what the officer is thinking or feeling, we find that usually this can be inferred from his behaviour as seen by the traveller. But on several occasions we are informed about the inner processes of the traveller for which there is no evidence – for instance, his awareness of the absence of something. In the third paragraph he is 'not surprised' at the indifference of the guard, since the latter would not understand French. On p. 120 we are told the traveller noticed that the faulty wheel did *not* squeak, and on p. 121 that the officer's blood was *not* mixed with water. We never get such 'inside' information about the officer's consciousness.

The soldier-guard and the condemned man also appear only when the traveller's attention is called or drifts to them, and their thoughts and feelings may always be adduced from their behaviour. Here too there are some slight anomalies, notably two passages of free indirect speech which will be discussed in due course.

With some slight anomalies, therefore, we experience 'In the penal colony' from the position and through the medium of the traveller. This perspective has the curious, even paradoxical effect of focussing our immediate attention upon the objects of the traveller's concern, the officer and the execution, ostensibly withdrawing it from the traveller himself, who may seem to remain in the penumbra of the recording observer. But there is a further factor which radically qualifies this relationship.

For in this third paragraph another decisive change occurs, which runs against the current of this simple relationship between observer and doer. As the officer places a cane chair on the brink of the pit, a ringside seat for the traveller, apparently thus affirming his role as a spectator, he at the same time turns him into a witness in a judicial enquiry. From this moment the manifest and express object of his speeches to the traveller, though these on the surface are explanations of the procedure and the machine, is essentially to win his approval and support, his intervention on behalf of the system. The traveller, by intention a sightseer, willy-nilly becomes involved. Or rather, from this moment the tension of the story lies in the contest within the traveller's mind between his desire to remain a spectator and the insistence of the officer that he should take sides. Thus, while the visual focus of the story is the officer, its mental and moral focus is the traveller. Even the ritual suicide of the officer is a demonstration and proof of his faith enacted before the witness. What the traveller makes of it, of it all, is the central issue, and the story ends, properly, not with the death of the officer but with the concluding response of the traveller.

Thus, there is a dialectical contradiction within this complex narrative perspective. The observer, apparently retreating out of the limelight and becoming the medium of the narration, at the same time becomes its central issue. Before we can suggest the influence of this structure upon the interpretation of Kafka's work, we need a closer examination of some of the textual problems. In passing, it may be observed that the vividness of this brilliant story, its tension that allows also for variety, for nervous action and for reflexion, is largely due to the double focus of these contrary main characters and to the contrasting relation that the reader, owing to the narrative perspective, has to them.[4]

TEXTUAL ANALYSIS

While there is a technical distinction between the narrator of 'In the penal colony' and the traveller, and we can sometimes decide one or other is the origin of some statement, in fact they coalesce to a remarkable extent. Not only is the scene throughout limited to what the traveller sees and experiences, but also the narrator is just as ignorant about the officer, just as dependent on intelligent guesses about his thoughts and intentions, as is the traveller. Since all the officer's lengthy explanations are addressed to the traveller, it is natural that these speeches, as reported, have the authority of fact, i.e. that the narrator reports them guarantees that this is what the officer said. Whether what he says is the truth is a different matter. There are numerous suggestions that we are hearing through the ears of the traveller, since we are told that the officer repeatedly turns to the traveller, appeals to him, watches the effect of his words on him etc. Even when he cries out in rage, as the prisoner befouls the machine with his vomit, 'it's all the fault of the commandant', he is cunningly grasping the opportunity of influencing the traveller, to whom he now turns with his impassioned appeal (pp. 110–13). The narrator never confirms or corrects what the officer asserts, and seems in this respect to be in the same situation as the traveller. We have no other evidence except the officer's consistency and his behaviour. He is clearly not utterly veracious, since he first tells the traveller that the new commandant 'acknowledges' that he can change nothing of the arrangements made by the old commandant (p. 101), though he himself reveals that things have been changed and further changes are threatened. The officer also tells the traveller that if he goes to the tea house on an execution day, he will find there adherents of the old commandant (p. 111), though when he actually goes, the habitués seem to him to find the prophecy on the gravestone 'ridiculous' (p. 122). The obsessional pride with which the officer talks of and manipulates his machine, his blind acceptance of the penal system that acknowledges no rights to the accused and punishes the slightest misdemeanours with torture to death, his brutal treatment of the victim, his almost deranged proposals to the traveller regarding his intercession with the commandant, all should make us suspect the truth of any of his allegations, even if, like the traveller, we may admire his conviction and his readiness to prove his faith by himself submitting to the torture of the machine.

Apart from the testimony of his own words and behaviour, the rare narratorial statements about the officer's thoughts or words are trivial and self-evident. While the traveller's thoughts may be given in free indirect speech, the officer's are often prefaced by an 'as if' that suggests they are guessed at by an onlooker: 'The officer smiled at the traveller as though he now expected him to . . .'; 'He looked sideways as though talking to himself' (p. 104); he watches the traveller 'as though he were seeking to gather from his facial expression. . .' (p. 109). Rather frequently the narrator provides us through small directions with authoritative information on the mental processes of the officer. When the traveller asks what the sentence against the condemned man is, we read: ' "You are ignorant of that as well" said the officer in astonishment and bit his lips' (p. 103). We are told he is 'astonished'. But actually the lip-biting tells us this, so that we understand an observer would know the officer was astonished because of the tone of the question and the biting of his lips. The statement is an induction from external evidence, not a fictional licence. When the traveller asks if the commandant is to be present at the execution, we are told that the officer is 'embarrassed', but again the evidence for this inference is added – 'and his friendly expression became distorted' (p. 105). This procedure of placing the inference before the evidence means nothing essentially different from the normal form of the description of the officer's annoyance with the squeaking wheel: 'as though the officer were surprised by this offending wheel he threatened it with his fist' (p. 107). It will be seen, therefore, that since the evidence for such conclusions is accessible to the traveller, we read them as suspicions or inferences drawn by him. As such they intensify the involvement of the traveller in the scene.[5]

One of the very few more elaborate descriptions of the officer's feelings is perhaps to be taken as a narratorial statement. When he has decided to subject himself to the machine, he goes to wash his hands in the water in which the prisoner has already washed his filthy shirt: '[the officer] went to the bucket of water to wash his hands, noticed too late the revolting mess, plunged them finally – this substitute did not satisfy him but he had to accept the inevitable – into the sand, and then stood up . . .' (p. 118). There are elements of free indirect speech in this; we hear the fastidious 'revolting mess' and the stilted 'accept the inevitable' as the officer's own words. Yet even here, the insight given into his mind, his revulsion, self-discipline, sadness, does not at all go beyond what the spectator would infer from his behaviour.

The same dependence on what can be seen and heard is evident in what is said about the prisoner and his guard. They appear only when the traveller's attention strays or is directed to them; like theatre clowns they enact, with extravagant gestures, all they think or feel, and therefore interpret themselves. Sometimes it is made explicit that we are told what *the traveller* was watching and how *he* interprets their behaviour. When the officer releases the condemned man and tells him he is free: 'For the first time the face of the condemned man took on real life. Was it true? Was it merely a whim of the officer that might pass? Had the foreign traveller obtained a pardon for him? What was it?' These rhetorical questions are typical, traditional free indirect speech, and it seems the narrator is granting us access to his hidden thoughts. But there follows: 'Such questions seemed to flit across his face. But not for long. Whatever it might be, he wanted, if at all possible, to be free, and he began to wriggle' (p. 117). So the expression on his face, his wriggling, is all that we truly see, his inner reactions are interpreted by the observer, the traveller – we cannot suppose the officer would bother himself with such thoughts. There is, however, a curious result from this. What is said about the condemned man's thoughts reflects upon the observer as well as the observed; it tells us about his concern, his capacity to observe, his attitude, whether of distaste, irony, or sympathy.[6] And if we review all the information given about the guard and his prisoner, we come to a striking conclusion, namely, that the objectivity with which the traveller sees and reports on these men, and in particular the torture of the condemned man, but also their greedy quarrel over the boiled rice, their comedy with the slit clothing, their zeal in fastening the officer to his bed of torture, all this objectivity reveals itself as moral detachment, as heartlessness, as incapacity for sympathy, that reaches its logical conclusion when the traveller refuses to take them with him when he escapes from the colony.

A single word may betray this inhumanity. When the officer delivers his nostalgic account of the great show-executions of olden times, and in his enthusiasm embraces the traveller, the latter looks over his shoulder in great embarrassment, and sees the greedy quarrel between the soldier and the prisoner (still strapped on the torture machine) over the *Reisbrei* that has just been placed within reach of the latter's mouth:

Kaum merkte dies der Verurteilte, der sich vollständig erholt zu haben schien, als er mit der Zunge nach dem Brei zu schnappen begann. Der Soldat stiess ihn immer wieder weg, denn der Brei war wohl für eine spätere Zeit bestimmt, aber ungehörig war es jedenfalls auch, dass der Soldat mit seinen schmutzigen Händen hineingriff und vor dem gierigen Verurteilten davon ass (p. 112).

(No sooner had the condemned man, who seemed to have recovered completely, noticed this than he began to stretch out his tongue towards the rice mash. The soldier pushed him away time and time again, for the mash was, after all, intended for later, but, even so, it was improper that the soldier plunged his dirty hands in and ate from the rice in front of the ravenous prisoner.)

It is the scene as the traveller sees it. The *schien* ('seemed') must refer to him, as also the particles *wohl* ('after all') and *jedenfalls* ('even so'). And that curious judgment *ungehörig* ('improper')? These hands, befouled by the prisoner's vomit, that are stealing the tortured man's presumably last comfort, are doing something called 'unfitting' or 'improper'! This is not objectivity in the traveller, but inhumanity, timidity, cowardice, whether the tone is ironic or shocked. We recognise the same voice in that jeering comment, in the first paragraph of the story, about the prisoner's 'doglike devotion'.

Actually, however, not all the incidents involving soldier and prisoner are so unequivocally referred to the traveller's experience and filtered through his mind. When the officer is undressing, the playful quarrel between the two soldiers over the handkerchief takes place. It is enacted only before the traveller's eyes, it is true, as the officer is preoccupied with his preparations for his own execution. But there is here no explicit reference to the traveller's attitude:

So, half in jest, they quarrelled. Only when the officer was completely naked did they pay attention. Particularly the condemned man seemed to sense that some great reversal had taken place. What had happened to him was now happening to the officer. Perhaps it would continue thus to the very limit. Probably the foreign traveller had given the order for all this. This, then, was revenge. Without his having suffered to the end, he was going to be avenged to the end. A broad, soundless grin now appeared on his face and never disappeared from it (p. 117).

The thoughts of the 'condemned man' are given in free indirect speech, though much of the language, the epigrammatic form, is not his, but the interpreter's. Who is this interpreter? It is not impossible to imagine it to be the watching traveller who, though he has no access to the inner processes of the other man, can deduce them from his expressions. But the style is actually not like his, and above all there is that odd phrase 'and never disappeared from it', a phrase that anticipates what is to come; for we have seen the narrative generally does not go beyond the immediate and limited experience of the participant. This is also very unusual for the Kafka narrator. Yet only this 'spirit' would have the right to explode the rigid immediacy of the events, though, if one must attribute it to the narrator, it would seem that this whole passage is a momentary lapse on Kafka's part into a more conventional narrative form.

However, apart from one or two 'lapses' of this and similar kinds, the question whether an observation is narratorial or subjective is, for the purposes of interpretation, rather an idle one, because the narratorial statements or judgments are always identical with what the traveller would perceive or think. Not only does the 'narrator', this imaginary ghost, always stand by the shoulder of the traveller, he also utters the same sort of judgments. The syntactical difference is not a difference of interpretation, and it is almost useless merely to point out where, syntactically, he exerts his presence over and above the participants. For the narrator never supplies a distinctive view on events, never corrects or enlarges the scope of the traveller, never in fact provides us with an authoritative key that will unlock the mysteries of events and exhibit an explicit meaning.

All the same, the narrator is not functionless. In the first place, he has a negative importance. If the story were presented as a first-person narrative, that is, as a direct report given by the traveller, its meaning would be radically altered. For it would appear as a memory, and hence would evoke a later time, when the traveller is able to contemplate and reflect upon the events narrated. This narrative method would therefore run the risk that attends all retrospective accounts, especially since it might suggest an outcome in which the traveller has come to terms with the dilemma and experiences narrated. It may be objected that Kafka wrote many first-person sketches and tales without falling victim to this risk. But all his first-person texts – among the most substantial are 'Der Riesenmaulwurf' ('The giant mole'), 'Investigations of a dog', 'Josefine die Sängerin' ('Josephine the singer') and 'The burrow' – describe a continuing and unfinished situation and dilemma, not a specific and concluded incident. They point not to a past, but to a present dilemma – and with the exception of 'The giant mole' (entitled by Kafka 'Der Dorfschullehrer', 'The village schoolmaster') all are told, very characteristically, in the present tense. The distinct and rounded event recounted in 'In the penal colony' could not tolerate this form, and Kafka had to adopt a different narrative perspective in order to reconcile the historical, complete event with the irresolution and questioning that belong to the present and explain the curiously inconclusive ending of this story.

As to the positive function of Kafka's narrator in this story, we have already seen that he as it were guarantees the 'truth' of his story, i.e. he is the poetic medium that invites us, allows us, to suspend disbelief and enter the world of his fiction. But it is clear that his relationship with the traveller differs from that with the other characters, for in regard to him he can inform us of complex mental processes. Repeatedly we are told that the actions, gestures, words of the other characters 'seemed' to mean this or that (to the traveller). But no gestures can tell us the traveller was 'determined' not to intervene (e.g. over the officer's preparations to immolate himself). If the officer is interpreted with an 'as if', we need no such locutions for the traveller, but are told he 'wanted', 'intended'. If a statement is made about the officer, the description of his gestures immediately demonstrates the grounds on which such a statement was made; and sometimes the same procedure seems to be used for the traveller: 'The traveller wanted to prevent the officer from seeing his face and looked aimlessly about him. The officer believed he was looking at the emptiness of the valley; so he seized his hands, moved round him in order to capture his gaze, and asked...' (p. 112). But there are many other occasions on which the traveller's feelings are directly communicated, and especially through free indirect speech. For instance, when the officer appeals for his sympathy for what the traveller calls 'the injustice of the proceedings and the inhumanity of the execution', a paragraph that begins 'the traveller pondered' gives in free indirect speech the arguments in his mind for and against taking sides and his surprise that he should even be tempted to intervene, since, as he says to himself, 'the intention behind his journey was to see – and in no sense to change the legal constitution of a foreign country, for example' (p. 109). None of this could be deduced from his behaviour. Or again, after the officer's final appeal, and before the traveller tells him he will report his disapproval of the system to the commandant: 'The answer which he was going to give had been unambiguously clear from the very outset; he had experienced too much in his life for there to be any room for hesitation now; he was basically honest and fearless. But nevertheless, as he looked at the soldier and the condemned man, he hesitated for a split second' (p. 116). The narrator is able to tell us, through the medium of free indirect speech, with what

73

clichés the traveller has to bolster up his resolution to utter a private protest to the commandant and forsake his cherished detachment.

This identity between narrator and hero is not unusual in narrative literature. It is the basic *Erzählhaltung* of Thomas Mann's *Death in Venice*. Here, not only is the narrator glued to the shoulder of Aschenbach and no more able than his hero to penetrate the secrets of the other characters, but also his judgments scarcely vary from those we can imagine arising in the character's mind had he survived. His retrospective account of the earlier life and ancestry of his hero is identical with Aschenbach's own references and judgments. But there is also something quite distinct in Kafka's narrator. For there is much that he does *not* tell us, motives and purposes that are clouded, especially what is going on in the traveller's head in his headlong flight from the colony, and of course anything about his past.

One psychological 'explanation' for this reticence on the part of the narrator may be suggested. It does communicate to us the unwillingness of the traveller to recognise or acknowledge his own motives, and thus it would illustrate in another form that near-identity of narrator and traveller that has been found elsewhere. But there is reticence with respect to other matters that does not yield to a psychological explanation, for instance, the lack of information about the traveller's past or about his purpose in attending the execution. He himself gives us some explanations, usually in the form of reported thoughts, but we can sometimes doubt his veracity, since he is usually trying to justify himself, perhaps delude himself. There is, I believe, a more general explanation, that links up with the same phenomenon in other works, and notably in *Das Schloss* (*The castle*), for here too we are left in ignorance of the true motives of K. and his past, and his actual statements are evidently very often misleading (he is no surveyor, he has no assistants, he is not married, though he makes these claims). It would seem that in 'In the penal colony', in contrast to the earlier tales, 'The judgment' and *The metamorphosis*, and also to *The trial*, Kafka deliberately blots out the traveller's past, his social connexions, his psychological motives, and discourages us thereby from looking for concrete motives and reactions, social or psychological, in relation to his behaviour. He does not denude him of all qualities, for he allows him a certain moral proclivity, not very marked, which we can call humanitarian, liberal, enlightened. Apart from this we know of nothing, except that he is a traveller, by his own definition one who travels to 'see' the world and is determined, if it is at all possible, to remain a detached observer. Thus, Kafka is able to eliminate from his story any personal, subjective responses on the traveller's part, just as in the officer he presents a man whose individuality has become submerged in his function of judge and executioner. The contest between reflexion and intervention is thus reduced to essentials, and we are not allowed to adduce psychological or social conditions to justify the traveller's behaviour – these would belong to the sort of 'alibi' that Sartre claimed we, in our existential freedom, must refuse to have recourse to when making moral decisions.

What conclusions may we draw from this review of the narrative perspective in regard to interpretation? There can be no doubt that the traveller is seen from inside and is the medium through which we see and experience the scene and events, while the officer is seen from outside. Clearly the officer is the more vivid of the two main characters, his actions are what we observe, his death is a sort of climax. The traveller wishes to be an observer, as it were indistinguishable in the background. But, as we have seen, the officer uses his utmost exertions to force this spectator to become a witness, and in so doing forces the conflict in the mind of the traveller into the mental foreground, the context which gives the actions and arguments of the officer their significance.

This narrative situation, in its fullness, does not permit us to consider the officer to be the 'hero' of 'In the penal colony'. The officer has anxieties, practical worries about the future of the system and machine to which he is devoted. But he *has* no problem; he *is* a problem, to the traveller. His faith and loyalty know no uncertainties, no doubts; there is nothing tragic about him. Rather, everything suggests that he is not simply, because of the narrative perspective, inaccessible to our deeper knowledge, but actually deprived of deeper resonances. He appears more and more as a monomaniac, with the slyness of such. So entirely is he pledged to an unjust law and an inhuman penal system that he meets the traveller's astonished enquiries only with irritation, as they hinder his entranced explanation of his torture machine (pp. 102–4). His victims are not human beings to him, but merely part of the penal apparatus. All the procedures established by the old commandant are for him *selbstverständlich* (self-evident), and when he acknowledges his faith in the universality of the commandant's attributes, his face becomes rigid, *starr* (p. 103). Thus, when he fails to win the traveller's support and recognises that his machine and system are doomed, his decision to subject himself to the power of the machine is condoned by the traveller as 'right'. It *is* a logical decision for a monomaniac who has identified himself with a machine and a system. The calm resolution that the traveller detects in his dead face – 'his gaze expressed calmness and conviction' (p. 121) – expresses not only moral courage but also the officer's incapacity for experience, for thought.

On the other hand, all that the officer does and stands for provides the traveller with problems. It is he who responds, puzzles, questions, half-sympathises, rejects, and who has to wrestle with a great decision. The mental movement, the moral struggle belong to the traveller, as the external incident and the speech belong to the officer (and, to a slighter extent, the soldiers). The narrative perspective ensures that we are literally *pre*occupied with the traveller, even before the nature of his problem has become defined. What happens to the others, the officer and the condemned man, comes to us through the traveller's awareness; through him we are imaginatively and morally engrossed in the story. The actions of the others are calculable, logical, foreseeable, and there is nothing that might alter their direction. But the responses of the traveller are not foreseeable, and hold us, throughout, in suspense, even at the very end. From the moment when, after his early indifference, we are told that 'The traveller was already a little won over to the machine' (p. 102), it is his attitude, his hesitancies, his rapt attention, his evasions and resolves that constitute the theme of the story.

It is necessary, therefore, that the end of 'In the penal colony' must bring us face to face with the traveller's experience, not leave us immersed in the officer's. But, it may be argued, Kafka himself did not seem very satisfied with his own ending, and projected two other endings. Is it not legitimate to doubt the aesthetic validity of the published ending? Yes, another ending might have been possible. But both the other, rejected endings also concerned themselves with the traveller, with his conclusions, and show Kafka still firmly attached to what seems to me to be the central issue.[7] Certainly there is nothing heroic about this ending, and it clears nothing up. The traveller, calling in at the tea house to see (apparently without much hope) what he will discover there, simply finds his puzzles multiplied. The habitués dispirited labourers, show no symptoms of revolt against the new regime, as the officer had promised, and the prophecy on the tombstone of the old commandant raises only sceptical looks. Even to read the tiny letters of the inscription the traveller has to debase himself by kneeling. (Why should so many critics consider kneeling must inevitably suggest religious worship? We kneel for other and often shameful reasons, too.) But the traveller has a way out of his puzzles. He can retain his role as a traveller, an onlooker, by escaping. The ship will rescue him from any necessity of intervening, and fleeing, he refuses to take with him those who would, by their mere existence, infect his own sheltered world with their problem and perpetuate his consciousness of failure.

Why is it most readers find this ending unsatisfactory and some think it a mistake? I believe it is because we have been led, in the tradition of story-telling, to expect finality, a decisive conclusion to a story, that will make its total structure understandable and utter a comprehensive judgment upon the main characters – whether this judgment be one of praise or condemnation. Such an ending Kafka himself provides in 'The judgment' and 'The metamorphosis' and sketches one for *The trial* too; in each case the uncertainties tormenting the 'hero' end with the annihilation of the uncomprehending victim. This tragic ending reflects back upon the incidents of the story and the attitude of the main character, and seems to suggest that his unconsciousness of guilt, his unawareness of the seriousness of his predicament, is a deep fault in him. 'In the penal colony' can provide a conclusive ending of this kind for the officer, whose death is thoroughly commensurate with his devotion and service; but not for the traveller. For him, caught between two conflicting ideologies both of which reveal their inhumanity, there is no finality available. This is the bitter lesson of the ending, that a conclusion is not available, only an evasion that merely perpetuates the doubts and problems that the incidents of the story have given rise to. And perhaps this is the maturity of this story, that it has an ending that does not clear up the meaning but prolongs the painful and humiliating uncertainty. This is perhaps morally unsatisfactory but it is truer to the experience of the story than would be a conclusive ending, and our aesthetic response must adjust itself to this truth.

THE TRAVELLER AND THE 'RELIGIOUS ALLEGORY'

How does the narrative perspective, as analysed above, effect the interpretation of 'In the penal colony' as a religious allegory?

The crudest result is a direct challenge to its validity in all its modifications. The religious status of the incidents of the story rests overwhelmingly on what the officer says and does and devises, and lacks any confirmation from the narrator or any other character. It is the officer who elevates his service to the torture machine to the rank of a holy ritual; it is he who, through his decision to immolate himself on the machine, deliberately provokes a comparison with the sacrifice of Christ on the Cross. It is his devotion to the old commandant, his strict observance of the old law, his belief in the Second Coming, that fortify these symbolic meanings. He uses the word 'commandment' in place of 'law', he invokes the concept of original and universal sin when he justifies his arbitrary power as judge–executioner and the brutal savagery of the penalty he imposes with his assertion 'guilt is always indubitable' (p. 104). It is only he who discerns a transfiguration in his victims, when after six hours of torture they begin to understand their sentence as it is being engraved upon their flesh, until after a further six hours of torture they are transfixed. Again, there is no confirmation of this from any quarter, and in the officer's case the traveller sees no such transfiguration.

It is clear that the reader must pay close attention to what the officer says and claims. But there is no reason for it to be taken as more than the evidence, the faith, of a particular character, from whom we are kept throughout at a distance, a critical distance. Yet it would seem that the whole religious interpretation has been built on the assumption that a character's opinions are to be understood as the author's.

To clarify my criticism, I will take a passage from Malcolm Pasley, certainly not an imperceptive or uninformed exegete. In his essay 'In the penal colony', Pasley writes of 'the godlike aura that invests the dead commandant' and adds: 'We are reminded of Jahveh as He is portrayed in the Book of Exodus.' The officer with his briefcase of holographs of the commandant 'calls up the figure of Moses'. The officer's hand-washing before he handles these papers 'reminds us forcibly of Jewish religious practices', as does the use of the word 'Gebot' for the law.[8] Now, Pasley is quite right, all these words and actions, like others, do conjure up religious analogies. They are meant to do so. They show the officer's interpretation of his functions and faith. But why take that *salto mortale* and assert that all these analogies convince us or reveal the author's own meaning?

There are contexts in which they might have this status, but also they might just as easily indicate a vicious or misguided parody of faith, a sublime or horrible delusion created to justify devilish cruelty. We have no narratorial confirmation of the truth or holiness of the officer's words and behaviour, and this is the first reason for refusing to equate the meaning of the story with the officer's faith. The only other grounds are those immanent in the story itself, the officer's reliability, credibility, as a witness, the inner consistency of his attitude, the conformity of events with his words, and, too, the response of the traveller.

There is no simple and explicit answer to our question. But we, with the traveller, are constantly made aware of the officer's unreliability, morally and in regard to the truth. All that he says is intended to persuade and win over the traveller. He misrepresents the attitude of the commandant, shows evident malice in the description of the latter's entourage, and his suggestions to the traveller become more and more fantastic and crazy. Still worse, he remains throughout completely callous towards the sufferings of his victims and utterly absorbed in the process and technique of torture. He worships the old commandant as the author of this penal system. I do not understand how this commandant and his representative, the officer, can be taken by a reader to be analogous to Jehovah or to Christ, for their only principle is punishment of the most savage sort. Why should we accept the officer's religious analogies as bearing the affirmation of the author, why should we see in him anything but a dehumanised fixation on cruelty, that in the end declares itself obsolete? – a view that the circle round the new commandant holds, if we are to believe the officer, and a conclusion the traveller comes to. Pasley refers in his essay to several items in Dostoevsky's *Memoirs from the house of the dead* that find parallels in 'In the penal colony'; it is surprising that he does not refer to those lines in which Dostoevsky writes of the brutalising effect of absolute authority upon the prison officers who wield it.

However, to stay at such a conclusion would not be enough, and it is precisely the narrative function of the traveller that creates a further dimension. For it is the traveller's attention, his watchfulness and his questions, that suggest there is some deeper mystery here, in the machine, in the devotion of the officer, in his pious veneration for the indecipherable scribble on the old commandant's papers, and above all, in his determination to accept the consequences of his faith and intrepidly to sacrifice himself to it. The traveller's attentiveness wins ours, and is only intensified by his doubts. After his early indifference he is 'a little won over to the torture machine', and he begins to ask questions. We are told by the narrator that the information he gets, the answers, do not satisfy him, but he remains engaged. And actually, the questions he does not ask seem indirectly to confirm some of the officer's views. For instance, after he has interrupted the officer's enthusiastic description of the machine with his question 'what does the sentence say?' (p. 103), the officer, somewhat uneasily, proceeds to explain that the sentence is incised upon the body of the condemned man and, as it were incidentally, speaks of the crime and punishment in terms that relate to the religious concepts of sin and expiation: 'The commandment which he has transgressed is written by the harrow onto the body of the condemned man.' After the traveller casts a glance at the condemned man, who evidently does not understand a word, there comes: 'The traveller had wanted to ask many questions but, faced as he was by the man, he only asked: "Does he know his sentence?"' It is a pertinent and humane question, but it lets the astonishing claims hidden in the words 'commandment' and 'transgress' pass without challenge. These terms have frequently been adduced as revealing the religious meaning immanent in this penal colony, and, as I have already pointed out, such an interpretation needs more justification than is provided by the mere words of the officer. But the fact that the traveller does not challenge them may seem to give them greater credibility.

However, there is another and more persuasive explanation

for this reserve of the traveller. While his curiosity is aroused, and replaces his first indifference or distaste, his sceptical and critical attitude never leaves him. He is shocked at the procedure of this court martial, as described by the officer, and thinks of the latter as a 'limited mind', not capable of adapting himself to a changing world (p. 105). He can hardly repress his horror at times, for instance when the officer, describing the means by which the victim's blood is channelled into a gutter, makes an expressive gesture with his cupped hands (p. 106). In his mind, we are told, he is convinced of 'the injustice of the proceedings and the inhumanity of the execution' (p. 109). When the officer presses him to declare his sympathy, we are told that his answer is not in question, he is 'an opponent of this procedure' and intends to report his opinion to the commandant. He acknowledges the 'honest conviction' of the officer, but his conviction cannot be shaken by personal sympathy (p. 116). To justify his refusal to intervene in the self-immolation of the officer, he argues that he has 'no right' to interfere and that the officer, from his own point of view, is acting 'quite rightly' (p. 119). In all this, there is no suggestion that the traveller in any way sympathises with or reveres the beliefs, the system that the officer worships.

How, then, does the traveller's attitude influence the readers' view of the religious meanings suggested by the officer and his sacrificial death? Clearly he remains sceptical, but at the same time strangely impressed. Can we find any comprehensive interpretation that would cover all the data? To accept the officer's own pretensions is not permissible, as I have argued, despite the chorus of critics who seem to me to misread with great determination. But yet, we cannot dismiss the religious dimension as mere craziness, since it has something impressive about it. What I believe so deeply and ambiguously shakes the traveller is the spectacle of a disturbing *parody* of religious faith, a parody, that is, that genuinely appropriates the features of religious belief but for a profoundly unchristian, unreligious object. To his alarm, amazement, and dismay, the traveller sees a man devoted to inhuman cruelty who attributes to the founder of this system powers and authority that are akin to those of God. The devotion of this man even to the most trivial aspect of the penal system claims the dignity of religious faith, his service to the torture of his victims is exalted by a visionary fantasy of some transfiguration that is supposed to dawn in the midst of the tortures, and when put to the test, he voluntarily submits to torture and death, a sort of image of the Son of God. The urbane, humanitarian traveller does not merely look on this with astonishment and distaste. He also must see in it something that his own pledges lack, the absolute devotion – 'absolute for death' – that only lives by faith and dies for the faith. For all his attachment to his civilised values, it is no wonder that the traveller is confused, overwhelmed, and daunted by what he observes.

Why are we, the readers, unable whole-heartedly to endorse the humane values of the traveller? It cannot be because of the officer's ridicule of the humanitarian motives of the commandant and his ladies, since we can easily recognise the bias and malice in it. Nor can we find reasons for abjuring the humanitarian values of the traveller in general, or for believing that the officer's creed is preferable – the narrator, as Thieberger writes, seems to be 'on the side of' the traveller. Yet we distrust the traveller and run no danger of finding in him an alternative to the officer. Why?

The fundamental reason is, I believe, the equivocal role he plays, from which his evasions and failure necessarily flow. Some critics have translated Kafka's word for him, *der Reisende*, by 'the explorer', but this is a serious misunderstanding. An explorer is a man with a precise purpose, determined to reach some goal, some specific knowledge, and usually equipped with the technique and expertise required to make his discoveries. A traveller is much more indeterminate, perhaps a sightseer on the look-out for anything curious, perhaps a philosophical observer, like Graf Keyserling. The explorer will disregard anything that might distract him from his purpose, the traveller hopes to find his purposes in the distractions. Perhaps this mistranslation (used by Gray) was induced by the description of the traveller as 'a great explorer of the Western world, a man committed to scrutinising the legal procedures in all countries' (p. 113). But these words are merely imputed to the new commandant by the officer, who thus ridicules his enemy's alleged inclination to inflate the significance of favourable testimony. The traveller himself explicitly denies any such function or authority; the commandant knows, he tells the officer, that he is 'no authority on legal procedures' (p. 113). No, he is a traveller, a visitor, a passer-by, who observes with some curiosity, some sympathy, some distaste, who carries with him his own civilised, enlightened, tolerant persuasions, but does not get involved; one might almost say, who maintains his civilised tolerance by virtue of not getting involved.

This is the traveller's role, and in many circumstances it can be an unexceptionable attitude. But what he sees in the penal colony does not tolerate the equanimity of the observer; he himself can scarcely maintain his role, is seduced towards fascination by the horror, assailed by the officer's importuning on the one hand and on the other his own shocked feelings, determined not to intervene until the catastrophe is irremediable, and fleeing in a tangle of confused shame. The story does not demonstrate that the traveller's humane principles are wrong; it demonstrates that they are only principles, since in the test of this experience he fails to act upon them – that is, in an experience in which the rational and humane observer, however high-minded, insofar as he remains an observer, is false to his humanism.[9]

This betrayal is repeatedly evident. It occurs notably with regard to the two soldiers, the guard and the condemned man. They appear to him throughout as sub-human, reduced to clown-like gestures. He seems to have no interest in the fate of the condemned man, except in his dissatisfaction with the legal procedure, and does not think of intervening on his behalf. When he is laid on the machine and subjected to the torture of the harrow, the traveller simply watches. When pressed by the officer, the traveller ultimately decides that he will inform the commandant of his disapproval of the procedure. Yet, before he tells the officer of his decision, he hesitates for a moment: 'But nevertheless, as he looked at the soldier and the condemned man, he hesitated for a split second' (p. 116). His thought is not spelled out, but I cannot think of any other grounds for hesitation than the questions arising in his mind, 'Are these sub-human types really worthy of a better treatment, do they justify the loss of my equanimity?'

Throughout, we find the traveller discovering reasons for refusing to intervene, even to judge. As the disproportion between the soldier's misdemeanour and his punishment becomes clear to him, he allays his troubled conscience with the reminder that this is, after all, a 'penal colony' under military administration, and sets his hope on the reforms that the new commandant may be expected to introduce (p. 105). A little later, in a long passage of free indirect speech, he persuades himself that a stranger is incompetent to judge the institutions of a foreign people. Also, he was travelling 'only to see' and not with the intention of altering foreign legal procedures. Yet he admits the situation in which he was placed was 'seductive', since the injustice and inhumanity in this case were 'undoubted', and the commandant had sent him to view the execution apparently with the object of receiving his opinion on it. The argument is fair enough, but the traveller leaves it in the balance. When, a little later, the officer graphically describes to him the powerful effect that the slightest suggestion of disapproval will have, the traveller seizes with relief on this theme, so much more manageable than the real question, and explains that, after all, his opinion, whatever it might be, is not important, a mere private opinion that will not influence the commandant at all (p. 113). But the officer will not accept his plea of impotence, and presses him to support him against the commandant. Only now does the traveller decide, and say openly, that he is 'an opponent of this procedure', though he hastens to add that, out of respect for the 'honest conviction' of the officer, he will report his opinion to the commandant only privately and not stay long enough to be drawn into more public statements (116–17). This is the climax of his commitment; a very muffled and subdued one, that shows much more consideration for the officer's feelings than for the life of the condemned soldier.

But there is still another test for the traveller. The officer proceeds to strip, and the traveller understands that he intends to die on the doomed death-machine. He recognises the logic of this decision, and tells himself 'he had no right to hinder the officer in any way' (p. 119). He watches the preparations and the behaviour of the two soldiers who zealously act as assistants, determined not to intervene. We can imagine he is under great tension, but he expresses it only by his fury with the busy and keen attention of the two soldiers, whom he orders to go away, while he will remain there watching the tortured officer. Only when the traveller notices that the machine is breaking up, that things are not following their due and expected course, does he begin to feel he must intervene; he bends over the harrow, and finds that the points are penetrating deep into the flesh; he realises 'that was in no sense a torture such as the officer had in mind; that was unmitigated murder' (121). Now he wants to intervene, but it is too late; he cannot even get the two soldiers to help him to release the impaled body. Once again, the traveller has failed to act, when the natural, spontaneous instinct to help his fellow creature has been too feeble to assert itself, and has allowed itself to be smothered by complex reflexions about what was right or logical or prudent or correct. Throughout he has been in the presence of a man pledged to abominable cruelty and inhuman authority, who carries out his revolting duties with a selfless devotion, raising them in his mind to the level of religious observance; while the traveller, pledged in principle to justice and humanity and never inclining to approve the savage authoritarianism of the officer's cult, fails at every stage to act in accordance with his own principles when

86

the circumstances require this, and even feels a certain awe before the unqualified devotion the other displays.

What does he conclude? We learn little from his words, more perhaps from his silence. As he views the tea house, we are told that it provokes in him something like 'a historical memory' and that he 'felt the might of earlier times' (p. 122). I suppose we are meant to understand that these impressions confirm that left in his mind by the officer's faith and dedication unto death. But otherwise the traveller now seems numb and dumb, only intent on fleeing from the colony and enacting, as he leaves, one further betrayal – forcibly preventing the two soldiers from joining him. His will not to be involved has become a necessity for him, since it is only this role that can make this failure bearable.

'In the penal colony' occupies an important place in Kafka's *oeuvre*. It is the first completed work in which he overcame the direct relationship between his personal life and his artefact that we find in 'The judgment' and 'The metamorphosis', which so vividly mirror his personal relationship with his father. But this means not only that there is no prominent or even significant reference to his private life in this new work but, more important still, it is not an allegory in any precise sense of the term, but a tale that embodies in a concrete form a whole group of experiences and thoughts. We cannot look for an original of either of the principal figures, for in their concrete abstractness they reflect numerous situations of personal and social life. The work seems to me to show a distinct maturing of Kafka's art, particularly since it is not related to one specific and limited source.

It is not, for that, detached from the world about him, and I am surprised that so little attention has been paid by critics to the hidden reference within it to the European war that, in the few weeks before 'In the penal colony' was written (October 1914), had transformed the world and the mental climate around him. Gray mentions the impact of the war but does not define it. But surely Kafka, whose explicit references to the war are few and reserved, must have felt himself implicated in that furious reorientation that swept over German intellectual life and brought so many leaders of humane and enlightened thought to proclaim their impassioned support of the war, of German authoritarianism, German faith, the German militaristic ethos, as against the allegedly enfeebled and decadent forces of enlightenment, humanitarianism, and democracy. This movement seized not only writers like Thomas Mann, Rilke and Hofmannsthal, including Jews like Friedrich Gundolf and Karl Wolfskehl and Kafka's friend Max Brod; it was not restricted to writers and artists but embraced all reflective men. Philosophers like Simmel and Scheler, theologians like Eucken and Natorp, all strove to justify and exalt the militaristic ethos and the national will to 'rescue' culture and the spirit by conquest, a sacred duty to which all other values must be sacrificed.[10]

Kafka did not join in this chorus, nor did he join the few neutral voices or share the naive faith in democracy of a Heinrich Mann. Without committing himself he remained, so far as we can judge from his rare references to the war and the great political issues, suspended between the different views in a 'neither-nor'. His diary entries illustrate this. After mentioning a great military parade in Prague he writes of himself (6 August 1914) as 'an empty vessel' and goes on: 'I discover in myself nothing but pettiness, indecision, envy and hatred towards the combatants on whom I passionately wish everything bad.' And expressing his distaste for the accompanying patriotic demonstrations, especially the loud enthusiasm of 'Jewish business people', he characterises his own painful detachment with: 'I stand alongside with my evil eye.' On 13 September Kafka mentions his grief and fear over reported Austrian defeats, but adds: 'The thought patterns which have to do with the war are of that tormenting kind which consume my substance in so many ways, just like the old anxieties about F. [Felice Bauer].'[11] To this dilemma, this unreconciled conflict between feelings and thoughts, this distaste for himself and self-denigration that accompanies the 'evil eye' with which he observes the passionate dedication of the believers, it seems to me 'In the penal colony' bears witness.

I am not suggesting that the 'real' theme of the work is the contemporary intellectual controversy about the war. The story contains no suggestion of national conflict, nor is there any implication that human rights and humanitarianism or authoritarianism and militarism are to be identified with one nation or another. Kafka presents us with a general moral problem that the war raised in its bluntest form. The traveller is the modern enlightened man, the man of 'Geist', whose distinction it is to have detached himself from action and material interests, from 'the ranks of the death-dealers', and whose calamity it is, too. For if reflexion rescues him from the partisanship of action, it also enfeebles dedication and spontaneity. And when an emergency occurs, when a choice between opposing actions becomes imperative, Kafka's traveller refuses to sacrifice his principles to a morality they condemn but at the same time, shrinking from intervening with actions that conform to his principles, also fails to feel intensely, and act upon, those natural human responses that are the ground and justification of these principles. He finds a third way that seems to him to preserve his principles and his character as an enlightened man of reflexion, the way of flight from the circumstances that made a choice necessary. The numbness that descends on him at the end, the blind panic of his flight, point only too clearly to his awareness of self-betrayal. There is no hero of 'In the penal colony', certainly the traveller is no hero; but the theme is embodied in him just as the narrative perspective is aligned to his viewpoint. What becomes of him is the important thing. If the ending is morally inconclusive, if it does not round off the story and resolve the problems it has set, it shows us something equally important, since its inconclusiveness tells us that these are problems that are not settled but still have to be wrestled with.

4 · THE BREAKDOWN OF THE IMPERSONAL NARRATOR: 'BLUMFELD, AN ELDERLY BACHELOR'

('Blumfeld, ein älterer Junggeselle')

A cursory survey of the stories that belong to Kafka's later years, after the writing of 'In the penal colony' in 1914, shows a marked predilection for a personal narrator who is either the chief participant or a modest associate, a bystander, who describes and reflects upon the main character and events. To the first group belong 'Eine kleine Frau' ('A little woman', 1923) and 'The village schoolmaster' (1914–15) and most of the animal pieces, 'Ein Bericht für eine Akademie' ('Report for an academy', 1917), 'Investigations of a dog' (1922) and 'The burrow' (1923), to the second 'Building the Chinese wall' (1917) and 'Josephine the singer or the nation of mice' (1924). Many of the later parables also are told in the first person as events or situations involving the teller, like 'Die Brücke' ('The bridge', 1916), 'Heimkehr' ('Homecoming', 1920) and 'Gibs Auf!' ('Give it up', 1922).

The impersonal narrator of the early tales is not completely or abruptly abandoned, nor was it always used in Kafka's early writing. Many of the separate incidents in *Observation* (1913), that embodied material from earlier years, were written in the first person and of the later pieces several are still in the impersonal form, such as Das Schweigen der Sirenen ('The silence of the sirens', 1917), 'Der Jäger Gracchus' ('The huntsman Gracchus', 1917) and 'Erstes Leid' ('First grief', 1922). In some of these however the message is borne on the direct speech of the main character and the narrator's function is reduced to a minimum, as is also the case in 'Kleine Fabel' ('Little fable', 1922). Two of the best-known and weightiest of the parables, 'The emperor's message' and 'Before the law', both of which are cast in the form of an impersonal narrative and were published by Kafka in *A country doctor* (1919), were abstracted by Kafka from earlier texts (respectively 'Building the Chinese wall' and *The trial*, 1914) and in their original context each is put forward by a person (the narrator or a character) to illustrate a view he is urging or suggesting. If there is no clear and decisive change of narrative form in the later stories, we cannot fail to observe a fairly marked preference for a specified personal narrator in them, sufficiently marked and in sufficiently significant stories for this form to be considered an important feature of the later Kafka. We have to limit this conclusion to the shorter tales, for Kafka adopted for all three novels the impersonal narrator, and while *America* and *The trial* belong to the years before 1915, most of *The castle* was written during 1922.

These later stories will be discussed in the later chapters of this study. As a preliminary, however, there are two stories of an intermediate character to which this and the following chapter are devoted, 'Blumfeld, an elderly bachelor' (1915) and 'Ein Hungerkünstler' ('A hunger artist', 1922). These are usually discussed as if their narrators conformed to the type of impersonal narrator we know in Kafka's early stories. But I believe it can be shown that they demonstrate, in quite different ways, peculiar features that may throw light on Kafka's growing preference for the personal, identifiable story-teller. Particularly in the first of these, 'Blumfeld', we can detect a subtle disintegration of that curious impersonal narrator that Kafka has earlier used with such skill, the narrator who mainly immerses himself in the consciousness of the chief character and emerges, though rarely, chiefly as an independent agent of the narrative structure. 'Blumfeld, an elderly bachelor', though only a fragment, is particularly interesting since this structural disintegration seems to have taken place without any conscious intention on Kafka's part. 'A hunger artist', to which chapter 5 is devoted, shows by contrast a conscious break with Kafka's earlier method, the adoption of a personal narrator, though still, and much to the confusion of critics, this fictitious narrator is not explicitly identified.

The opening of 'Blumfeld' reminds one of that of 'The judgment'; an apparently conventional, artless narratorial opening leads immediately into the mazy jungle of an inner monologue out of which the narrator can scarcely emerge. The little work is too much of a fragment to encourage much effort at interpretation. It consists of two episodes or chapters. In the first Blumfeld, a cranky, lonely bachelor, is coming home from the office wishing he had some companionship to welcome him at home, a pet dog perhaps, though he dreads the fuss and trouble a pet might cause him. On this day he receives the strange visitation of a pair of bouncing balls, that dance him attendance in his flat. Irritated by their irrepressible tap-tap, he spends an unhappy and restless night, but in the morning manages to shut them up in a cupboard. On his way to work he despatches the landlady's son to take charge of the unwelcome visitors. In the second chapter Blumfeld arrives at his office, where he shows himself to be a surly, opinionated and tyrannical manager, at war with his boss and his juniors, full of self-importance, spite and suspicion. That is all. Obviously there is here a grotesque satire of the dehumanising routine of office work and managerial authority, enhanced in Blumfeld's case by his crabbed bachelordom, his crushing obtuseness, his incapacity to give affection to others, his lack of any generous feeling or impulse. His deepest longing is for a pet who will give him devotion but not require any tending, any affection, so that he does not recognise that the dancing balls are in fact exactly what he wanted. But I do not think the fragment reads as satire in any serious sense. It is a grotesque, a fantasy on the theme of bachelorhood. Perhaps Kafka was thinking of the lonely loveless old age he himself, with his inhibitions, might have to suffer, but if so there is more than a touch of Mephistopheles' mocking response to Martha in Goethe's *Faust*, when she warns him of the fate of bachelors: 'with horror do I see that from afar'.[1] But I am concerned here only with the narrative method.

The opening is traditional:

Blumfeld, ein älterer Junggeselle, stieg eines Abends zu seiner Wohnung hinauf, was eine mühselige Arbeit war, denn er wohnte im sechsten Stock.

(Blumfeld, an elderly bachelor, climbed one evening up to his flat, which was a wearisome business as he lived on the sixth floor.)

This is normal straight narrative in which the impersonal narrator informs us what Blumfeld's status is and where he lives and, using the past tense, indicates that we are to hear a story told retrospectively. The only curiosity is the slightly clumsy syntax of *was eine mühselige Arbeit war*; it sounds colloquial rather than literary and suggests, perhaps, that this phrase forms in Blumfeld's mind rather than a narrator's.

The next sentence actually does tell us what Blumfeld is thinking, though the form is still narratorial, since the thoughts are introduced by *er dachte* and are given in the subjunctive mood, that distinguishes the thoughts sharply from the narratorial account:

Während des Hinaufsteigens dachte er, wie öfters in der letzten Zeit, daran, dass dieses vollständig einsame Leben recht lästig sei, dass er jetzt diese sechs Stockwerke förmlich im Geheimen hinaufsteigen müsse, um oben in seinen leeren Zimmern anzukommen, dort wieder förmlich im Geheimen den Schlafrock anzuziehen, die Pfeife anzustecken, in der französischen Zeitschrift, die er schon seit Jahren abonniert hatte, ein wenig zu lesen, dazu an einem von ihm selbst bereiteten Kirschenschnaps zu nippen und schliesslich nach einer halben Stunde zu Bett zu gehn, nicht ohne vorher das Bettzeug vollständig umordnen zu müssen, das die jeder Belehrung unzugängliche Bedienerin immer nach ihrer Laune hinwarf. Irgendein Begleiter, irgendein Zuschauer für diese Tätigkeiten wäre Blumfeld sehr willkommen gewesen. Er hatte schon überlegt, ob er sich nicht einen kleinen Hund anschaffen solle.

(As he was climbing up the stairs, he thought, as so often of late, that this entirely lonely life was really a great burden, that he now had to climb up these six floors in what amounted to complete secrecy in order to arrive up there at his empty rooms where, again in what amounted to complete secrecy, he would put on his dressing gown, light his pipe, browse a little in the French magazine to which he had subscribed for years, while sipping at his home made cherry brandy, finally going to bed after half an hour, but not without previously having completely to rearrange the bedclothes which the cleaning woman, who was impervious to all instruction, threw down as it suited her. Any companion, any spectator at these activities would have been welcome to Blumfeld. He had already wondered if he should not acquire a small dog.)

The account seems perhaps disarmingly simple and clear, at least syntactically. But there are small jolts that disturb the placid surface of the narrator's account. The reader grows fully suspicious, perhaps, when he reads that Blumfeld's daily help is *jeder Belehrung unzugängliche* and makes the bed *nach ihrer Laune*, for these phrases express Blumfeld's irritation and are not narratorial. If we return to the beginning we see that this supposed indirect speech (*ratio obliqua*) is full of 'quotations' from Blumfeld – like the emphatic *vollständig einsame Leben* in place of the simple *einsame Leben*; or the repetition of the colloquial *förmlich im Geheimen* with its exaggeration; or the statement that *any* companion would be welcome (the dancing balls soon prove this to be Blumfeld's thought, not the narrator's); or the rather pallid expression *sehr willkommen*, feeble and rather pedantic, that would be rather inept for a narrator to use, but if Blumfeld's own term is highly characteristic of his cautious, reserved personality. Even the great length of this central sentence thus comes to have meaning, since it interprets the dogged pedantry of the character.

Readers familiar with Kafka's work will not be surprised at this passage. It is another example of what we have seen in earlier chapters, that the narrator aligns himself with the main character and sees things from his angle and with his preconceptions. But now even the experienced Kafka reader receives a shock. The final sentence *Er hatte schon überlegt, ob . . .* prepares him for reported speech, and he is therefore not surprised to discover that the rest of the long paragraph and the whole succeeding paragraph present Blumfeld's reflexions. But there comes something new.

Without warning the character's reflexions are now given in the present indicative, in place of the past tense and subjunctive mood. That it is still reported speech is clear since Blumfeld is referred to throughout in the third person, but the normal syntax of reported speech, especially the normal sequence of tense that requires the past tense when the narrative is composed in the past tense is otherwise disregarded. Indeed, if we were to change the third person used for Blumfeld and the corresponding verbs into the first person and put these long passages within inverted commas, they would scarcely be different from direct speech. There can however be no doubt that we have here, and continuing throughout the fragment, a species of free indirect speech in which the present tense has taken the place of the past. Many indications confirm this. Throughout, words and phrases that are characteristically Blumfeld's recur and construct our image of his nature and way of thinking. 'Such an animal is amusing and above all grateful and loyal', reveals both Blumfeld's pedantry and his longing for unconditional devotion. He takes pleasure in the thought that the dog would be his exclusive possession. Stilted phrases like 'exceptional benefactor' are meaningful only if they are formed in his mind, not the narrator's, and it is his pedantry, a scrap of classical education, that appears when he thinks of fleas as 'the constant companions of dogs'. So, likewise, his bullying nature and self-complacency appear when the text speaks of his school-masterly strictness towards his daily help. The account is pitted with the verbs and particles that indicate an inner argument – *allerdings, doch, aber, dann, muss, will* etc. – a typical feature of free indirect speech.

There are one or two difficulties. Occasionally the past tense is used:

Flöhe, die standigen Begleiter der Hunde, würden sich einstellen. Waren aber einmal Flöhe da, dann war aber auch der Augenblick nicht mehr fern, an dem Blumfeld sein behagliches Zimmer dem Hund überlassen und ein anderes Zimmer suchen würde. Unreinlichkeit war aber nur ein Nachteil der Hunde, Hunde werden auch krank und Hundekrankheiten versteht doch eigentlich niemand.

(Fleas, the constant companions of dogs, would appear. But once there were fleas, then the moment was not far off when Blumfeld would have to abandon his comfortable room to the dog and look for another room. But dirtiness was only one disadvantage of dogs: dogs also fall ill, and nobody actually understands dogs' ailments.)

But the first 'waren' is really a conditional 'if'; and 'Unreinlichkeit war' seems a result of linguistic contamination. As we shall see later, when reflecting about the past the thoughts of Blumfeld are sometimes given in the past tense also. Another slight difficulty is the frequent reference to Blumfeld by his surname, instead of *er*, and a reader may think it an improper form of thinking of oneself. But this arises often in classical free indirect speech from the reduction of all first and second persons to the third, when, as I have pointed out in my study, *The dual voice*, the person whose thoughts are given may use his name in order to distinguish himself from other persons.[2] In German, where other creatures including dogs may be masculine too, the distinction is more urgent: 'a colleague of Blumfeld's has such a dog; he will not go with anybody else' is a case in point. Actually the rather frequent repetition of Blumfeld's name produces another effect, namely, an emphatic and clumsy self-assertion, and it seems to be indulged in in order to bring out Blumfeld's crude self-importance and his underlying pathological insecurity. 'So Blumfeld will remain alone after all, he doesn't have, as it were, the lusts of an old maid' is a typical case, where his arrogance towards old maids is bolstered up by his aggressive self-assertion. Whatever incidental problems arise, there can be no doubt that the character of Blumfeld speaks throughout, in the officialese, the assertiveness, the nervous apprehensions, the fussiness, the crudities; what would be a bad style if it were narratorial becomes vivid and functional as expressing the character's nature.

The last sentence of this second paragraph illustrates this, a

sentence that syntactically might belong to the narrator or to
the character, in which Blumfeld's hankering after a canine
companion is summed up:

Etwas derartiges will Blumfeld, da er es aber, wie er einsieht, ohne
allzugrosse Nachteile nicht haben kann, so verzichtet er darauf, kommt
aber seiner gründlichen Natur entsprechend von Zeit zu Zeit, zum
Beispiel an diesem Abend, wieder auf die gleichen Gedanken zurück.

(Blumfeld does want something like that, but because he cannot have it,
as he realises, without excessive disadvantages, he will do without; but,
in accordance with his thorough nature, from time to time he comes
back again to those same thoughts – for example on this evening.)

Allzugrosse Nachteile is Blumfeld's pedantic term for the
imagined pet's need for care and love, *gründliche Natur* is his
euphemism for his inflexible plodding slowness of mind, and
the clumsy, broken sentence communicates the same clumsy
heaviness. If we ascribed the sentence to the narrator, the only
compensation for the clumsiness and inexactitude would be a
suspected and not very subtle irony.

What is the significance of replacing the past tense of
reported speech by the present? This is much more than a
question touching Kafka's style, for it is a frequently met
feature of modern free indirect speech; in *The dual voice* I gave
the example of a passage from Saul Bellow, in which in the
middle of a passage of free indirect speech the author switches
from the past tense to the present.[3] The meaning of such a
switch is clear. Its advantage is to give us direct access to the
thinker, abolishing in part the mediation of the narrator who is
there simply to tell us that the passage concerned presents the
character's thoughts. The preservation of the conventional syntax, in this case of the past tense, would make the reported
speech sound rather literary as opposed to natural, rather stilted.
The object of free indirect speech is to present the character's
thoughts much more directly than normal reported speech
does, and yet the normal complex syntax counters this objective
and removes it to a distance, preventing the reader thus from

entering fully into the consciousness of the character. In the nineteenth century and before, readers were so unused to such shifts of consciousness that all these syntactical and other signs were necessary; but the modern reader is capable of extraordinary gymnastics of this kind and the author can use almost any means to convey directness and authenticity of experience. So, after the shock that Kafka's introduction of the present tense administers, the reader rapidly adjusts to the new situation. But, having acclimatised ourselves, we are in for a second and more unusual shock. For, when the narrative perspective of the opening of the story is resumed, in order to describe Blumfeld's arrival at his door, here too the present tense replaces the past; and from this point onwards, throughout the story, the account is in the present tense (except of course where events that have occurred before the time of the story are referred to):

Als er oben vor seiner Zimmertür den Schlüssel aus der Tasche holt, fällt ihm ein Geräusch auf, das aus seinem Zimmer kommt. Ein eigentümliches klapperndes Geräusch, sehr lebhaft aber, sehr regelmässig. Da Blumfeld gerade an Hunde gedacht hat, erinnert es ihn an das Geräusch, das Pfoten hervorbringen, wenn sie abwechselnd auf den Boden schlagen. Aber Pfoten klappern nicht, es sind nicht Pfoten.

(When, arriving at the door to his flat, he takes the key from his pocket, he is struck by a noise which comes from his room. A peculiar, rattling noise, but very lively and regular. As Blumfeld has just been thinking of dogs, it reminds him of the noise which paws make when they strike the ground alternately. But paws do not rattle. It isn't paws.)[4]

Typical is the almost indistinguishable merging of the narratorial statements and those presenting the character's responses. The first sentence, that implies distance from the scene, is narratorial. But *ein eigentümliches klapperndes Geräusch* suggests already the attentive listening of Blumfeld. It is then the narrator who explains why he attributes the noise to paws; but the final sentence is clearly Blumfeld's self-argument and conclusion. This close, intimate, interweaving of what traditionally would be defined as the objective narratorial statement and free indirect speech is now maintained throughout the piece. And though free indirect speech traditionally does allow for such alternations of objective and subjective statement, the use of the present tense for both seems to reduce their separateness. I believe this is so because, while the narrative past tense usually serves to indicate events, significant elements of a story-structure, the present tense here follows every small motion of Blumfeld and enfolds us in every insignificant action or movement of his mind; we lose the sense of a story and become engrossed in a situation, or perhaps it would be more correct to say, in a state of mind. The general type of composition is:

Blumfeld bückt sich zu ihnen [den Bällen] hinab, um sie genauer anzusehen. Es sind ohne Zweifel gewöhnliche Bälle, sie enthalten wahrscheinlich in ihrem Innern noch einige kleinere Bälle und diese erzeugen das klappernde Geräusch.

(Blumfeld bends down to take a closer look at the balls. They are, without doubt, ordinary balls, but probably inside them there are other, smaller balls. These produce the rattling sound.)

The narratorial first sentence and the second, clearly Blumfeld's thought, are not at different levels of authority; the second answers as authoritatively as is necessary, the question implied in the first. The same is true of the account of Blumfeld's preparations for going to bed and of his stratagems with the restless balls, as also of his behaviour when the daily help arrives in the morning.

The present tense has only one substantial interruption, in a long passage (pp. 278–81)[5] that tells of Blumfeld's misfortunes and resentment in the earlier part of his career in the factory, and here the preterite, pluperfect, and compound past are used. Grammatical analysis of the traditional type is not easy, for it is often very difficult to distinguish narratorial from subjective statements, though occasionally we are helped by Kafka's use of the subjunctive for reported speech; but often enough the subjunctive is replaced by the indicative, and we have to guess whether we are still meant to be reading Blumfeld's thoughts –

for example, the account of his interview with the boss, Herr Ottomar (p. 278):

Und wie sei gerade dort [in Blumfelds Abteilung] die Arbeit angewachsen! Als Blumfeld eintrat, an diese Zeiten könne sich Herr Ottomar gewiss nicht mehr erinnern, hatte man dort mit etwa zehn Näherinnen zu tun, heute schwankt ihre Zahl zwischen fünfzig und sechzig... Nun lehnte Herr Ottomar niemals Blumfelds Ansuchen geradezu ab, das konnte er einem alten Beamten gegenüber nicht tun, aber die Art, wie er kaum zuhörte, über den bittenden Blumfeld hinweg mit andern Leuten sprach, halbe Zusagen machte, in einigen Tagen alles wieder vergessen hatte, – diese Art war recht beleidigend. Nicht eigentlich für Blumfeld, Blumfeld ist kein Phantast, so schön Ehre und Anerkennung ist, Blumfeld kann sie entbehren.

(And in this particular [Blumfeld's] department how the work had increased! When Blumfeld entered the business – Herr Ottomar could certainly no longer recall these times – there had been roughly ten seamstresses to cope with; today their number hovers between fifty and sixty... Now Herr Ottomar never went so far as to reject Blumfeld's requests outright – he could scarcely do that to an old administrator. But the way in which he hardly listened, talking to other people over the head of the petitioning Blumfeld, offering at best partial consent to what he wanted, only to forget everything a few days later – this behaviour was very offensive. Not actually to Blumfeld, Blumfeld has his feet on the ground; however fine honour and recognition is, Blumfeld can do without it.)

The switches of perspective here are almost bemusing, certainly hard to pin down and consciously register; at any moment, for short or longer periods, in the middle of a sentence, through the slightest variations of tone and phraseology, we shift from the narrator's voice to the consciousness of the character. The even flow is without dramatic pause or emphasis, even exclamations are damped down, and the subtle modulations are perilously full of mockery, irony – perilously for two reasons: the first, that one cannot be sure that one grasps all the modulations of meaning; the second, that one loses the sense of direction of the story. The difficulty of precise analysis is great, but perhaps the most important and simplest fact about this prose is that the narrator's and character's voices are so close as to be almost identical; or perhaps better, these voices do not correct one another but indirectly confirm the other.

To some extent this is true of the earlier Kafka stories, where as we have seen the narrator abandons his traditional right to independent observation and judgment in favour of the chief character. But in 'Blumfeld, an elderly bachelor' this development seems to have gone to the extreme possibility, if a narrator is to function at all. We can try to sum up our observations.

1. Since the narrative is now related in the present tense, we have lost a formal feature that communicates a significant distinction between the character and the story-teller. For the past tense conveys a temporal distance from the events related and hence allows for two time levels: the evocation of the present, namely the time of the events portrayed and of the consciousness of the characters, and the evocation of some point in time from which the whole of these events, and their outcome, can be surveyed as a completed past. These two levels form a basic dialectic of traditional story-telling which of course is not affected by the use of the so-called historic present as a narrative form, for this is only a disguised preterite. But in this story there is, after the opening sentence or two, only a present, and such narratorial intrusions as there are belong as much as Blumfeld's actions and thoughts to the fleeting present.

2. This absence of a temporal differentiation is paralleled by that of a spatial differentiation. While the narrator of the earlier stories from time to time offers another view of a scene, perhaps completing the view given by the character, perhaps from a perspective not available to the latter, here the narrator seems incapable of an independent view – in other words, the reader is never presented with any more objective view than Blumfeld's. There are numerous striking examples of this. Take for instance the description of the landlady and the children as Blumfeld leaves his home and gives instructions as to the disposal of the dancing balls. We see the persons involved only

through Blumfeld's eyes, whatever the actual form of the sentence may be, in a passage that is impregnated with the hatefulness, resentment, inhumanity that is Blumfeld's (p. 274). There are no statements to qualify the single impression the reader receives; if we are to criticise and revise this impression, the only evidence we can rely on is Blumfeld's character as a whole as we evaluate it in the course of the story. Is the land-lady's son so repulsive, has he rickety legs and a goitre, is he 'unbelievably dense' and the image of his mother? We can never know and it has no relevance for this story. We are similarly barred from any knowledge of the factory and office except that communicated, directly or indirectly, through Blumfeld's mind.

3. This subjectivity of the narrative perspective is of course a feature of all Kafka's early tales; it might be thought that the difference of 'Blumfeld, an elderly bachelor' is only one of degree. But if so, the change of quantity entails a change in quality. For we swiftly recognise in the earlier tales the function of the narrator, even if he is largely swallowed up by the chief character; the narrator clearly retains important functions of story-telling, most notably the power to determine the phases of the action, to sum up periods from a distance and to elaborate on a particular moment, to create a beginning and an end. But in the 'Blumfeld' story we really ask, what is the function of this narrator? We know he is needed to open the story, and he retains an important function in describing Blumfeld's morning preparations to set off to work, even though his role is chiefly that of Blumfeld's mouthpiece. But after that point we are scarcely aware of his guiding hand. We follow Blumfeld's arrival at the office, his thoughts and memories, we see the place and the other persons through his eyes, but the reader feels him-self lost in the maze of thoughts that circle round the same resentments and envies, that lead nowhere, that do not take the story into any new phase but turn our attention to the most trivial problems or incidents; when the fragment breaks off it

can scarcely surprise the reader, who will have been wondering how all these details can lead to any end.

Of course we understand the psychological function these random trivialities have. It is through them that one understands the obsessive triviality of Blumfeld's character, and one experiences this all the more profoundly since the reader, like the narrator, is submerged in the character's perspective. The monotonous fluidity of the writing, with the shifting variations of gray tones – no vivid colours, no brilliance, nothing startling – exercises its fascination; but it has no onward movement. The cause, I believe, is the submergence of the narrator. For at no point are we released from his serfdom, or from the present tense that ties us to the here and now. He can never release himself sufficiently from the character – as he does in the earlier stories and the novels – to view events from a more distant point, to sum up a process, foreshorten the lapse of time, or even to imagine what is to become of Blumfeld. There are passages in the other works, notably in the novels, when the reader becomes enmeshed in the endless random reflexions or speech of a character in a somewhat similar manner; I think particularly of Olga's explanations in *The castle* or the speculations of the two chief characters of *The castle* and *The trial*. But in these there is always a narrator available who can put an end to a chapter and leap to a new situation and stage. But in 'Blumfeld' no rescue looms into sight, the narrator has submitted to his creation.

If we take it that the narrative method of 'Blumfeld, an elderly bachelor' is the logical fulfilment of the tendency already marked in the earlier stories, then we must conclude that it demonstrates the impossibility of constructing a story upon this basis alone. The instrument Kafka created is a wonderful agency for a certain part of story-telling – for the evocation and experience of the workings of a mind, particularly a complex, suffering, distorted mind. But also it threatens the creation of story and the understanding that depends on a story i.e. on a connexion, material and psychological, of persons and events in a time sequence that has a beginning and an end. It would seem that in this fragment Kafka was trying to strip away from a story as many as possible of the traditional artifices that have made story-telling possible in order to be able to present to the reader the naked truth of a mental situation. He reduces the function, the intrusions, of the narrator, the mediator, to a minimum, in particular avoiding as far as possible the syntax (the tense) that suggests his function as a reporter – and we can suggest that the lack of an ending belongs to this endeavour and is not an accident. But for all the fascination of this text, its subtle, cunning texture, we feel baffled and dissatisfied by this lack of structure, this boneless wonder. And we ask a question that we do not ask in the case of the earlier stories. Why is there in this story a narrator of this kind at all? Why is he necessary? Could the story not be told with even greater authenticity by the character himself?

There is no sign that Kafka asked himself this question in this form, yet in many of the later pieces an autobiographical form with a personal narrator is adopted, which means that the mode of the story changes and in particular the quality of the ending. These pieces we shall examine in chapter 6. But there is another possibility. Greater authenticity might be achieved if the impersonal narrator of the earlier stories and novels were replaced by a personalised third-person narrator who, while he knows enough to tell a story, has no claim to the comprehensive retrospective knowledge and authority that clings traditionally to the impersonal narrator. This option Kafka also adopted, and it is this that first demands our attention.

5 · THE IDENTIFIABLE NARRATOR OF 'A HUNGER ARTIST'

('Ein Hungerkünstler')

If 'Blumfeld, an elderly bachelor' can be discussed as an artistic failure 'A hunger artist' stands right at the opposite extreme of Kafka's achievement. It is one of his most accomplished, flawless creations, with respect to its structure from its beginning to its close, to the proportions of its different phases, the interplay of characters, settings, and events, and to its narrative style. It is also a highly characteristic work, continually inviting us to see its incidents and characters as symbols of some universal predicament and always teasing us with its ambiguous complexity.

These features alone would make a rather full investigation of its narrative structure desirable. But there is an additional reason for a close examination. Most readers acquainted with 'A hunger artist', and especially those who have some knowledge of critical studies of this work, will be surprised and sceptical over the suggestion in the title of this chapter that the story is told by an identifiable personal narrator. For almost every published study of this work accepts or assumes that it belongs to the narrative type of the early stories and the novels; that is, that the narrator is impersonal and his account authoritative and factual, except where this narrative agent temporarily adopts, as we have seen in the other stories, the perspective of the main character. Among all the critics there is I believe only one who detects the hidden hand of a personal narrator, though this one, Brigitte Flach, fails to find any significance in this fact. So my analysis goes against the stream of opinion, and for that reason requires substantial justification.[1]

Yet even a superficial survey of the style of narrative in 'A hunger artist' reveals a striking difference from that of Kafka's earlier tales. For here the narrator, whoever he may be, clearly stands outside the characters and events portrayed and remains throughout at a distance from the chief character. He describes events as he sees or knows them, not through the mind of the character. He in no sense identifies with or merges in the 'hero' – the situation we have observed repeatedly in the earlier works. This narrator does not have unlimited direct access to the mind of the hunger artist, he knows him in the same way (though more intimately) as other bystanders would and describes his gestures, behaviour, words as an observer. He is not debarred from telling what the character's thoughts and feelings are, but for this, he relies, as other witnesses would, on information he can glean and words he hears – often indeed he gives the legitimisation for his assertions. For instance, he claims to be an 'initiate' and thus to have access to information not widely known (p. 164);[2] or he qualifies a statement with a 'perhaps' or supports a speculation with a defensive 'thoroughly believable' (pp. 165, 169). Most strikingly, in comparison with the narrators of earlier stories, when he describes the hunger artist's thought in reported speech, he uses his own idiom for this purpose, scarcely ever adopting the hunger artist's idiom. Free indirect speech is used very rarely, and when it is – e.g. in a series of exclamatory questions (p. 166) – he still keeps to his own style and jargon. Indeed, we would be hard put to it if we were to try to define the hunger artist's characteristic mode of expression, for the only words of his that are reported are meagre, bare, expressionless; it is the narrator who has the temperament and a taste for rhetorical devices. In every respect the story remains firmly in the hands of this narrator and this fact is mirrored also in its firm structure and the smooth coherence of the narrative movement from beginning to end that distinguish it from the earlier stories.

However, merely to demonstrate that we are faced with a different type of story would not be a very profitable undertaking. I hope to show that the formal structure has much bearing on the interpretation of 'A hunger artist', that it rules out certain hypotheses just as it opens up others. Kafka does not identify in any explicit terms a narrator of the story, but this (fictitious) agent does indeed proclaim himself through a very distinctive and personal style and through judgments that are peculiarly his. It is as if this 'person' were hiding behind the mask of an impersonal narrator and trying to usurp an authority that would pertain to the latter, only repeatedly to betray his true and all-too-human features through the threadbare mask. If this is so, radically new interpretations are clearly required for textual statements that have lost the right to be considered authoritative and reveal themselves as proper to this person, to his capacities and motives; indeed it is only under this condition, I believe, that the work can claim to be flawless.

It is my object here, therefore, to show by means of a textual investigation how a personal narrator imposes his presence in this story, and to suggest the effects a recognition of his signature causes upon interpretation. Since I am aware that it is an illusion to believe that a Kafka text can yield a definitive, final meaning, I am less concerned to offer a comprehensive interpretation of this elusive story than to establish the coordinates within which an evaluation must be located. Attention will be primarily directed upon the opening paragraphs of the story in which these narrative coordinates are firmly established. The uncovering of a rich vein, almost a riot, of humour will compensate, I hope, for the sometimes wearisome labour of following a close stylistic analysis.

Almost all studies of Kafka's 'A hunger artist' see it as an allegory of either the artist in the modern world or the saint. Most recognise some obstacles to any simple meaning and Ronald Gray, pointing out numerous examples of obscurity, inconsistency, and caricature in the story, believes it is an artistic failure that reveals Kafka's incapacity to control his mounting neurosis.[3] But Gray no more than others takes account of the narrative structure, and none submits it to a rigorous examination. It would be an excessively tedious undertaking to discuss all these studies, but we are here concerned with a question prior to interpretation, namely, how is the text to be read? And for this purpose we have for this story a handy tool. There is a thorough and detailed analysis of the text, the style, of 'A hunger artist' carried out by Eberhard Frey, in which sentence by sentence every word and phrase is examined and weighed.[4] This analysis is in most respects observant, acute, and helpful, and since Frey agrees with most critics in his interpretation of the story as an allegory of the artist, I think that in general one can assume that his reading of the text corresponds pretty closely to that of most critics, most readers. Like the other critics Frey, while sometimes noting the technical functioning of the narrator of 'A hunger artist', does not attribute to him either a personality or a significant role. He normally uses the term *Erzähler* in a very abstract way, as if his functioning were self-evident and did not require critical attention. I therefore propose to refer continually to this published analysis of Frey's, since his reading can be taken as characteristic of a widespread approach to the text and gives a concrete basis for understanding upon what the normal interpretation is based and for putting a finger on the source of misunderstandings.

The circumstances of the publication of 'A hunger artist' throw a little light on one or two puzzles. It is one of the few works that Kafka himself published. Written in early 1922, it first appeared in *Die neue Rundschau* in October of that year. Before his death Kafka prepared to publish it again in a small volume containing three other short pieces, all written in these last two years of his life, and this volume appeared posthumously in 1924 entitled *A hunger artist: four stories*. The other stories are 'First grief'; 'A little woman', and 'Josephine the singer or the nation of mice'. 'A little woman' is the story of an unnamed woman's irrational distaste for an acquaintance, told by the latter, who is sublimely unaware of his own obsessional concern with the woman. 'Josephine' tells of the mysterious influence and encouragement exerted by a mouse-bard over her people, whose great pretensions are accompanied by a feeble voice and capricious whims. 'First grief' is nearest to 'A hunger artist' in theme, since its subject is also a variety artiste – its first words are 'A trapeze artist. . .'; and here too the performer is the victim of an obsessive devotion to his art that withdraws him from almost all human contact except his impresario, who sympathetically indulges all his whims. The mode of narration is different in each story. 'A little woman' is told by the chief participant; 'Josephine' by a reflective observer among the mice; and 'First grief' by an impersonal narrator. If there is a common theme it is that of the obsessive. Of the three so-called 'artists' only Josephine is a true artist, and she through her singing creates a unity in and with her people, while the two variety artistes are cut off from normal life and the community. In English we should hardly use the term 'artist' for such circus performers, even though we might use it to distinguish a particularly graceful and expressive one; we might speak of the 'art' of such performances as juggling, tight-rope dancing, balancing etc., but the term 'art' is much more capacious than 'artist'. German can use *Künstler* with less embarrassment, and *Trapezkünstler* (trapeze artist) would not seem amiss, though we would not be likely to read into the term in this context anything more than skill, graceful strength; it does however add an aura and dignity to the profession that a circus management or impresario would eagerly appropriate.[5]

At the opening of his examination Frey rightly points out the clumsy challenge within the term *Hungerkünstler*, since while we might imagine an artist in fasting, hunger is only something we suffer and lacks the creative ingredient belonging to the concept of artist (pp. 155–6). He therefore suggests that Kafka deliberately uses the strange compound in order to draw our attention to the true but half-hidden theme of the story, namely, the lot of the true artist. If Frey had taken into account the term *Trapezkünstler* used in the other story, he might have found the term less provocative; but the context will convey quite a different implication.

THE FIRST PARAGRAPH

Kafka's story starts as if it were to be a treatise on hunger artists and their decline in popular esteem, and it is with some surprise that we find that 'the hunger artist' of line five switches acrobatically from the meaning of the class to that of a particular performer. But, from the start, the language is anything rather than academic or scientific, for we experience shock after shock. There are the crude emphases of *gut lohnte* ('it was well worth one's while') (instead of *lohnte* simply); 'completely impossible', 'the whole town'; clumsy constructions like *grosse derartige Vorführungen* ('great performances of that kind') and later, *der Mode halber* ('for the sake of fashion') and *der Sicherheit halber* ('for safety's sake'); show-business jargon like *in eigner Regie* ('under one's own management'), *Abonnenten* ('those with subscription booking') and *Besichtigungen* ('tours'), used nonchalantly as are 'hunger artist' and 'hunger day', as if there was nothing strange about this profession and a human starver could be looked at in the same way as a performing ape. It is odd that the cage is mentioned only incidentally, as if we must already know the performer is so confined and find nothing disturbing in this.

All this Frey comments on (pp. 156–66). He notes 'the mixture of self-important pseudo-scientific observation and gawping curiosity', the crude and semi-literate officialese, the stereotyped sentimentality of the description of the children. He notes too the switch from the general subject to the particular performer, though he does not comment on a similar inconsistency when the lively engagement of the children is contrasted to the frivolity of the adults. (The narrator says that the latter visit the hunger artist just for fun and because it was a fashionable thing to do, though at the beginning of this long sentence he has told us of the intense interest of 'the whole town' in such shows. What are we to make of such self-contradiction and inconsistency?)

Despite the accuracy of his specific comments, Frey does not try to explain the meaning of this style. His summing up properly directs our attention to the self-contradictory behaviour of the *Hungerkünstler*, alternating between appeal for the approval of the public and withdrawal into himself, but Frey discusses this and other matters without any regard for the medium of description (pp. 164–6). On the style itself he refers to 'examples of unpleasant officialese, which however for the most part fit the situation – with the possible exception of the repeated use of a somewhat fusty construction' (p. 163). But what is the 'situation' he refers to? Is this bad German sometimes 'unsuitable' and the occasional 'fusty construction' regrettable? Does Frey mean that Kafka's German is in places rather poor?

Once such questions are posed, the answer is not hard to find; indeed it seems astonishing that it could be overlooked. It is clear that in this story Kafka is adopting a narratorial mask. And even from this first paragraph we can give this mask a recognisable character. It is the mask of a showman or someone who identifies himself with show business, in the sense that he has 'inside' professional knowledge, understands and commends the skill of the performer and his manager (the impresario we are soon to meet), and is enthusiastic about their success as measured by their popularity. He is not a cultured man nor a practised writer and finds some difficulty in expressing himself. That is why he sometimes falls into slang and for his more weighty pronouncements has recourse to the officialese and clichés he has acquired from the trade and the newspapers. He is a man more acquainted with speaking than writing, and thus we can explain his strong emphases like 'completely impossible', which are superfluous in writing but natural in speech. His lack of concern for logic or consistency is that of a speaker, a showman, who knows he must win the attention of his hearers by ever new devices: thus he can gain significance for his account by promising general thoughts on hunger artists, but knows that his hearers will listen with a livelier interest to the concrete case and not bother if his promise is unfulfilled.

Similarly his self-contradiction over the attitude of the adult public will be scarcely noticed by hearers but serves to enhance the appreciation of the children's thrilled fascination. We can even say that this showman–narrator does not clearly distinguish the readers of print from the listening crowd at a circus; his matter-of-fact manner of referring to the performance, his merely incidental reference to the cage, are appropriate to the latter, since they can be assumed to be acquainted with the show. We can already see in this first paragraph that once the narrator gets over the 'pseudo-scientific' opening, his object is as much to commend and admire as to describe; this aspect will become stronger, but already we detect an advertising showman rather than an objective enquirer.

If we imagine public readings of Kafka's works, we should expect that most of the texts, including the novels, would have to be read in a somewhat toneless, subdued voice, one that conveys the subtleties of irony and suggestion through slight shades and pauses; colour would enter only for passages of direct speech or mimicry. But it would be quite different with 'A hunger artist'. Here the tone is highly coloured, highly personal, pompous, emphatic, banal, vulgar, always varying; the voice with which it is read must enact this narrator, otherwise the sentences do not make sense.[6] A characteristic voice of this type would also be necessary for a few other Kafka tales, like 'A report for an academy' or 'Investigations of a dog', but nothing so flamboyant and emphatic as for 'A hunger artist'.

This sketch of the narrator is of course only adumbrated in the first paragraph; it is filled in and elaborated in the succeeding pages. But his features are already distinguishable and we can already say what that 'situation' is that Frey refers to. It is not simply the *Hungerkünstler*, but the presentation of this 'artist' by a showman. Once this is established, then everything fits in and, in particular, we can see how brilliantly appropriate the style with all its crudities is. We are now able to understand the puzzles that Frey properly recognises but cannot explain.

The first of these puzzles is the term 'hunger artist' and the

nonchalant use of related terms like 'hunger day'. It is natural
for the showman to enhance his client by appropriating the
prestige of the artist; and for him, professionally, there can be
nothing strange or distasteful about the art he commends. He
therefore exploits the term to the limit, and it can be added that
he wins his reward, since he has taken in even observant readers.
Frey also thinks it curious that the title of the piece is 'A hunger
artist' when we would have expected 'The hunger artist'
(p. 156). He perhaps has not noticed that the titles of books,
even of chapter headings, often express an authorial view upon
the events narrated as distinct from that of the narrator, even
an ironic interpretation.[7] In the volume of which 'A hunger
artist' formed a part, 'First grief' and 'A little woman' are such
ironic titles, and with 'A hunger artist' Kafka himself gives us
a nudge, perhaps even ironically using the term his narrator
adopts but at least, through the indefinite article, suggesting
the uniqueness or oddity of this 'hunger artist'.

A smaller puzzle is presented by the strangely flat, unemphatic third sentence of Kafka's text that purports to explain
why hunger artists are no longer popular – 'they were different
times'. Frey rightly says that the reader would expect a more
emphatic expression, perhaps nostalgic, but believes that its
simplicity gives the phrase 'a deeper, more serious meaning'
(p. 157). The context does not confirm this conclusion, but
there still remains the question, why this simple phrase in a text
studded with overemphasis? First, these words conclude the
'pseudo-scientific' theme of the opening, and are the narrator's
explanation (of course, it is not an explanation but only a
tautology). Second, here the business man reveals himself, for
it is not the showman's business to dwell on misfortunes; he
has to recognise the state of the market and adapt himself to
the new conditions. The flat phrase therefore anticipates that
rather astonishing last paragraph of 'A hunger artist', that has
embarrassed many critics, in which, after the hunger artist's
remains have been swept up and buried, our attention is won
for his magnificent replacement, the younger panther. Frey

writes, correctly, 'the narrator seems to be enthusiastic about this panther' (p. 263), but cannot fit this change into his interpretation since he has not recognised in the narrator the personal characteristics outlined above.

When we recognise that the 'situation' established in this story is the hunger artist as seen by this narrator, we deepen the ambiguity governing the whole. For we know the hunger artist only as he is reported by the narrator and what we have to evaluate is not just the hunger artist's doings and words but these as reported and evaluated by the coarse showman. Everything the latter says has to be assessed critically in regard both to truth and to judgment. This does not mean that he only evokes our disbelief. His character and profession enable him, as it would an impresario, to appreciate, admire, and understand the art of the hunger artist; as what he boastingly calls *ein Eingeweihter* ('an initiate') he has inside information. Though he does not distinguish the technical skill of the performer from the art of showmanship, and though his description always becomes advertisement, his qualities make him an appreciative observer of the performances he is to describe. Besides this, if he has the wiles of a showman he also has the naivety of one, so that unwittingly he betrays the tricks of his profession. As we shall see, for these reasons his description of the great showpiece staged by the impresario at the end of each fasting period is fully reliable. Nor need we doubt the truth of the hunger artist's words as the narrator reports them. But where he interprets the hunger artist's thoughts or intentions we have to be sceptical; we have every right to doubt that this narrator is competent to understand fully this strange obsession.

Since Frey is unaware of the dialectics of the situation, he like many critics fails to appreciate its humour. He is indeed at times aware of a narrator and he attributes to him 'touches' of irony and humour. But the humour lies not in the consciousness of the narrator, who throughout remains true to himself, serious, admiring, advertising, struggling with this unfamiliar medium of the written word. He himself is the chief object of

humour, through the contradictions within his confused conception of art, the clumsy combination of pompous and slangy
style, of wiliness and naivety – sources of humour that are
reflected also in the impresario and the hunger artist himself,
since both are also engaged in two arts, that of starving and that
of showmanship. Once Frey even calls the narrator 'omniscient',
on the meagre grounds that the narrator knows something
hidden from everyone namely, that starving was easy for the
hunger artist (p. 196). Now it is true that the narrator here
writes:

Er [der Hungerkünstler] allein nämlich wusste, auch kein Eingeweihter
sonst wusste das, wie leicht das Hungern war. Es war die leichteste
Sache von der Welt.

(For he [the hunger artist] alone knew – no other initiate knew that –
how easy it was to hunger. It was the easiest thing in the world.)

But the narrative continues:

Er [der Hungerkünstler] verschwieg es auch nicht, aber man glaubte
ihm nicht, hielt ihn günstigstenfalls für bescheiden.

(He [the hunger artist] did not even make any secret of it, but nobody
believed him, they took him – to put it at its most favourable – for
modest.) (From paragraph 3.)

This is a typical example of Kafka's humour. It is a maze of
'Kauderwelsch', clumsy, illogical, absurd. *Auch kein Eingeweihter sonst* is absurd; he must be counting the hunger artist
himself as an initiate! 'The easiest thing in the world' is helplessly banal. The superlative *günstigstenfalls* is so uncouth a
tongue-twister that Frey cannot copy it correctly. And in one
breath the narrator tells us no one knew about this fact, in the
next he tells us that people did know but did not believe what
the hunger artist told them. Here and elsewhere we have the
reverse of an omniscient narrator. All our very limited narrator
knows he picks up from what he sees and hears, doctoring it in
his report so as to appeal to the reader's credulity and love of

sensation; since his account is retrospective, he also draws on his knowledge of the outcome.

If through the acknowledgment of the presence of a specific narrator we find a troubling further ambiguity is involved in Kafka's story, we are very fully compensated by the humour which, as we are now free to recognise, breaks out all over the place. In Frey's reading – and that of most critics – the text is an earnest, sober, unattractively written puzzle with an elevated meaning; Gray, who notices the prominence of 'grotesques and caricatures', cannot find any justification for them. But now it breaks into life. Laughter begins with the first sentence in the obvious contrast between the pompously announced intention and the inadequate linguistic and intellectual tools. Every piece of clumsy construction is fun, for we measure it against the pretensions of its originator, as is the case in *Bleak House*, where we register both Mr Chadband's venality and his spiritual pretensions. At times, as we shall see, there develops an outrageous, side-splitting, grotesque fun, at its height in the description of the show-spectacles staged at the end of each fast-period. But all this is true humour, not arbitrary caricature, because it is all integrated in the theme of the story and ultimately in the 'problem' of the hunger artist.

My sketch of the narrator's function and character has ranged beyond the information to be gleaned from the first paragraph. But before we turn to the second paragraph one more question can be broached: is satire of the narrator a prime objective of Kafka's story? An answer to this question can be given only when the whole story is considered, but it is clear that if that were Kafka's object, it would reduce 'A hunger artist' to something merely jocular. At this stage one can say such a purpose is very unlikely, and that Kafka's attitude to the variety theatre and similar popular entertainment, as evident in his other works and diary, is the opposite of satirical. From his diary-comments on the Yiddish company that visited Prague in 1910 we can see what delight the sensational plots and extravagant acting and speech gave him, and the amused affection with which he writes of variety or circus 'turns' and their impresarios, for instance in 'First grief' and 'A report for an academy', is unmistakable. K.'s two alleged assistants in *The castle* are transposed pierrots. Kafka's delight in this naive, expressive type of theatre has complex roots, no doubt, but I think for our present purposes the most significant aspect is the naivety and transparency of the illusions it creates, so that the sophisticated spectator can watch the whole process of artistic presentation with its hoary tricks unfolded without disguise before him. Kafka enjoyed this as much as Brecht does, and like him with appreciation, not ridicule or satire. In this story the crude, spluttering showmanship of the narrator is a coarsened magnification of the more subtle art of the impresario and the hunger artist himself, but still may claim our amused appreciation.

THE SECOND AND THIRD PARAGRAPHS

The second paragraph is devoted to the watchers who are 'elected' (!) to keep a twenty-four hour guard on the hunger artist to ensure that he does not cheat. These three-man groups are 'strangely enough, usually butchers'. Frey appreciates the effective contrast that such beefy, greedy, cheerful butchers make to the emaciated and ascetic hunger artist (p. 176). But he finds nothing curious about the word *merkwürdigerweise* ('strangely enough') and so misses both the point and the tone. For the word is slipped in to allay the reader's suspicion of 'elections by the public' that usually settle on these bulky *Fleischhauer* ('hewers of flesh'), and in fact it only betrays that it is all a trick of the impresario's. The grotesque situation, in which, to the despair of the hunger artist, the good-humoured card-playing watchers give him every opportunity to cheat, is made more farcical by the narrator's overemphatic assurances of the hunger artist's probity. He protests that the latter would not eat 'even the smallest amount – under no circumstances, not even if one used force'. He flatters his audience by saying the inspection was introduced 'to pacify the masses' though 'the initiates' (with whom the reader may identify himself) know it is unnecessary. The laxity of the watchers tortures the hunger artist: 'nothing was more of a torture for the hunger artist. . . they made him melancholy; they made hungering dreadfully difficult for him'. He tries to prove he is not taking nourishment surreptitiously by singing for long spells, but this only makes the watchers admire his ability to sing while eating. He prefers, we are told, the suspicious watchers who keep him under the light of electric torches, and we find this moody, taciturn artist is then ready to listen to their anecdotes, exchange jokes, tell stories 'from his years of wandering', anything to keep his guards awake. The situation is made still more grotesque by this sudden invention of a quite new hunger artist, garrulous and with tales to tell of his varied past, like any popular hero of romance. The narrator closes this sentence with a typically bathetic statement of praise, to the effect that the hunger artist could starve 'as none of them could'. Frey believes the phrase suggests the contrast between the artist and the ordinary man (p. 173) and does not see that the showman-narrator readily sacrifices a more impressive comparison for the sake of drawing the spectators (and his readers) into the experience. The absurdities climax when we are told that the hunger artist is 'happiest' when the watchers consume at his expense a plentiful breakfast. But, with his usual taste for superlatives, the narrator calls it *ein überreiches Frühstück*, just as he calls a full room *ein übervoller Saal* ('a room full to bursting'). But here he overdoes it, for *überreich* means 'excessively rich' only in a pejorative sense; no wonder credibility is strained when he says our sensitive ascetic hunger artist, with his anorexia, rejoices to see these stout butchers 'throwing themselves' at this super-lavish meal! Even then the hunger artist's tribulations are not ended, for doubters suspect the meal is a bribe.

Frey comments on the superlatives in the description, 'the heavily emotionally loaded speech'. He recognises that the narrator at least seems to 'identify himself' with the hunger artist and perhaps at times gives the latter's feelings through free

118

indirect speech, though he also believes he 'distances' himself from the hunger artist through occasional touches of 'fitfully appearing humour' (p. 175). But we do not experience touches of humour, but massive grotesque comedy. Once we recognise the person of this narrator we do not need to read his clumsy clichés and officialese as free indirect speech of the hunger artist.

The following paragraph slides rather clumsily from a discussion of the hunger artist's dissatisfaction with his success to the description of the spectacles staged at the end of each fasting period. In the discussion we come across another series of showman's clichés and verbal tricks in his defence of the hunger artist, that culminates in the loud assurance of the latter's genuine reluctance to break off his fasts with 'one had to issue him with a testimonial' – as if such a testimonial, from such a salesman, had any trustworthiness. In the following description it is the impresario who takes over, the narrator scarcely does more than describe his magnificent showmanship, including the little tricks of sleight-of-hand by which he captivates his public.

Each fasting period is limited to forty days by the impresario, 'and in fact for a good reason' adds the narrator, giving the reason that experience had proved that popular interest always declined after forty days (he uses the excruciating business jargon 'a significant reduction in demand'); characteristically he ignores the danger to the starver's life of a longer period. Frey hears in this forty days an unconscious religious overtone, since the period links up with the forty days of Christ's fast in the desert and of Lent (p. 183); together with other religious references that we soon meet, it betrays, in Frey's view, the story's real, deeper meaning, the artist's sacrificial devotion to his task. Now it is true the narrator only notices the business grounds for the forty days. But the impresario? Surely he is aware of the power of these suggestions, as we shall see; and it is his skill to be able to exploit them, a skill that goes beyond that of the narrator. It would seem that the many critics who have detected in these allusions the hidden deeper meaning of the story have simply fallen victim to the impresario's wiles.

The spectacle that now follows is described with admiration and enthusiasm, as indeed it should be since the impresario, whose work it is, is as it were the refined embodiment of the narrator's prose style. Preparations and events are presented in his spirit. The 'room full to bursting' now becomes an *Amphitheater*, the cage is wreathed in blossoms, a military band plays, two doctors are present to examine the hunger artist, a megaphone is used to announce their findings, and two young ladies are chosen to lead the hunger artist from his cage to a small table where a delicate sick-room repast awaits him. The hunger artist takes the proffered hands of the ladies but refuses to leave his cage. A series of grandiloquent rhetorical questions interpret through free indirect speech the grounds of his refusal, 'not only to become the greatest hunger artist of all time, which he probably was, but also to surpass himself and achieve the incomprehensible' – we recognise the narrator's ponderous search for superlatives. The impresario has to intervene and, with a mute but expressive appeal to Heaven to look on this 'pitiable martyr', catches hold of the hunger artist round the waist and transfers his fragile frame into the keeping of the ladies. Even the narrator notices, though with approval, the showmanship involved, for he writes of the 'exaggerated caution' the impresario displays, 'in order to make credible that he was here concerned with such a frail object', and he tells us too that he hands the feeble body over to the ladies 'not without secretly shaking him a little so that the hunger artist's legs and torso shook uncontrollably this way and that'. The result is that the hunger artist supports himself on one of the ladies, his nerveless legs dragging on the floor, embarrassing both her and her friend, all to the huge delight of the onlookers, whose roars of laughter cause the lady struggling with the hunger artist to burst into tears. The tension is relieved by a 'servant who has been in readiness for some time'. He takes the collapsed hunger artist off their hands and sets him down at the table. There the impresario gives the half-fainting artist a little liquid refreshment, cheerfully chatting in order, we are told, to distract the public's attention from the hunger artist's state. But the latter manages to whisper a toast to the public, so the impresario informs them, and all closes with a fanfare from the band, so that 'nobody was entitled to be discontented with what had happened, nobody, except for the hunger artist – always except for him'.

In his analysis of this scene Frey (pp. 184–98) notices most of the features and the deliberate showmanship of much – the band, megaphone, the two doctors etc. – though he attributes it solely to the impresario; that the assistant is standing there, ready to take the hunger artist out of the hands of the ladies, betrays it all as a 'prearranged game'. The narrator is thought to be only a reporter, here and there adding a touch of irony or 'bitter humour', for instance when we are told the impresario's care in handling the hunger artist was 'exaggerated' or that he shakes the passive body 'on the sly'. But this interpretation cannot explain the active support that the narrator's language gives to the whole spectacle, to the tricks that he sometimes detects and the successful effect. But even in regard to the impresario Frey is taken in. He seems to think the narrator is quite right in saying that the impresario tries to distract attention from the hunger artist by his 'cheerful chatter'; but of course this is an old stage trick, in fact the impresario *draws* attention to the hunger artist by this means.

Much more hangs on his comments on the religious associations suggested by this scene, and Frey's view here corresponds to that of many critics. The impresario's mute appeal to Heaven, to look with pity on the 'martyr', is thought by Frey to infuse 'profound irony' into the situation (p. 190), as does the description of the collapsed wasted body and the supporting ladies, which recalls a realistic late-medieval Deposition from the Cross (pp. 191–2, 197–8). Now, there is no doubt that these religious associations are awakened. But are we to take them, as Frey and other critics do, as the secret theme of the story – 'the martyrdom of the artist' – behind the ostensible events? What is overlooked by this interpretation is that this meaning is devised by the impresario, it is his intention to gain prestige for his client by summoning up these powerful analogies; are we to join his spectators as his dupes? For his appeal to Heaven is a deliberate (and rather stagey) gesture. He takes excessive pains to make the hunger artist seem to be in an utter state of collapse and, as we have seen, he gives the inert body a shake to emphasise its helplessness. Yes, by contriving the scene, placing the two ladies in that position, supporting the emaciated body, he deliberately invokes the familiar image of the dead Christ. So this is not the esoteric message of the spectacle, but the deliberate one contrived for public consumption. Can therefore these 'echoes of the Passion of Christ' have as Frey says 'a mystical resonance' (p. 197), when they are devised by an impresario whose chief object is effect and whose means include the trickery of the showman? We have every reason to be sceptical.

But perhaps even more unfortunate is Frey's failure to grasp the hunger artist's role in this spectacle. Like most other critics Frey takes him to be a 'marionette' in the fingers of the impresario. But there is a recurrent adverb in the account that Frey totally disregards, and that makes the hunger artist's conscious participation in the showmanship indisputable. It is the word *immer* – 'always'. So far I have discussed this scene as if it occurred once and was a unique event; but the narrator tells us at the beginning that this ceremony was repeated at the end of every fasting period, and by the use of the word *immer* he emphasises that it is always the same. The hunger artist 'always' protests against leaving his cage, though he places his bony arms in the hands of the ladies. Then follows: 'and then there happened what always happened', i.e. the comedy with the impresario and the ladies, the appeal to Heaven etc. The narrator repeats 'always' as he uses superlatives, to emphasise that this great scene is not a flashy success, but solid, well established, a masterly piece of art, and as in other cases, e.g. with his 'überreich' earlier, the effect is not exactly what he intends and does not simply increase our admiration. For it tells us that this scene is a carefully rehearsed act in which the hunger artist is a full participant, not a marionette. If it had occurred only once, it might be genuine; but as it is, it is an enacted show. The hunger artist's refusals, his collapse, his dangling legs, his desperate grip on the lady, his helplessness at the table where, though only semi-conscious, he still manages to suggest a toast to the public: all is a clever act. This the narrator's description tells us readers, so that what we see is different from what the spectators saw. Our response is not simple, for the narrator's intention is ambiguous. On the one hand he wants us to admire a genuine feat of starvation, on the other a great piece of show-manship. The conflict between the two, both within the hunger artist and the narrator, turns the scene into a magnificent grotesque comedy, in which the unrehearsed portions – the reactions of the ladies and the public – are beautifully fitted into the rehearsed.

But there remains a residue that this reading does not account for. So far we have seen the narrator as a sort of echo of the impresario. But there are moments when, as Frey finds, the narrator distances himself from the impresario, whose concern is solely success, showmanship. The first is the emphasis on the hunger artist's desire to break all records, to surpass himself, his longing for greater difficulties to overcome, irrespective of the showmanship value. The second is the fact that his reluc-tance to leave the cage, his feebleness etc. is not entirely played, since we are informed that the very thought of food makes him feel ill. The third arises when the impresario is using all his tricks, including his mute appeal to Heaven, to show that the hunger artist is a 'pitiable martyr', to which the narrator adds: 'which, admittedly, the hunger artist was – but in quite another sense'. And lastly when in the last sentences of the scene every-one is described as content with the show except the hunger artist 'always except for him'.

Frey like other critics thinks that the suggestion within these last two cases is that the hidden source of the hunger artist's suffering and discontent is his devotion to the holy cause of art and his willing embrace of the martyrdom this involves (p. 190). But there is another and more practical way of reading these hints, a different interpretation that would better fit the narrator's character. It seems to me that we have no right to read into his hints anything more than: 'He was not a martyr to starvation, as the impresario conveys, but an involuntary victim to his distaste for food, which was so extreme that it drove him to ever higher achievements.' This corresponds to what the narrator informs us of the hunger-artist's death-bed confession. This judgment however, if it seems the appropriate one for this narrator, need not satisfy us, for there are factors which go beyond his understanding.

THE ENDING

Now that the narrative angle of 'A hunger artist' has been established, there is no need here to examine the rest of the story in such detail. We are told of the failing popularity of the hunger artist and assured that it arises from an unfathomable change of fashion, not at all from a decline in his powers of starving. He is forced to dismiss his impresario and enlists in a circus, where he is given a miserable stand in a corridor leading to the stables. He rarely has a visitor except those who pause before his cage on their way to see the animals in the stables, and he realises he is 'strictly speaking only an obstacle on the way to the stables'. His ambition is still to starve but even the attendants forget him until the manager, one day observing the cage, asks what it is doing there. When the attendants rake through the rotting straw they find his emaciated body at the point of death. He manages to whisper to the manager that they should not admire him since he had starved only because he could never find any food that appealed to him, and dies. His remains are swept up and buried and his place in the cage is taken by a young panther, an image of vivid life, that attracts many visitors.

The story of these years of decline is told briefly and sparsely;

the narrator who had thrilled with effervescent enthusiasm over the hunger artist's successes seems anxious to pass over his painful decline as swiftly as possible. There are still the same lame phrases, the same pompous claims. The narrator still defends the hunger artist's great fight and like a good salesman tries to make his misfortunes seem more tolerable. Thus he tells us that the cage's position in the corridor is 'incidentally a pretty accessible place'. When children no longer show any interest for the hunger artist he consoles us with his familiar sentimentality that he can see 'in the gleam of their questing eyes something of new, coming, more compassionate times' – Frey (p. 225) takes this absurd self-deluding cliché as 'something prophetic and sententious', though it comes from the same source as had just attributed the children's lack of understanding for 'hungering' to 'insufficient preparation both from school and from life'. Likewise a little conventional religious comfort must be served up, to reconcile us to the hunger artist's sad fate, so we are told the hunger artist 'worked honestly, but the world cheated him of his reward'. Frey rightly says that the phrase suggests that he will reap a heavenly reward but once again, separating the words from their source, he considers they present us with a profound authorial verdict on the 'paradoxical situation' of the hunger artist, forced through his devotion to art to serve two masters, the world and the spirit (p. 237). No: this is what *the narrator* wants us to believe; the author is veiled. As earlier, the narrator always stresses the great difficulty of starving, and brings the reader into the argument by direct address – 'try to explain to somebody the art of hungering! Whoever does not feel it will never be brought to understand it.' The logical confusion of an *ad hominem* argument is smothered by the prestige of a garbled Goethe quotation. It is strange that Frey can consider this direct appeal to the reader to contrast with the normal 'dispassionate narrative style' of the story (p. 232). On the contrary, the writing is never 'dispassionate', it is always directed at winning over the reader, at commending, persuading, thrilling etc.

In the account of the last days of the hunger artist the narrator is less prominent and the hunger artist's final conversation with the manager (*Aufseher*) is given in direct speech. In this exchange Frey rightly hears something new, for it is a stylised exchange with something of the formal character of a litany (pp. 248–54). At one point the dying hunger artist uses a famous phrase of Luther's – 'I can do no other.' But it is far-fetched to suggest that the manager recalls a priest giving absolution (pp. 240–7) – a curious sort of priest indeed, who immediately gives the order to sweep up the remains and bury the hunger artist and his rotting straw! It is certainly not easy to understand, but I think the simplest explanation is the best, namely that the solemn, elevated style expresses the narrator's feeling, soon to recover as we shall see. The content of the exchange between the hunger artist and manager is, if we do not know our narrator, surprisingly meagre and bathetic. For he asks forgiveness, and when the *Aufseher*, indulgent and heartless like an impresario, comforts him by saying 'certainly we forgive you' (such forgiveness costs nothing and is worth nothing), the hunger artist explains what he wants to be forgiven for. They are, namely, not to admire him as a hunger artist, since he starved 'because I could not find the food which I like'. And his last words are: 'if I had found it, believe me, I would have made no fuss and I would have eaten my fill like you and everybody else'. It would seem that the hunger artist is annihilating the sense and purpose of his whole art, and the narrator's description of the dead man that follows, though meant to have a solemn meaning, is also empty: 'those were his last words, but in his sightless eyes was the firm – if no longer proud – conviction that he would continue to hunger'. That is our narrator all over. He knows a death requires a solemn epitaph and he provides the right terms ('sightless eyes') and the impressive cadence, but what he says is crushingly banal.

He is himself too in the final paragraph. With an almost audible sigh of relief the salesman turns from the distressing topic to the new attraction, the panther, sweeping away the memory of the hunger artist with his body. ' "Now clear things up", said the manager, and they buried the hunger artist together with the straw.' Characteristically he can write: 'Even for the dullest of minds it was a palpable relief to see this wild animal hurling itself about the cage which had been desolate for so long.' In the alchemy of our narrator's judgment only the most obtuse mind would refuse to throw off the memory of his former hero, and the remainder of the paragraph is devoted to the panther, an image of the opposite of the hunger artist, in implicit contrast to whose bodily feebleness and distaste for food he extols the panther's fierce teeth and 'joy in living'. With his last words however he speaks of the fascinated spectators, a salesman to the end.

All critics who understand the words of the narrator of 'A hunger artist' to be authoritative expressions of Kafka's 'true' meaning find these last paragraphs extremely puzzling. Frey is no exception. While he can enumerate the various twists to the story given by the 'confession' of the hunger artist, he rescues his own interpretation by reading *Speise* as 'spiritual food' (pp. 248–51); but this is mere clutching at a straw.[8] In his comments on the last paragraph Frey rightly sees that the *Aufseher* and his assistants want to get rid as quickly as possible of the memory of a man who disturbed their 'order', but finds nothing puzzling or significant in the narrator's attitude (pp. 261–3). To the end Frey's recognition of the narrator is fitful and selective, and his interpretation, like those of most critics, can be maintained only by this fault in reading.

THE HUNGER ARTIST AS SYMBOL

The hunger artist's life ends with the sort of *pointe* that concludes many a humorous anecdote, an abrupt cancellation of the deeper implications and problems that we have been encouraged to harbour. I do not think, however, that any reader is likely to accept the hunger artist's 'explanation' of his profession and ambition. The narrator may well do so and gladly turn to a more rewarding topic, but by now his judgments and enthusiasms only rouse our scepticism and amusement. Just as we have been able to see through his pretensions and advocacy on behalf of the hunger artist, so also we cannot find his abandonment of the hunger artist has any greater persuasiveness.

At the same time, we cannot disregard the narrator even in his final dismissal of the hunger artist. It is he who has directed our concern towards the hunger artist and who, voluntarily or involuntarily, wins it also for himself, so that throughout we are occupied with both. We have to take into account this fact, that Kafka interposed such a character between us and his hunger artist: why should he have done this? I do not know of any critic who has asked this unavoidable question.

It cannot be doubted that we are meant to enjoy the comedy of this narrator, a comedy which arises out of his character, in particular out of the contradictions between his literary pretensions and his vulgarity, between his claim to truth and his interest in showmanship, his confusion of technical artistic achievement and popular success, of sentimentality and its exploitation, as we have seen in our analysis. This humour is echoed in the behaviour of the showman characters that appear in the story, the impresario and the manager (*Aufseher*). It is the basic form of Kafka's humour which Felix Weltsch defined as arising when 'a supposed unity reveals itself as a duality'.[9] This humour has often an ominous, sinister character, as, for example, in *The trial*, where we are made aware of the intervention of unknown and hostile forces. But here, in the humour aroused by the words of the narrator and the actions of the actual theatre or circus persons, the humour is not frightening, bottomless, since the opposed elements are both readily recognisable. The humour seems to me always to be good-natured, sympathetic. That there is deception intended, self-deception enacted and displayed, is not sinister, for it belongs to the profession that lives by deception, to the showmen and the theatre, but that uses such deception to charm and amuse, to cater for the public's delight in delusions and skill; a profession that also admires these things, that admires and tenderly cultivates its artists. If it also does it for money, for gain, who would take that as a cause for repudiation? It is the most harmless sort of deception imaginable; and like Dickens Kafka loved such entertainers. If he could see through their tricks, he did not because of that mock at them; rather he loved their tricks and those of the performers, and it increased his delight to see through their professional wiles. So, in the self-portrayal of the narrator of 'A hunger artist' and in his description of the other circus personnel, there is no satirical intention on Kafka's part. We are invited to have fun, to laugh and enjoy our laughter. I do hope readers will not be persuaded to believe that such an attitude on our part is improper or even blasphemous, as some critics would have us think, and will not deny themselves the great pleasure of reading this story in this way.

It is against this background that we see the hunger artist; or rather, he belongs to this world. Like his impresario he is suspended within this contradiction of skill and showmanship, and he participates, as we have seen, in the great spectacle of his show, the tricks that ensure popular success. But he does not fit in like the others and we do not feel, I think, the lively pleasure in his contradictory situation that we find in that of the narrator. For he is truly a skilled performer, he undertakes the arduous discipline, he truly suffers, while the showmen only exploit his suffering. Thus we do not doubt the narrator's insistence on the hunger artist's true devotion to his art, even though we may or must doubt the interpretation the narrator puts on it. So there is also something within the hunger artist that is unique, that is not explained, that occupies us, and this something is strong enough from the start that we recognise it, not the burlesque of the narrator, to be our central concern.

The hunger artist is not only a showman. Like the trapeze artist of 'First grief' he is an 'artist' in the sense that he is devoted to his 'art', the starvation feats to which he devotes his will; for its sake he is ready to suffer, to set out to beat all records. When his act loses popular interest, his impresario or the narrator can find alternative clients and interests. He however is set on one thing only, and his devotion is so entire that when nothing is to be gained by it he starves himself to death. The manager and the narrator can sweep his remains away and get on to a more profitable line; but the reader remains with the hunger artist, with his problem.

It might seem that he himself has 'solved' this problem, since with his last words he explains his fasting by his anorexia and forbids admiration; if he had taken a normal pleasure in food, he says, he would never have made any fuss (*Aufsehen*) and would have eaten his fill like everybody else. Why is it we do not believe him? Not by a verbal trick, like Frey and others who suggest he meant spiritual food when he spoke of food. But we know his own explanation is not sufficient. If he did not like food, there were many other ways in which he might have managed. It was not inevitable that he became a hunger artist, that he imposed on himself this arduous discipline, that he drained himself of strength and ultimately of life. It is not difficult to understand his desire to achieve a record, to win admiration, whether we take this as evidence of a simple desire for fame and popularity or, more subtly, of a need for a manifest affirmation of his self-fulfilment. But how does it come about that he is ready to pay such a price – not just the price of his death, but continually the price of isolation, of utter loneliness in his cage and in between his shows? The narrator, failing as often to understand him, tries to persuade us that if the public had fully appreciated his powers he would have been very sociable and cheerful; but the truth is that, like the trapeze artist of 'First grief', our hunger artist *chooses* loneliness, an isolation that is almost mute. None of this was required by his anorexia.

If anyone were to explain this choice of his as merely making a virtue of necessity, this only veils the actual great achievement, the triumph of mind over body, or will over inertia. And such an objective has no definable bounds, so we can accept as true the narrator's report that the hunger artist was always dissatisfied with his achievements and anxious to outdo himself, even if the narrator is unable to understand why. We can understand that he always becomes irritated with the spectators when they do not trust his sincerity or ability, and we condone his participation in a bit of trickery, showmanship, since we understand that he needs his achievement to be made manifest if it is to provide him with some objective reassurance. If popular and box-office success is the aim and criterion of the impresario and narrator, for him this is only a symptom of his achievement.[10]

Such considerations have no doubt been in the minds of those many critics who see Kafka's hunger artist as a symbol of the artist in general, or even of the saint. But neither analogy does justice to the concrete particularity of the character, let alone of the character as mediated to us by the narrator. If we may apply here the test of Goethe's definition: 'That is true symbolism where the particular represents the more general...',[11] we have to say that these interpretations blur and distort the particularity of the work.

In the first place the hunger artist's devotion to his 'art' is found in many types of professions in which a particular ability is linked not only with an innate gift but also an associated innate failing; this applies to Kafka's trapeze artist and may apply to a good sportsman, a good mechanic, a good housekeeper etc. If a famous footballer says that he has devoted himself to football because he was 'no good' at anything else, he does not say this in order to depreciate his footballing genius, nor do his hearers come to any such conclusion. The hunger artist's profession requires much less skill than does the footballer's or trapeze artist's, and if it is to be called an 'art', fasting is a singularly unattractive one, utterly lacking in subtlety, ingenuity and charm, and remarkable only for the performer's power of endurance. What art there is in it is the showmanship, something quite different from fasting. It was the showman element in the true artist that led Thomas Mann to compare the latter with the illusionist, the confidence-trickster. But Kafka's hunger artist participates unwillingly, unjoyously, in the showmanship of his turn and the staging and effects are all the work of the real theatre artist, the impresario. The strongest argument for the artist analogy is perhaps the non-utilitarian nature of the hunger artist's pursuit. But this too, on closer inspection, is shown to rest on very frail grounds. For his occupation is not merely non-utilitarian, it is utterly valueless, has no relation to life at all, is absurd in the fullest sense. And the defenders of art as a spiritual, non-utilitarian and non-materialistic activity do not justify it as absurd but always claim for it some deep spiritual significance. If Kafka meant his starver to stand for 'the' artist, one can only say that it was a most unhappy choice; he might at least have chosen a trapeze performer! But in the text the only suggestions of such an interpretation come from the narrator, who imposes such terms as *Hungerkünstler* and *Hungerkunst* on us, for it is his métier.

Even more unsatisfactory is the analogy with the saint.[12] The showman aspect is here, obviously, much more of a stumbling block, but so is the absurdity of the hunger artist's obsession. The voluntary starvation of a saint is worthy only if the motive is worthy; a religious fast is not a mere test of oneself, it is a religious sacrifice.

THE NARRATOR AND THE MEANING

There are many difficult puzzles in this story. But our purpose here is not to propose a definitive solution; it is to ask: why are these puzzles, why is this story presented through the medium that Kafka chose, through a personalised narrator? All the material we are presented with comes to us through the imperfect, flawed lens of this reporter for whom I usually have not found an apter name than 'showman'. What we are told is not all for that reason necessarily false or distorted, though much may be, especially his interpretations and judgments; but something is true and all may have a kernel of truth. But if Kafka chose an imperfect instrument of this kind, perhaps his intention was to warn us against expecting clear and final interpretations?

This narrator is a comic character – comic in his literary and philosophical pretensions, his irrepressible showmanship, his confusion of art and popularity, his clumsy self-betrayals. He involuntarily devalues the 'Hungerkünstler' since he can only evaluate him in his own terms. This does not mean that the hunger artist is not a tragic character; but it does mean that the tragic theme is continually interrupted and disrupted by comedy, at times infected by it and reduced to tragi-comedy. Even in Kafka's early stories and the novels there are often moments when tragedy slips into grotesque absurdity and into comedy, when devotion appears as obsession or self-assertion, spiritual aspiration or scruple as poverty of spirit or wily stratagem; but the narrative provides a corrective to such distortions. In 'A hunger artist' however there is no such corrective, no remission from the narrator, who constantly keeps open for us, against his will, another mode of considering this tragic fate, namely, of seeing the flaws, the comedy in it. We see through this narrator clearly enough not to become his victim and not to content ourselves with cynicism; but his influence is pervasive enough to make us hesitate over final judgments.

This situation of the reader is much more like a life-situation than that in the earlier tales, indeed than that in any stories with an impersonal narrator. Not only does the object of the story – the hunger artist in this instance – offer a number of problems, but also we see him only in a distorting mirror. We are not immersed in the consciousness of the chief character as we are in Kafka's earlier tales, but are almost violently hindered from identifying with him, forced to see him in a caricatured likeness. A great obstacle is placed in the way of our understanding, it would seem, so great that it has led, I believe, to a general unwillingness to recognise the fact of its existence, i.e. to recognise the personal character of the narrator of this story. But I believe that this is its significance and function. Kafka does not tell us what the 'real' truth and meaning of his story is. What he is saying is that the truth of experience comes to us only in veiled and complex, even dubious forms, that it has many facets, and that we too share in the sort of limitations that his narrator here flaunts. So that the reader's experience of the desolate fate of the hunger artist is not pure and unambiguous but complex, contradictory, offering other possibilities of evaluation among which humour is prominent. One should add that this humour itself is never pure, wholehearted, restorative; the grotesque element throughout the story, the distortion and caricature, so magnified by the vulgarity of the narrator's mind and style, sow unease, not relief, in the reader's mind and themselves testify to the painfulness of the world of the story.

It seems to me, then, that the personalisation of the narrator of 'A hunger artist' suggests a deeper reflexion upon the complexity of life and suffering, of judgments, of verdicts, than we find in the earlier work of Kafka. It qualifies what might have been a statement of catastrophe by viewing it in a specific perspective that allows us, not to ignore the tragic element, but also to consider it from various sides, sometimes with snatches of light-hearted amusement even, sometimes with a bitter irony that extends to the sufferer himself. In this respect the story anticipates a general change of attitude that we shall observe in Kafka's work of his last years, a change that is significantly linked up with a tendency to adopt a personalised narrator.

An obvious question still sets itself. Why, if a personal narrator is employed, did Kafka not name him, make him into an explicit participant; why did he leave him so anonymous and unidentified that most readers fail to observe his presence? Should we have lost anything if the narrator had been so identified? I do not think so for it seems to me that our judgment of the totality of this brilliant work only gains from our awareness of the various 'witnesses' to whom we owe our knowledge of the events, since thus we can better evalute the quality of their evidence. I can only hazard an explanation for the lack of an explicit identification of the narrator. It would seem that Kafka could not as yet throw off the narrative form that had served him so well in his earlier work and that he had employed just at this time for 'First grief', his story about a 'trapeze artist'. Perhaps he thought he could introduce an ironical note into the style – so obviously present from the first sentence onwards – without changing it essentially. But such a change can hardly be introduced with impunity, and actually it rapidly consolidates into the massive presence of a personal narrator who imposes himself upon the story and differs from an impersonal narrator so fundamentally that he cannot be reckoned a mere modification of the latter. I dare to make so speculative a suggestion only because Kafka himself, in nearly all the significant stories of these last years, does take this step and use an identified personal narrator – and also because this medium is not a mere formal trick but is associated with a new type of story (if one can still speak of 'stories') and with a new attitude towards the fears, anxieties and suffering that still remain Kafka's theme.

6 · THIRD-PERSON AND FIRST-PERSON FABLES AND PARABLES

FABLE AND PARABLE

In my first chapter it was claimed that Kafka's stories have 'meaning' on two levels, one the familiar one that belongs to any structured story in which a number of uncertainties are resolved in a fulfilling ending, the other the symbolic meaning that in several ways they incite the reader to seek. That is, in this latter respect Kafka's stories have something of the character of a fable or parable. We have noted in them several formal elements that drive us to look for some such symbolic meaning, notably the apparent incoherence of events and of the behaviour of the characters and the baffling effect of the ending. But repeatedly the theme itself evokes such a search. For this theme is not suffering pure and simple, suffering that arises from circumstances, but suffering that repeatedly is understood by the central character and alleged by others to be a punishment. And punishment is not a simple fact of existence unencumbered by moral implications, but a concept that implies and exists within a whole ethical and perhaps legal system of which it is a member; it belongs to a code-family the other members of which are related concepts like innocence, guilt or sin, expiation, justice, verdict and trial and judge. In two of these stories – 'The judgment' and *The trial* – there is an explicit framework of a guilt and a verdict, an accused man and a condemning authority, while 'The metamorphosis' and the other two novels, *America* and *The castle*, suggest a comparable nexus of guilt, protest, and implacable authority. 'In the penal colony' is the only one of these stories in which the hero is not involved as a victim in a case brought against him, but as we have seen his behaviour pronounces his consciousness of guilt in failing to intervene in the punishment of which he is a witness.

When he reads these stories, therefore, the reader is faced

with the operation of a penal or moral system to which the characters pay tribute in their consciousness and their behaviour. But a Kafka story is distinguished also by a second characteristic that we do not find, for instance, in Dostoevsky's *Crime and punishment*, namely, that the nature of the guilt and punishment, their cause, the ethical or legal code to which they belong, perhaps the justice of this code and the legitimacy of the authorities who administer it, remain tantalisingly obscure. We can indeed very properly use the term 'code' for the underlying ethical system, for in Kafka's work it remains a code in the other meaning of the word, a secret language that has to be deciphered before we make a judgment on its morality. If we wish to grasp the very structure of the story, the coherence of events and thoughts, the relationship of the ending – perhaps its relevance – to what has preceded it; if we are to see seemingly arbitrary contingencies transformed into articulated significance: then we are forced to read it as a codified message. There are other elements in the texts that force us to look beyond the surface story, such as the irruption of unrealistic events and grotesque figures into the everyday world that surrounds these stories, the nightmarish effects like the strange foreshortening of time or the endless bewilderment of corridors. But the main feature that we have to wrestle with is this repeated insistence on some system of meaning that is of a different order than ordinary mundane concerns.

However, though these stories bear in this respect some similarity to the fable or parable, one would not call them such. They are too much the stories of specific individuals in specific situations, social and material, to be felt to be written as illustrations of some lesson. There is too much of a story in each, that is, there is too much change of situation to allow for any single lesson. Above all, the narrative form is strikingly different from that found in the fable or parable, since the reader is drawn into the experience of the main character, participates in it emotionally and imaginatively to such a degree that his participation suspends or even obstructs the sort of objective judgment that a fable seeks to inculcate. Many of Kafka's most fable-like shorter pieces tend to the quality of a story and many of them make us hesitate what to call them, fables or stories; and if we do call them 'stories' we must mean that they contain much more, and more than can be formulated, and involve the reader more intimately and mysteriously than do fables or parables. Even when, like 'The huntsman Gracchus', they seem to conclude with an interpretative 'explanation' – 'My boat has no rudder, it drives before the wind that blows in the nethermost regions of death' – the vivid scenes of the brief story are not all contained within this moving conclusion that itself raises more questions and associations than it settles. And yet, contrariwise, one can invert this opinion and observe that many of Kafka's later stories, and especially those with an animal subject – the ape's report, the dog's investigations, the badger's (?) ruminations, the mouse's singing – all seem to be extended fables and to seek some 'moral' that would explain their existence. Artistic and literary genres do not have sharp frontiers: here, with Kafka story–fables, we are not concerned with lines of demarcation but with tendencies and approximations. It is perhaps unnecessary to explain that I here use the term 'fable' in its most common meaning and am not concerned with its other meaning as a 'fabulous' i.e. far-fetched or incredible story or legend.

What is a fable or parable? Is there any difference between them? In structure they are very similar, in content and reference there is considerable difference. Both aim at supplying a lesson about human behaviour, perhaps a moral injunction, and create an incident, a story, the purpose of which is to illustrate the lesson. Both belong originally to an oral tradition and in the great examples, in Aesop's fables and the parables of the New Testament, this oral character is strongly marked in the form. Both are short, capable of being assimilated and understood by the surrounding listeners. The story must be simple, without elaboration, so that it can be immediately understood; it must have the sole aim of one particular lesson and not offer the distraction of other issues or ambiguities. The context of that aspect of the story to which the speaker draws particular attention must be familiar to the listeners, close to their normal experience and thought, so that the specific incident and its meaning stands out prominently against a background that provides no surprise or puzzle. Neither the scene nor the characters are individualised since the greater the individualisation, the greater is the risk of disparate and confusing responses. The style must be bare, objective, so that the reader will not identify with the character but remain at a critical judicial distance. The characters are always types. When animals are used in these illustrative anecdotes they can be so used because they are reduced to single well-known characteristics on which the moral turns – the cunning of the fox, the might of the lion, the timorous speed of the hare, the innocence of the lamb and the foolishness of the sheep, the greed and obstinacy of the pig etc. In the same way the human characters are generalised into types – the father and the son, the good housewife, the sower, the master and the servant, the good neighbour. In order to isolate and emphasise the lesson of his fable the teller must share, or at least adopt, certain common assumptions which he is not concerned to challenge and for this reason, in a later age, problems and issues will be discerned that were not intended earlier. Thus the parables of Jesus about the unfaithful steward or the prodigal son are read quite differently in an age when the ancient conception of the master–servant or the father–son relationship is no longer accepted.

If the fable and parable share these features, in other ways they are different. Traditionally the fable is distinguished by the use of animal characters while in the parable we expect human beings. This distinction is not so great as might be inferred since the animals speak and think like human beings and are like them not individualised; it is clear that they are meant to illustrate human predicaments, faults and virtues and they have the extra attraction that in spite of this glaring anthropomorphisation the behaviour of these humanised animals reflects shrewdly enough their observed appearance. But, perhaps because of this, the wisdom the fable teaches is above all practical and useful, for an animal would be an unsuitable vessel for a subtle spiritual truth. And the greatest and characteristic distinction of the parable is that it is concerned with spiritual principles and attitudes, and with behaviour as it flows from these. It creates simple practical models of God's ways with man and teaches what are the right and wrong human responses: it is essentially an instrument of religious instruction.

The central purpose of fable and parable has not changed greatly over the centuries. Both have remained above all media for the use of moral and religious teachers and preachers, and they were extremely popular in the later Middle Ages and Renaissance, when the concept of an independent art of literature scarcely existed. The most prominent of the changes they underwent arose from the effort of the tellers to bring the circumstances of the tales up to date, to attach an anecdote to a particular town, profession, or even person. Since at the same time, with the development of printing, the fable lost its oral character and was written for readers, there was opportunity for developing this sort of local colour at greater length, to win the attention of remote readers as well as near neighbours. But though this didactic literature was extremely popular in the Europe of the sixteenth and seventeenth centuries, it became a sort of sub-literature, for its themes remained mostly domestic and humble in an age in which 'high' literature was engaging in the grandest and deepest of human concerns. The fables of La Fontaine, the literary peak of the fable, are indeed an oddity in his time, the later seventeenth century. In form they are brilliant. Vivid images evoke his animals, the narrative is terse and swift, the dialogue lively and full of wit, the moral comments pointed, humorous, and often full of humane feeling. But it is strange to find so sophisticated and subtle a narrative skill and linguistic mobility married to so humble a morality, and it would seem that these entrancing fables were read for their charm rather than their explicit message. In the succeeding centuries the fable fell out of fashion in the higher culture, pursuing its modest way in quieter regions; perhaps only in Russia was it possible for a Krylov to win a high literary status for his shrewd versions. European literature did not forgo moralising, even preaching; but more and more it was felt that the 'moral' must be implicit in the story, and as stories filled with more and more life, any 'moral' came to be inadequate and misleading.

Parable and fable must be distinguished from allegory although all arise from a similar purpose, to instruct in or exhort to right thought and behaviour. Allegory indeed became one of the main literary and artistic forms from the Middle Ages to the eighteenth century, whether harnessed in the interest of religion, like *Piers Plowman* or *The Pilgrim's progress*, or of courtly love like the novels of Mlle de Scudéry. But the method of allegory is different from that of parable. Whether it offers a story of many episodes or few, allegory is built out of elements – situations, events, characters – that stand for something else, for some vice or virtue, some temptation or ideal, and their function in the story is this spiritual one that dominates and often obliterates their natural character. It is true that in the most living of allegories, such as Bunyan's *The Pilgrim's progress*, the actual living characters of the allegorical figures keep to our delight always breaking through their formal function, as in the conversations of giant and giantess at Castle Despair. But usually the relation of each item to a specific meaning destroys the living unity of characters and events and, if the lesson becomes plain, the aesthetic experience is pallid. By contrast we can see how important it is that the parable is limited to a very simple theme and situation, since this can be presented to us as a whole event in its own terms without the need for allegorical hints and props. Its religious or moral meaning arises from the totality of the event, not out of the particular meanings of its parts, and it is this totality that evokes not one but many life-situations in which similar problems, faults, choices are to be found and made.

The modern history of the parable is similar to that of the fable, though its close association with doctrinal teaching has placed sterner limitations on its survival in the secular civilisation of modern times. While the ancient biblical parables retained their significance within and without the churches, few new ones arose except in the context of the sermon. The limitless greed for incident and adventures, for the excitements of war and love, contributed to the growth of an extensive allegorical literature during and after the Middle Ages, and even the pious retelling of biblical stories, such as we know in Philipp von Zesen's seventeenth-century novels based on such popular stories as those of the biblical Joseph, shows a predilection for incident and dramatic tension that is the very opposite of the parable. As a genre, the parable in these centuries shows its most pertinacious vitality in the closed Jewish communities of Eastern Europe, where a rabbinical literature of religious anecdote, often verging on allegory, served until modern times to elucidate the faith in terms of the life-situations familiar to these communities.

The great crisis of religious belief in the nineteenth century, that in the case of the Jews was exacerbated by their social emancipation, led to an almost frenzied search for substitute faiths, and the first decades of the twentieth century bear witness to this search in various ways.[1] Just as in Christian circles there was a revival of interest in the medieval moralities and mysteries, so in emancipated Jewish circles there grew a lively interest in the mass of religious anecdote flourishing in the Eastern European rabbinical literature, notably in the Chasidic tradition, of whose spiritual value Martin Buber made his contemporaries appreciatively conscious. For most of the emancipated, educated Jews in Germany and other Western cultures these rabbinical stories held a nostalgic attraction enhanced by their alienation from the ancient communities and beliefs. We can see from Kafka's diaries that he too, living in a great centre of traditional Jewish orthodoxy but philosophically and socially divorced from it, felt at times something like this nostalgic affection for these products of a more primitive and closer community. This was not unusual. What was unusual was that he found in the ancient tradition of exegetic story and parable not a sentimental comfort but a means to express his own spiritual situation. He created a modern type of parable, not by modernising its formal elements or building out its descriptive detail, but by returning to its original simplicity of structure as a means to express, with excruciating simplicity, a message that is the very opposite of the faith that inspired the traditional parable. Several of Kafka's brief parables have indeed been shown to have arisen from Jewish stories to which he supplies a new ending and message.[2]

It was Heinz Politzer, in his important study *Franz Kafka: parable and paradox*, who firmly established the parabolic character of Kafka's stories and their formal connexion with the Jewish tradition of parabolic anecdote, and on this basis could define their peculiar character as 'code ciphers conveying indecipherable messages'.[3] But in his first chapter, 'A discourse on method', Politzer fails to distinguish Kafka's parables from his stories and because of this approaches the parables with, I believe, false premises. He applies to Kafka's parables the pious ingenuity of rabbinical biblical exegesis that finds in the sacred stories, the myths, of the Old Testament never-ending possibilities of meaning, scrutinising every word, every turn of phrase, for some secret message. Now, this method has its justification for the biblical stories, those about the patriarchs for instance, as it does for myth in general, since such texts reveal layers of meaning deposited by successive ages, who add to and subtract from original versions in order to meet their need. Round the great figures collect a group of variable meanings that together construct the significance of the hero for the subsequent life of the people. Politzer looks in Kafka's parables for a similar fullness of meaning that reaches out beyond the confines of the actual situation presented. Instead of recognising the abstract character of the figures of parable, Politzer sees them as having a real individual life that is hidden from us and that holds perhaps the clue to their meaning; the events of such a parable, Politzer says, 'seem to be the last visible signs of invisible chain reactions which originate in the unknown, the not-knowable'. Since these remarks are made specifically in relation to Kafka's parable 'Give it up!', I defer more precise discussion of them till I discuss this parable. But it seems to me a grave error, that raises innumerable irrelevant questions and needlessly magnifies the uncertainties that Kafka texts provoke. Kafka's parables are much more akin in form to the parables of Jesus. Like these they are about imaginary, typified figures, cut off from any past or future, from any reality except an imaginative one, and built round a particular theme; they are not accretions but are deliberately composed and completed. If they are baffling, we should understand that this is their intended effect, and we should not look outside them for clues or explanations.

At the same time, a baffling parable need not be an 'open parable' in the precise sense that Politzer gives this term. By it he means a parable with an infinite number of possible meanings, and Ingeborg Henel is certainly justified in saying that this would imply that every interpretation is 'equally meaningless'.[4] Here we shall use the term in a more restricted sense.

I. THE THIRD-PERSON PARABLES

Kafka's parables and fables belong essentially to the years following the publication of his early tales 'The judgment' and 'The metamorphosis', to the years when we find abundant evidence in his diaries and imaginative work such as *The trial* and *The castle* that the problem of religious faith (or unbelief) was deeply occupying and tormenting his mind. I use both terms, parable and fable, to indicate that in these pieces he used sometimes animal, sometimes human characters, but in fact there is in this context little profit in distinguishing the two forms. From the beginning it is clear that Kafka's work in this genre belongs to the tradition of parable, and Heinz Politzer quite rightly spoke simply of them all as parables. What this term means is that Kafka's parables, including those that, like 'Little fable', seem closest to the form of the fable, are concerned with spiritual attitudes and problems, not with practical morals; one might almost say, indeed, that viewed in relation to the ancient tradition of fable they strangely and alarmingly lack all concern for practical behaviour, for interpersonal and social obligations. One may legitimately wonder whether Kafka thought of his animal tales as fables; even the title 'Little fable' was invented by Max Brod for a story that in Kafka's manuscript has no title.

In some ways Kafka's parables (henceforth this term will include what might be called fables) are in form closer to the ancient type than the modern. There is a minimum of description, no brilliance of imagery or subtlety of dialogue, no verbal sparkle or elegance; nor does he seek the local colour, the characterisation that is an attraction of the rabbinical anecdotal parables. In the bareness of his settings, the lack of individualisation of his characters, the abstractness of his situations, he echoes the serious simplicity of the ancient parable, with its universalistic reference. In many Kafka also adopts the traditional narrative medium of the non-personal narrator, who stands at a distance (technical and moral) from his characters and whose unchallengeable authority guarantees the significance of every item in the story. But if in these ways he seems to associate himself more with the ancient tradition than with modern variations, in another he is startlingly modern. For though he invites us to read these parables as we would ancient parables, with the same expectation of a simple moral lesson that will illuminate the meaning of the events related, in fact the reader finds his expectations cheated, for there is no formulated moral and the conclusion of the incident is obscure and ambiguous, leaving the reader baffled and distressed. Politzer gave the name 'open parable' to this type of Kafka parable, but I do not think he admitted to what a degree such a term is a forbidding paradox. For the essence, the *raison d'être* of the fable or parable is precisely a clear, defined moral inference or injunction; and here, in Kafka's parables, this essence is absent. We can easily imagine 'morals' that are more open, less precise, less narrow than the Aesopian; but if a story does not allow for any conclusion, and yet invites us to expect one, it runs the danger of seeming mere cynical play – unless its object is to attack the whole tradition of believing that moral rules can be formulated. Yet the simplicity and transparency of these Kafka parables are such that they do not at all seem to be intended to be cynical parodies; they are not like Brecht's parodies of popular hymns. Rather, they seem to be forced from him in his effort to find an image for the human situation, and he himself is distressed by what comes into being.

In addition to these parables there are other, even contrary tendencies in Kafka's parabolic writing which include both the individualisation of a situation and the use of a first-person narrator. There is no sharp difference of date between the different types, but we will start our examination of a few examples with the type I have defined and leave to the end the first-person parables, which are more frequent at the end of Kafka's life.

'Little fable' ('Kleine Fabel', 1920)

'Alas', said the mouse, 'the world is growing smaller every day. At first it was so wide that I was afraid, I went on running and was glad that at last I saw in the distance walls to right and left, but these long walls are hurrying so swiftly towards one another that I am already in the last room and there in the corner stands the trap into which I am running.' – 'You have only to change direction', said the cat, and ate it up.

This is disarmingly similar to a traditional fable and Max Brod's title is appropriate enough. Speaking animals invoke all the associations of the fable and we read in it a symbolic message. Mouse and cat symbolise human qualities, stand for weakness and power, the hunted and the hunter, victim and victor, timidity and ferocity, harmlessness and pitilessness, panic and calm. The weak mouse, hynotised by its fear, runs irresistibly towards the doom prepared by man, only to succumb to the cat who calmly and with relish tells its victim, before she is eaten, how to escape.

But what is the lesson? Is it that of Aesop's wolf and lamb, that there's no arguing with power? Or is it: 'Don't surrender to your fear'? Or: 'Don't fear the world merely because it is open'? Or: 'Don't always keep on in the same direction'? Or: 'Don't complain to the powerful, who are your enemies'? Or: 'Have you asked whether this doom is deserved'? Or is it a fable about a cat – 'Power disguises itself as friendship' or 'Power likes to humiliate as well as destroy' etc.? Some or all of these 'lessons' may be drawn, but surely one loses oneself in endless speculations if one expects there to be a clear lesson to be drawn from this example from life. Simple in its outlines the story has indefinite implications. The function of fable was to allow us to understand life, to order and label its manifestations, to teach us practical wisdom that will serve to guide our behaviour. But this fable of Kafka's does not illuminate the mind but terrifies and confuses.

Its apparently so simple form powerfully contributes to this result. It is composed of two statements followed by a conclusive 'and ate it up'. But actually this simplicity is highly sophisticated. The mouse's successive phrases start as reflexions upon the past but end in the present tense, the recognition of the threat to its life. These successive phrases pour out tonelessly, breathlessly, without a true pause, without distinctions of emphasis or feeling, communicating the helpless panic that has seized the creature. The transfer of activity from herself to the walls which close in on her intensifies the reader's feeling of the paralysis of will and mind that is overtaking her. The relaxed ease of the cat's remark and the last words are brief and sudden like the deadly spring that we imagine. And the simple finality of 'and ate it up' confirms the ending with the authority of the objective narrator.

This narrator hardly appears. But he ensures that we read the words of the mouse and the cat as their partial view, not as general truths, and above all he holds us at a distance from the characters and thus allots to us the role of impartial judges. This narratorial stance, so different from that in Kafka's stories where the narrator normally evades authoritative judgments and viewpoints and, adopting the perspective of the character, continually submerges the reader in the character's experience, is characteristic of the religious teacher, the composer of parables. In the stories, as we have seen, the impersonal narrator's dual function, to establish the events of the story and to evoke the experience of the character, is shared in very unequal proportions, since the experiential side dominates in quantity and quality of significance the record of events. In 'Little fable' and the other third-person parables these proportions change drastically or, rather, the role of the narrator as an independent recorder of incident and describer of situation becomes very large and important. He can still tell us of the experience of the character but he does so from outside, not through the medium of free indirect speech which in the stories often implies the subordination of the independent objective view to the subjective view of the character. Or, as in 'Little fable', direct speech is used by the characters to express their thoughts and feelings, and this means that we take note of their views as something distinct and personal, something towards which we may stand in a critical relationship. Thus the most characteristic feature of Kafka's narrative style in the stories, the submerging of the objective narrator in the character, is absent from the third-person parables. It is this independent objective authority that we recognise in all the items of 'Little fable', though in this mini-fable these are of course very few, and for this reason the shock of reaching not a religious message and lesson but a disaster and a puzzle is all the more disconcerting.

'Before the law' ('Vor dem Gesetz', 1914)

'Little fable' belongs to 1920, but its spirit is close to Kafka's perhaps most famous parable, 'Before the law', which was written in 1914. This forms part of the unfinished novel *The trial*, and in its context is proffered by the prison chaplain as a 'holy' text that belongs to the documents of the law and should overcome Josef K.'s febrile resistance to the charge laid against him. Since Kafka himself published it separately we can first consider it as an independent work.[5]

Again the work proclaims its genre from the opening words – 'Before the law stands a door-keeper.' The identity of law with a place is biblical, though Old Testamentary rather than New, and we are immediately in the mental region in which the law is God's word and its decrees worshipped as the tables were once in the ark. Throughout, the term law is used without explanation, in its bare dignity, and worship of it belongs unquestionably to it. So we expect a parable within a normal religious framework, and the second sentence confirms this: 'To this door-keeper there comes a man from the country and begs for admission to the law.' We understand the door-keeper is a servant of the law and the 'man from the country' is a simple believer seeking the fulfilment of his faith; all the terms are traditional, all simple and abstract. When the believer is told by the door-keeper that he cannot be admitted now, though he may be later, the man accepts the refusal; but he is bewildered when the door-keeper taunts him with the account of the hierarchy of numberless door-keepers that will bar his way to the law, for, he tells himself 'the law must be accessible for all and at all times' – and he now notices what an alien 'tartar' appearance his door-keeper has. The simple man settles down to wait, tolerated by the door-keeper but treated as an inferior and a nuisance; he grows old and senile, all his thoughts obsessed by this one obstacle, the door-keeper. As he falls blind he becomes aware of a radiance that 'unquenchably' issues through the forbidden doorway. Before he dies he is allowed to ask one final question: 'All strive towards the law; how is it that in these many years no one but me has asked for admission?' And the door-keeper 'bawls' at him: 'No one else could gain admission here, for this entrance was appointed for you alone. I am now going to shut it.'

Just as the terms of this story belong to parable, so also does the narrative form. For it is told with complete authority, the authority of a narrator who knows the place and function of each item in his exemplary tale, that is to say its meaning in the whole; who therefore is leading the reader to an ending that will reveal the meaning of the whole. This narrator concentrates our attention on the 'man from the country', since he is the subject of the story, and we are informed about his thoughts and feelings whereas the temple of the law and the door-keeper are described from outside (there is no external description of the main character). But though this narrative perspective is superficially parallel to that in Kafka's early tales, the independence of the narrator's objective perspective is always retained and repeatedly emphasised. It is he who describes the arrival of the man, explains that he bends down in order to peer through the door, that after he settles down to wait he tries to bribe the door-keeper etc. The tale of the long wait is securely in the narrator's hands, especially clearly so in the foreshortening of time, for it requires the retrospective narrator if the passage of days and years is to be summed up in a brief sentence. This external authority appears when we are told that the man deludes himself with the belief that this door-keeper is 'the only hindrance' preventing his admission to the law or again when we are told the man is becoming 'infantile' and blind, matters the man cannot himself know of or be sure of. In the last sentence, when we are told that the door-keeper 'sees the man's end is near', we stand, with the narrator, outside the action. At no time does this narrator suffer from any of the conditions limiting a personal narrator, never does his report subordinate itself to the subjective experience of the man. And this means that we too, the readers, are placed in this position, are spectators of a situation and event the significance of which we are led to believe is to be made manifest and which we are called on to understand.

Since the form of this story is indubitably that of a parable most critics consider that, in spite of the cruel deception of the man from the country, there must be a religious meaning for his rejection, and this must lie in some sin attached to him. Some critics suggest this must be the barbarism, paganism that belongs to men from the country, though this would run utterly against its normal meaning of simple faith. Others suggest that his unpardonable sin was his patience, his readiness to sit and wait, to obey the menial door-keeper, when he should have taken the law by storm (this would be a curious lesson for the chaplain to give Josef K., for his intention in telling this parable is to dissuade Josef from his protests and persuade him to admit his guilt; and the K. of *The castle*, who does try to take the castle by storm, comes to no better end than the patient 'man from the country'). But no ingenuity can obliterate the massive simplicity of this tale, and we have to come to terms with the idea that Kafka is saying that so cruel a punishment may be visited on simple trust. We might allay our horror by transferring the blame to the humble servant of the law, but this too would be a mere evasion.

The error of the religious interpretations is very understandable because the form of the parable and its whole manner invites the reader to expect some such lesson. But we learn that this invitation cannot be fulfilled, and we have to learn to accept this. It is not that Kafka is using the parable parodistically, in order to make fun of a genre that defined spiritual values and a spiritual order within the world. He sought these himself and always clung to the hope that they might exist and create a meaning to life that it does not have on the everyday plane. But the situations his mind imagined always led him into bewilderment and despair. For his generation Georg Lukács wrote in 1916, before he became a Marxist: 'The abandonment of the world by God is evident in the incongruity of soul and achievement. Human endeavour lacks transcendental coordinates.'[6] Lukács overcame this dilemma by embracing Marxism; Georg Simmel by shearing the supernatural attributes from the concepts of soul and God. But Kafka could never renounce his longing for a spiritual meaning and authority even though it always eluded him and at best tantalised him as an uncertain gleam through a doorway or a misty outline on a hill. If the heroes of *The trial* and *The castle* persist in seeking some metaphysical authority, they never reach it nor find their hopes confirmed; they are cheated as the 'man from the country' in 'Before the law' is cheated. But in every case the author does not triumph over their failure; in it he embodies his own grief and despair. The form of the parable enables him to express his persistent hope as well as its grievous disappointment.

In *The trial* this parable is followed by a discussion on its meaning between the chaplain and Josef K. The latter, finding in it a parallel to his own treatment by the servants of the law, or to the chaplain's all-too-ready assumption of his guilt, takes it as an indictment of an unfaithful servant, the door-keeper; and when the chaplain defends the latter's behaviour as 'necessary', Josef K. bitterly remarks: 'A melancholy inference. Lying is made into a universal principle.' The chaplain's own attitude and argument seem to be underpinned by the dignity of his office and of the cathedral in which he stands in the pulpit, yet if we assume this we are perhaps being misled much as we may be by the parabolic form of the story about the 'man from the country'. This chaplain is hollow; his credit lies only in his office and the circumstances in which he speaks.[7] He assumes Josef K. to be guilty before he has come to trial; when Josef maintains his innocence the chaplain's rejection, 'So speak all the guilty', means that in his view all men are guilty; and he skilfully uses all the resonance of the cathedral and the authority of the preacher to urge his views. Finally, when he begins to elaborate on the possible meanings of the parable he has told, he finds such a variety of problems and tackles them with such a zestful volubility that we recognise here a bureaucrat for whom these spiritual issues are enjoyable intellectual playthings and who is quite incapable of understanding that for Josef K. they are matters of life and death. If Josef K. is dissatisfied with his own conclusion, he and we are even less satisfied with the chaplain's empty dialectics. So that in the novel, as well as when we read 'Before the law' as a separate parable, we find its 'meaning' is its lack of meaning, the deceiving of love and faith; though the reader may well go further than Josef K. and the chaplain in their argument and find the cause of the failure of meaning to lie not in the servant or the petitioner but in the power they serve and worship.

'The huntsman Gracchus' ('Der Jäger Gracchus', 1917)
Several of Kafka's parables are richer in detail and individualisation even than 'Before the law', and the richer they are the more they inevitably tend to story; that is, the richer the suggestiveness and the more specific the characters, the less clearly will they serve an unambiguous meaning. Often the elements may have such stray radiance and point in such different directions, may be so unfulfilled within the framework of the work, that one does not know what to call them, parable or legend or story. I use 'parable' only when the various facets of the story, by fusing into a meaning, require us to seek it. To this borderline type belongs the mysterious and fascinating 'The huntsman Gracchus'.

The opening describes a still, dreamlike scene, the almost deserted little harbour on the Lake Garda (it is Riva that Kafka knew well). A strange barque arrives, seemingly drifting before the breeze, and a sailor leaps out and moors the boat to the quay, and two black-coated bearers carry on to the quay a bier on which a covered human figure is lying. They wait there till the skipper has secured the sail and then the three proceed with the bier to a nearby house which they enter. A man in formal mourning clothes, top hat and black gloves, comes down from the town and after knocking is admitted to the house, where fifty young boys form a welcoming double row. The barque skipper greets the visitor and takes him up to a room on the first floor where lies the man on the bier, lighted candles at his head; his wild matted hair and beard and brown skin seem to refute the impression that he is a corpse. When the two bearers and the skipper leave the room, the prostrate man opens his eyes and with a painful smile asks the visitor who he is; the latter answers, 'The mayor of Riva', and adds that he knows the other is the huntsman Gracchus, for a pigeon had woken him in the night and whispered to him that he was officially to welcome 'the dead huntsman Gracchus'. Gracchus asks the mayor whether he thinks he is to stay in Riva, and the latter answers that he cannot say, but asks: 'Are you dead?' Gracchus then explains who he is.

Long before, Gracchus was a great huntsman, the famous huntsman of the Black Forest, who had fallen to his death when hunting chamois. But the death-barque that was to have taken him to the other world (*das Jenseits*) had by some accident or negligence of the skipper lost the way, and for centuries now they have been crossing the seas, never able to find the way; sometimes he thinks he is near the goal but his hopes are always cheated and he is doomed to travel for ever in the dismal barque of death, his 'wooden cage', still alive 'in a way'. He had always enjoyed life and was glad too to welcome death, and he does not understand why he should have suffered such misfortune. When the mayor asks him whether he had incurred any guilt, Gracchus answers that he knows of none and surely there is no evil in being a huntsman. The mayor agrees that so far as he can see there is no evil in it. Putting the fault on the skipper, the huntsman complains that he can find no help: no one knows of him, nor of his whereabouts, nor of how he might be helped; people hide under the bedclothes in order not to hear of him – 'The idea of helping him is a disease and must be healed under the bedclothes.' And when the mayor asks him if he intends to stay in Riva the huntsman answers, with a smile that mitigates his mockery: 'I have no intentions. I am here, I do not know more and I cannot do more. My barque has no rudder, it drives before the wind that blows from the nethermost regions of death.'

The message of this strange parable, summed up in the huntsman's last words, is clear enough: the alienation of man, falling upon him without cause, pursues him even after death, forbidding him the peace of oblivion. As the author postulates a mythical underworld and ferryman, the story is full of mythical or fairy-tale elements, more than I could include in my brief synopsis, and from the beginning, the still scene in the harbour, the reader is entranced in a magical spell. Many of the details are difficult to understand and might seem mere decoration or mood-creators. But the brilliant researches of Hartmut Binder have uncovered the source of almost every puzzling item and have done the great service of clarifying the specific importance of Kafka's composition.[8] Some of the descriptive items, like the harbour at Riva, come from other contexts, even from contemporary stories; the boys who greet the mayor are reminders of an earlier version, and so on. But Binder's chief discovery was to link Kafka's main theme, usually till then accepted as an original invention, with the ancient myths of the Wild Hunter and the Flying Dutchman, of which the former appears in a collection of legends in Kafka's library, the second would be known to him through Heine's account and perhaps through Wagner's opera which was based on Heine. Both these legends are built round men who cannot die and are forced endlessly to roam the woods or seas; the legend of the Wandering Jew also contributed to Kafka's story, as Binder suggests. But these sources also throw into relief the peculiarity of Kafka's conception. For the Flying Dutchman and the Wild Hunter are condemned to wander because of a sin or crime, and both are permitted to return to life at seven-yearly intervals with the hope of winning redemption through the love or intercession of a human being. This double source explains the connexion of Kafka's huntsman with the sea and the landing at Riva; it explains too the reference of the huntsman to the 'help' he can never hope for, which in Kafka's story is puzzling. But above all, these sources, which bear a familiar message of guilt, punishment and redemption, make it all the more remarkable that Kafka's huntsman is guiltless and that his suffering is incomprehensible, a theme that is so profoundly Kafkaesque and so disturbing that few readers can acknowledge its presence. To cap his discoveries Binder points out that the apparently mysterious name *Gracchus* is the Latin for 'daw, jackdaw' (Kafka would have known the Italian *gracchio*), and this is also the meaning of 'Kafka' itself. So that under this code lies Kafka's message: 'this is my fate, too'.

There can be no doubt that the multiplicity of motifs in this parable threatens to bury the message, or better, to disperse the message in a brilliant shower of possible associations that lead away from the central issue. We are here on the borderline of a story, which is not only more complex in motif and setting than the parable but also is not so tightly bound up with a meaning, a message. Faulty as a parable, 'The huntsman Gracchus' may serve however to close this review of parables written in the third person, partly in that it illustrates the claim this form makes to present an imaginative general truth and partly in that, through the name that makes 'Kafka' the hero, this particular parable slyly disclaims a general validity and becomes a personal confession. It links with the first-person parables, as with the later tales, in another important respect since it does not present us with a closed incident but leaves the reader suspended in an uncompleted puzzle.

2. PARABLES IN THE FIRST PERSON

The third-person parables so far discussed all have that non-personal narrator who is a function not an identity. The lack of third-person parables with a personal narrator is not accidental. For the role of the narrator is here authoritative, he bears the authority of the religious teacher, and any personal identity could only diminish this unquestioned authority. This authority Kafka claims even for parables that offer dismay and puzzlement instead of comfort and guidance.

For a similar reason the first-person parables do not include any in which the personal narrator is only at the periphery of the action, a bystander; always the narrator is the main character himself. Only this character has an authority equal to that of the impersonal (often called omniscient) narrator, though his authority comes from a different source and applies to a different field. It is the authority of authentic experience, inward experience, as contrasted with that of religious conviction and truth; to neither of these could a bystander lay claim with such power. Because of this, these first-person parables of Kafka have a different structure as well as a different quality; they describe the character's experience of events rather than the events and situations themselves. And while they are like the third-person parables in that they present the reader with a fearful and puzzling situation, they are different in that the story, the action, is not rounded off with a conclusive ending, but ends as it were without a conclusion.

'Give it up!' ('Gibs Auf!', 1922)

It was early in the morning, the streets were clean and deserted, I was going to the railway station. When I compared a tower clock with my watch I saw that it was much later than I had thought, I had to hurry, the fright over my discovery made me uncertain about the route, I did not as yet know my way about in this city, luckily there was a policeman at hand, I hurried up to him and breathlessly asked him the way. He smiled and said: 'Are you asking *me* to tell you the way?' 'Yes', I said, 'since I can't find it myself.' 'Give it up, give it up' he said and turned on his heel with a flourish, like people who want to be alone with their laughter.

Brod gave this parable its title.[9] The narrator tells how, trying to find the way to the station in a strange city, and pressed for time, he asks the way of a policeman – the German word *Schutzmann* emphasises the latter's function as a 'protector'. The policeman, aggressively addressing the stranger with the familiar 'du' that a superior uses to an inferior, jeers at the very idea of expecting help from him and turns away triumphantly to enjoy a good laugh. One can see a relationship between this parable and 'Little fable'. The central figures of both are caught in a trap, the stream of pauseless sentences conveys their

growing panic, and cat and policeman rejoice in their helplessness. But while 'Little fable' ends in catastrophe, 'Give it up!'
breaks off in bewilderment, bewilderment over being lost and
bewilderment over the failure of expected help.

The first chapter of Politzer's *Franz Kafka: parable and
paradox* is devoted to an exhaustive analysis of 'Give it up!'
that provides a model of Politzer's critical method, and since
this method has great advantages as well as significant faults I
take the opportunity of giving a critical summary of much of
its argument, especially that part that is relevant to the nature
of parable.

Recognising that 'Give it up!' is an example of a Kafkaesque
type to which he gives the term 'open parable', Politzer considers it to be an image of 'the insoluble paradox of human
existence' (p. 22) and rightly rejects all those types of interpretation that would read into it as a whole, or into particular
elements in it, some clear, unequivocal meaning. Amongst
these are the view that the parable presents the position of the
Jew in the Habsburg empire; that which sees it as an image of
pathological angst and the policeman as a father-figure; that
which detects in it a moral lesson on the evils of impatience;
that which sees the policeman as a messenger from a higher
realm (pp. 9–13). Demonstrating the insufficiency of these
'explanations', Politzer concludes that while the parable clearly
centres upon the uncertainty of the individual in a world of
'disorder', it does not present any religious interpretation of
this disorder; nor does it bear an existential message, he argues,
since we do not know whether that 'Give it up!' demonstrates
a real power of choice nor whether such a choice would free the
man from his uncertainties.

But though Politzer rejects certain positive interpretations,
he himself lays false trails. For he sees almost every item of the
little story as a riddle, as posing a question, even if this question
cannot find an answer (pp. 3–8). The story is for him the tip of
an iceberg and everywhere he sends down probes to find causes
and motives. When the man looks at the public clock on its

tower, Politzer says: 'We feel strangely compelled to ask for the motivation of his trivial action. His watch was slow; he must have sensed that he was behind time.' And Politzer goes on to suggest that we are presented with a contrast between subjective and objective time; the clock on the high tower means a 'higher' order of reality, and the shock the man experiences is due to his realisation that 'he is no longer in step with a higher order of things'. On the other hand the question arises, why does he accept the clock's time as true, why does he not check it? Perhaps his own time, his watch, is right?

Or again, since his insecurity arises from his unfamiliarity with the city, perhaps the cause of his discomfiture is his impatience; he should have waited till he was more at home there. It is impatience that brings him to want to leave, that causes his haste.

Or questions regarding the policeman. I pass over a set of suggestions that the policeman 'towers' over the man and is thus mysteriously related to the tower clock, since these clearly go beyond the text. Politzer also makes an unnecessary mystery of the presence of the policeman in the deserted street and asks why the man does not question why he was there. With more justification he suggests that the policeman's arrogant and jeering question really may indicate diffidence, uncertainty on his part, that it is only a question not an affirmation and is misunderstood by the man. The policeman's use of 'way' may indicate something deeper than merely the way to the station. And what does 'give it up' refer to? Does it not mean more than just 'give up your effort at finding the way to the station', perhaps give up your haste and your travels? Politzer goes so far in his exegetical enthusiasm as to write: 'We hasten to substitute an "everything" for this "it". "Give everything up!" the policeman seems to be saying, "let all hope go, abandon the way and the desire ever to find it, give up your quest, your drive and your yearning, your very existence – yourself!"' These few syllables, Politzer concludes, 'can mean anything from benevolent advice to the most sinister urge to self-destruction'.

We can see that by the term 'open parable' he means, not a parable embodying a tormenting scepticism, a despair of meaningfulness, but one that offers a choice of many interpretations, all indiscriminately possible.

My primary concern here is not to point out how far-fetched some of Politzer's suggestions are, but to show that they indicate a false conception of the parable genre. When we read Jesus' parable of the Prodigal Son, we do not ask, what did the father cultivate on his farm? What work did he require of his sons? What were his relations with his wife? What upbringing did he give his sons? What quarrels caused the son to leave home? etc. etc. We understand the parable to present a generalised case, representative figures and conflicts, the great and central theme alone being unique: the son's confession of sin and prayer for pardon, the father's forgiveness and joy. So here, in 'Give it up!', Kafka provides a concrete image of a general situation, concrete enough to have a recognisable outline, but generally applicable for the very reason that the man concerned has no character except his wish to get to the station in time, his fear of being late, his confusion about the way. This is a situation everyone has experienced, both in this precise form and in other forms for which it can serve as a model. All those questions that Politzer asks are irrelevant, about subjective and objective time, about haste and fear. On the background of this normal situation there stands out the one, unique event: the policeman to whom the man naturally turns in his difficulty refuses to help, jeers at the very idea that he (or anyone else) will help, and tells the man to give up his attempt. That is, the normal assumption of order, upon which we build our daily existence, is suddenly shattered, and we are left baffled. I suggest that this is the direct 'message' of the parable and it is in this way that we are intended to read a parable.

Thus Kafka's parable is 'open' not because it offers an infinite number of possible and perhaps contradictory meanings, but because it describes an event that suddenly, mysteriously, without cause, shatters our innocent expectation of order and meaning. This is the immediate content of this parable of Kafka's. Like all parables, however, it has innumerable applications and the reader tests its truth against other types of experience through which a familiar and understood world suddenly reveals unexpected disorder and threats. The fault of many Kafka critics is to see some particular experience as the meaning of this parable, while the task of the writer was to create a model for many experiences.

There remains the question of the form of this parable, in that it is written in the first person, the 'man' being 'I'. This is not considered by Politzer. If this parable had been written in the third person, I believe the reader would feel he had the right to know what came next, he would require the anecdote to be completed – as the story of the mouse is completed in 'Little fable'. But I do not think we in fact look beyond the end of 'Give it up!', and I believe the reason is that it is written in the first person. We understand it as a symbolic statement of a general experience of incipient lostness and isolation and bewilderment, a condition which affects most of us. This experience does not necessarily lead to catastrophe nor to any conclusion; most of us survive it without conquering it. How we survive is in this parable not at issue; its essential theme is the repeated experience of being abandoned. The use of the first-person narrative places the reader more precisely in the position of the character than does the third person. That is, it places him in the position of a man who is reflecting on his experience and still remains baffled and suspended within the uncertainties and vague threats that are suggested. The first-person form is admirably fitted to communicate this continuing situation; perhaps, even, one might suggest that this form frees the author from the obligation of inventing an end, catastrophic or not, for a situation that in its essential nature is endless.

'Testimonials' ('Fürsprecher', 1922)

'Testimonials' belongs to the same year as 'Give it up!' yet its situation and theme are closely related to the world of *The trial*.[10] The writer, a man suffering from an undefined accusation, is searching in a crowded law-courts building for witnesses to his character, guarantors, and he can nowhere find anyone suitable. It is clearly a hopeless search and the accused man himself almost gives up in despair. It is the situation familiar to us in many Kafka texts. Professor Stern has shown that *The trial* explores an issue arising from the persecution of the Jews and a response on Kafka's part that has frightening implications.[11] Its essence is that the crime the accused faces is not something he has *done* but something he *is*; thus, though he may feel that everyone joins in this condemnation, he can never find the formulation of this law nor the law courts in which he can stand trial, and the more he protests his innocence the more his guilt-feelings accumulate. Thus, in this short text 'Testimonials' the accused man is not looking for witnesses to his innocence of an alleged offence but for people who can give a favourable opinion of his character. Probably we should understand an implicit reference to antisemitism, which is certainly indicated in another short parable called 'Community' ('Gemeinschaft', 1920), in which five friends decide irrationally to exclude a sixth from their friendship.[12] The theme of 'Testimonials' has however a wider bearing than the situation of the Jews, for it is a common misfortune to imagine a charge or a guilt of this nature and to consume one's energy and happiness in a necessarily vain effort to protest one's innocence.

However 'Testimonials' (I prefer this translation of 'Fürsprecher' since 'guarantors' has unwanted implications) does not remain in this sphere of *The trial*. The story-teller describes how tempted he is by his failure to give up the search for witnesses and retrace his steps, submit. But then something in him rebels, for to retrace his steps would be a confession of error, of failure. And the piece concludes with a remarkable injunction he directs to himself:

Once you have started on a path, keep on, under all circumstances, you can only win, you are running no danger, perhaps in the end you will fall to your death, but if you had turned back after your first steps and had run down the entrance stairway you would have fallen at the very outset and not perhaps, but certainly. So, if you find nothing here in the corridors open the doors, if you find nothing behind these doors there are more floors above, if you find nothing up there do not worry, hoist yourself up new stairs. As long as you do not stop climbing the steps will not give out, under your mounting feet they will grow upwards.

This is a most unusual ending for a work by Kafka, for it is a moral injunction, an exhortation with regard to behaviour. As such it brings 'Testimonials' closer to the traditional fable or parable than we should expect, even if the precept does not belong to the practical wisdom or altruistic principle that form the staple of the ancient parable. Nor does this work, with its ending, negate the image of a hostile, baffling world that recurs so insistently in Kafka's stories and parables. The writer remains engaged in an apparently hopeless search, there is no end in sight, no resolution of his puzzles and problems; we can even observe, in the hurry and anxious articulation of his sentences something akin to the panic of the mouse or the man lost in the city. That is, the uncertainty and suspense of the ending is a common feature of Kafka's imaginative world. But here, though suspended within uncertainties, the tone is hopeful, not despairing, and the last sentence itself emerges from the restless flow of the preceding one to form a precise, shaped, significant image, a shapely and balanced sentence. It is the Kafka world we have become familiar with, but Kafka's attitude towards it has changed. Instead of despairing he formulates a means of surviving in the midst of threats.

There is even more in this attitude than survival. One might say, all his exhortation to himself means is that he must persist in seeking those guarantors who will bear witness to his character – yet the writer has already admitted the hopelessness of such a search, just as Josef K. in *The trial* bears unconscious witness to the hopelessness of his endless rejection of the undefined accusation. But this ending contains a message, we feel, that is not limited to his misguided search. If he can really 'keep on', he will really transcend the guilt that he is charged with and that by acknowledging he persistently renews. His resistance becomes an attack, his effort will create new conditions, new 'stairs', and becomes a model of the whole creative effort of mankind.

We have something here that is extremely rare in Kafka. That it is possible at all seems to depend on its being a first-person statement. For this injunction is delivered by a man to himself in a situation that is full of insecurity. The parable starts in the past tense, describing the searcher's quest and questionings as if they were the preliminaries to some decisive event. But in the middle it switches to the present tense as his helplessness and self-questionings torture him. There is no resolving event, only a resolve that takes shape in the midst of all the uncertainties; it is a resolve to persist that does not dispel the threats and uncertainties but does re-shape his attitude. Whatever hope and energy there is in this injunction, they are no more than is permissible for the character to assert in his challenge with circumstance. As a summing up made by an authoritative objective narrator, an objective moral commentator, it would surely be or seem pretentious, unfounded, deceptive wishful thinking, and would scarcely fit into Kafka's *oeuvre*.

'The emperor's message' ('Eine kaiserliche Botschaft', 1917) The nearest approach to this ending of 'Testimonials', both in form and message, is found in the earlier parable 'The emperor's message' which Kafka published in the collection *A country doctor* in 1919. It was abstracted, as 'Before the law' was abstracted from *The trial*, from a larger unfinished work 'Building the Chinese wall', which belongs to 1917.[13] Like 'Before the law', too, it is a parable told by a character to illustrate the latter's point of view, though in this case the teller is the fictitious narrator of the whole work, a Chinese scholar who sets out to explain why the Chinese wall was built and, more generally, what the attitude of the widely scattered Chinese people is to an authority, an emperor, who lives so remote from most of his subjects that his capital itself, Peking, 'is much stranger to us than the next world'. When published separately the parable perhaps would not seem to belong to the first-person group, though the humble subject (*Untertan*) of the emperor, with whose attitude it is concerned, is addressed in the second person. But the context bears repeated references to the position and thoughts of the person composing 'Building the Chinese wall' and throughout he puts his arguments, including the parable itself, as his modest attempt at explaining the nature of the relationship of the Chinese people to their emperor, the source of their unity as a people and of what we may call their awareness of their political identity. We can thus take this parable as belonging to Kafka's first-person parables; it describes how the typical humble citizen wins this sense of identity.

This is the legend: on his death-bed the emperor calls his messenger and whispers in his ear a message he is to carry 'to you, an individual, a mean subject, a tiny shadow cowering in the furthest distance from the imperial sun'. The messenger sets out, fighting his way through crowded rooms and ante-rooms. Beyond there are endless other crowded rooms, stair-ways, courts – 'he will never get through them; and if he did, there would be still more in the great encircling palace, and so forth through millenia'. And were he to burst out of the precincts – 'but never, never can this come about' – there would still be the capital city to traverse 'clogged high with its dregs' – 'He will never get through, let alone with a message from a dead man.' And then comes the unexpected startling sentence that ends this 'legend': 'But you sit at your window and dream it [the message] into being, as evening falls.'

Up to this last sentence the legend seems to repeat, in a new and moving image, the theme of many of Kafka's tales and parables. Man longs for some recognition from a revered authority some task, some assurance that his person and his life have some significance, some meaning behind the mere fact of existence; but though the authority exists, and even if a message has been sent to him, the obstacles are such that the message will never get through, the longing and the faith are unrewarded and have been in vain. But the astonishing ending, as in 'Testimonials', transforms despair into hope. It does not deny the material facts, that is, it does not say the emperor makes contact with you or the message gives you a significant task to fulfil. No, the emperor remains no more than an image in your head and the message will never come. But the parable asserts that you can turn the supposed message into a reality by the ardour of your need and the power of your faith, you can 'dream it' into reality – Kafka uses the verb *erträumen*, and the prefix *er* means to bring the dream to completion, to fulfilment. And in his surrounding commentary the Chinese scholar explains that it is through this power of the mind that the authority of the emperor itself comes into being, that the imperial power, the unity of the nation, and the individual's sense of identity, of a worthy task, all depend ultimately on this subjective act.

When the theme of 'Building the Chinese wall' is reduced to this level of abstraction, some violence is done to the fragile little work. For all its arguments and conclusions are put in a tentative and modest form, hedged in by a sort of Chinese delicacy and politeness. It is not the work of dogmatic self-confidence but of a prudent yet tenacious search through the complexities and obscurities of existence for a basis for sufficient confidence to ensure a worthwhile existence. Our scholar retreats indeed when he finds his thoughts becoming too dangerous, especially when he might be charged with undermining the objective reality of the political authority. Kafka must have smiled to himself when he composed the scholar's prudent principle: 'Seek with all your powers to understand the instructions of the authorities, but only to a particular limit, then put a stop to your reflexions.' A gentle humour of this kind often appears in this little work, a recognition of the modesty with which, in the face of all the gigantic problems of life, a means of survival, of spiritual survival, can be discerned.

To this sense of modesty we can attribute the first-person form which presents its conclusions in a personal, hypothetical way, not as a dogma.

'Homecoming' ('Heimkehr', 1920)

Very few of Kafka's parables have the consoling or encouraging ending that 'The emperor's message' and 'Testimonials' offer, even if the consolation is only one of hope and attitude, rather than anything more concrete and tangible. However in these later parables there is a lessening of the absolute despair and angst that we usually associate with Kafka, and as my last example I take his 'Homecoming', so perfect an expression of an attitude that we frequently meet in Kafka's last years that I allow myself the indulgence of giving a translation of the whole little work. It is one of the many works that were not published during Kafka's lifetime and it was Max Brod, who first published it, who gave it its title:[14]

I have come back, I've come through the gateway and am looking round. It is my father's old farmyard. The puddle in the middle. Old unusable implements, driven into a tangled heap, clutter up the approach to the loft-steps. The cat is crouching on the landing. A ragged cloth, once draped round a pole in fun, stirs in the wind. I've arrived. Who will receive me? Who is waiting behind the kitchen door? Smoke is coming from the chimney, the coffee is being made for supper. Do you feel at ease, do you feel at home? I don't know, I'm very uncertain. It is my father's house, but one thing stands cold beside another as if each were busied with its own affairs, which I have partly forgotten, partly never knew. Of what use can I be to them, what am I to them, even though I be the son of my father the old farmer? And I don't dare to knock on the kitchen door, I only listen from a distance, standing upright, not in such a way as to risk being caught out eavesdropping. And because I am listening from a distance I make nothing out, I hear only a faint chime of a clock or perhaps only imagine I can hear it coming over from childhood. What else is going on in the kitchen is the secret of those sitting there, that they are keeping from me. The longer one hesitates outside the door, the more one becomes a stranger. How would it be if someone were now to open the door and ask me a question. Shouldn't I myself then be like a man who is intent on keeping his secret?

More than once I have criticised Hartmut Binder for referring us too emphatically and exclusively, in his commentary to Kafka's writings, to Kafka's biography and hence for singling out their autobiographical significance. In his commentary on 'Homecoming' he mentions only biographical implications.[15] But the most striking and significant feature of 'Homecoming' is that it is clearly a parable, which must mean an attempt to create a generalised situation and symbolical event; and as striking is the fact that it conjures up one of the most loved and profound of the parables of Jesus, the parable of the Prodigal Son, that embodies Christ's message of God's love for sinful man, the power of repentance and the joy in Heaven over the repentant sinner. It is only in the context of the genre of parable, and specifically in relation to the story of the Prodigal Son, that we can understand Kafka's 'Homecoming'. The explicit association – the father as a farmer, the hesitation and doubt of the returning son – and the implicit – the utterly different outcome – both surely suggest that Kafka was deliberately composing an alternative to the theme of Jesus' parable.

In Kafka's parable we do not know what the son has been doing, we are told only that he has been away, clearly for a long time. The farmyard is much as it used to be, only neglected, disorderly. There is no one there to welcome him, a cloth attached to a pole, which seems once to have been a flag, is ragged and stirs listlessly. Once familiar objects seem now unrelated to one another and to him. There are signs that people are at home, but the returning man asks himself what he can mean to them; he clearly is not returning with a mission, to take up his inheritance, restore the homestead, support his father in his old age. Whoever it is that is there, behind the kitchen door, will always possess a secret he can never penetrate; the more he hesitates, the more insurmountable this barrier between himself and his family appears to him; and he realises, as he waits outside the door, that he himself does not wish to open himself to the others, to emerge from his own isolation.

Like so many of these later Kafka parables, it is an image of a situation, not a story. There is no decisive event, the character remains poised in the midst of laming questions. There is no catastrophe as in 'Little fable', but also not the positive injunction of 'The emperor's message' or 'Testimonials'. The implicit contrast with the welcome of the Prodigal Son's father, the self-cleansing of the son's confession and prayer for forgiveness, the joy of the feast, make the return of Kafka's son sombre, hopeless. If we believe, as I think we must, that Kafka is also evoking the religious meaning of Jesus' parable, then we can recognise that he is sadly admitting that the son is alienated from his Heavenly Father's house and will never enter into his inheritance.

But the tone is one of grief, not of catastrophe or rebellion. It is the son who tells this parable, he describes his return, the farmyard, and his thoughts. The mood the account creates is his mood. It is not that of a rebel or a sinner, but of a man who half wishes to return, perhaps longs for the mutual trust and confidence of childhood, but recognises that this has gone and that return has no meaning. The account is throughout in the present tense so that the reader passes with the character through the various responses the return arouses. What it will lead to we do not know, it is not a retrospective account, and in this way too the character, with the reader, remains poised in the midst of uncertainties. Yet this lack of an ending, and the lack of decisive event, do not mean that the character is racked by anxiety. The stillness the unemphatic, undramatic scene evokes, the reflective self-questioning that the absence of question marks makes undramatic, the steady pace of the self-communion, all suggest not a sudden dilemma but already a coming to terms with his alienation, mournful but not tragic.

Jean-Paul Sartre, in an interview shortly before his death, was asked about the 'despair' he had written about in *Being and nothingness,* and he answered that he had never really felt despair; man cannot live without hope, he said, and hopes cannot be fully realised, but what he had called 'despair' should better have been called 'a lucid view of the human condition'.[10]

His comment on himself has an important bearing on Kafka (whose work Sartre greatly admired). Of course, Kafka had a long and profound experience of despair, itself commensurate with the intensity of his hope, and his early parables demonstrate the angst and despair accompanying cruelly frustrated hope. But in 'Homecoming' and some other of the later parables we find not a tragic despair over the inaccessibility of the faith, trust, reconciliation that would bind him to life, but what Sartre calls 'a lucid view of the human condition'. The very composure of the style breathes this calm insight that comes to terms with the world as it is, beyond horror and panic.

3. KAFKA'S PARABLES IN REVIEW

We have not considered all those works of Kafka's that might be considered to have the form of the parable. I have confined my choice to those that approach most clearly to the form, that is, that combine a story-situation and characters sufficiently generalised to suggest a 'lesson'. What we have been able to observe is an evolution in the character of Kafka's parables, or better, a marked tendency that separates many of the later parables from the earlier.

At first the theme of the traditional parable seems to be violently inverted. In place of the encouragement, hope, faith of the traditional fable, Kafka offers disaster, the cheating of hopes, despair. He uses the familiar form of the parable, which rouses in the reader the expectation of a revelation of meaning and significance, only to shock all the more severely with a proclamation of disillusionment. The profound contentment that lies in the mutual love and trust of man and man, man and God, that forms the atmosphere of the traditional parable turns into the desolation of loneliness, alienation, abandonment. The traditional parable enables us to understand a spiritual world, Kafka's parables veil it in a baffling uncertainty. But in the later parables of Kafka, while the opacity of the world, its hostility or indifference to the helpless individual, are no less, he finds a new way of contemplating the human situation. Kafka does not provide better endings to the problems his characters face, but he shows that in the midst of uncertainties and threats they need not despair. They can summon up, perhaps, courage still to hope from the depths of their own spirit or recognise the inaccessibility of home and shelter as the natural condition of man which they may learn to endure. Neither happy endings nor catastrophic tragedies are our lot, this older Kafka seems to say, but survival in which our alienation may be quickened by an undefined hope.

To this different emphasis in the theme correspond changes in the form of the story. While the early parables have a recognisable story, i.e. an event that comes to an end, the later present almost only an unresolved situation; the character does not emerge out of his confusions through a terrible end, but remains poised in the uncertainties, changing only in his attitude towards them. Further, Kafka uses more frequently the first-person mode, so that the stories, while they seem to claim a universal validity, ultimately rely more on the note of personal experience that speaks in them; there is a winning humility in this form that accords with the modesty of the 'lesson'. And often the present tense is used and strengthens our awareness that we are invited to reflect on ever-present experience in its inconclusiveness, without the somewhat suspect wisdom that retrospection comforts us with.

I have reserved for this moment, when the main features of Kafka's parables have been reviewed, a consideration of the only attempt known to me to make the narrative perspective the feature that separates Kafka's stories from the parables. For this purpose W. H. Sokel has relied in the main on a comparison of the parable 'Before the law' with the novel to which it belongs, *The trial*, though his article of course considers several other parables and stories.[17]

Professor Sokel accepts the structural distinctions between parable and story that Hillmann makes, which correspond roughly to those formulated in the early part of this chapter and to which I refer in note 4 of chapter 1. But to these he adds 'the relationship of the narrative perspective to the events related'. In Kafka's stories, Sokel says, adopting Beissner's view, the narrator presents only the hero's experience, there is only one perspective, that of the hero, and hence 'seeing and experiencing are identical'. In the parable, on the other hand, there is an independent narrator, distanced from the characters, who may see events from various viewpoints and is not locked within the perspective of the main character. The meaning of this formal difference is that while in the stories and novels the reader is offered only the experience of the hero, in the parables he is directed towards reflexion about events; in the first his objective is experience, in the second it is knowledge, understanding. There is some truth in these definitions, but they do not hold for all Kafka's stories and parables; and since this distinction is called 'essential', a large assumption is made regarding the nature of literary genres.

In my earlier analyses of the narrative perspective of the stories I have shown that the monoperspectival view, even in the less rigid form that Sokel adopts, fails to do justice to the structure of these stories; it is equally unsatisfactory to read that where a story presents more than the hero's perspective it is tending towards the parable. Though Sokel's definitions are applied only to Kafka, one is uneasily aware that they are not valid for story and parable in general. But here I am chiefly concerned with Kafka's parables and leave other questions on one side.

It might be thought that the first-person parable would propose difficulties for Sokel's definitions, since here 'seeing and experiencing' are one. Sokel does not shirk this problem. Taking 'The emperor's message' and 'A report for an academy' as typical, he shows that in these parables the first-person narrator is distant from the events, even if only as a creature looking back over his life, so that seeing takes precedence over experiencing and the reader engages with the narrator in a search, an enquiry. It is indeed very helpful when Sokel calls this parabolic manner of writing a 'life-saving projection of an inner problem', as opposed to the dangers of submersion in experience. But of course what he says does not apply to other first-person parables like 'Give it up!' or 'Homecoming'. And since in these, which Sokel overlooks, the reader is immersed only in the perspective of the 'I', they shatter the foundation of his distinction between story and parable – for no one would dare to call these works anything but parables.

There are differences between stories and parables, as I have indicated in the opening pages of this chapter. There is also a case for arguing that all Kafka's stories have something of the parable about them in the sense that we are often aware of two levels of meaning, one explicit and one 'in code'. We are aware too of many instances where we hardly know whether to call a work a story or a parable. Here Sokel makes what seems to me a faulty assumption since he believes that there are features which 'essentially' separate the two genres. For the literary genres do not have the rigid identity and characteristics of biological species, and it is useful to adopt Wittgenstein's suggestion of 'family resemblances' as an analogy of the features that establish membership of a genre. That resemblances and differences are various and fluid does not mean that there is no reality or usefulness in the concept.

I said at the outset of this chapter that in his parables Kafka returns to the simplicity of form of the New Testament parables. He eschews the elaboration, the individualisation of character and situation, that usually marks modern variations of the older fable or parable. His own are abstract and simple. But this does not mean they are artless, even if sometimes they seem so. The story element, bare, using well-understood motifs, constructs without emphasis a meaning, and the lack of emphases, the unpretentiousness of events and connexions serves to drive home all the more surely the perhaps forbidding or baffling conclusion. The language of narrator and of characters is usually rather colourless in itself, not imaged or epigrammatical, and does not need to contrive great effects for, closely consonant with the action, it brings out both the disturbing message and the helplessness of the victim in the face of suffering and confusion. Every statement is doubly charged since, while each parable describes a situation, it also conjures up at the same time, through its evidently parabolic form, suggestions and expectations that are to be flouted, cheated. These compositions are very subtle and can reveal, on examination, a host of possible meanings. As such, they are the very reverse of oral parables. We do not feel, as with the parables of Jesus, the presence of a crowd of listeners seeking and receiving guidance; it is rather the opposite, since we feel as it were the reluctance of the author, in many of them, to offer his understanding or problem, his unwillingness to urge on his readers his painful lessons. They seem to be wrung from him, their terseness, the lack of exposition and argument seem to suggest this. The non-oral element is even more appreciable in the first-person parables. If these were actually autobiographical fragments they might well invite the attention of listeners. But they are not. They too have a generalised form, the 'I' is a stylised medium, a means to offer a general experience in a way that allows us to feel all the uncertainties that surround and weigh on the character. They require therefore a more complex attention than the traditional oral fable, ask the reader to place himself imaginatively in the role of this 'I' and not confuse him with the real-life author. Above all, when the first-person is allied with the present tense we have a highly sophisticated form of parable, that asks us to experience a situation without asking for an ending or solution, something that seems to reject the very essence of the ancient parable. In all these respects we have in Kafka's parables a very subtle and very modern art-form, fascinating and deeply disturbing, involving our imagination and our minds without giving the comfort of definite conclusions, a form that, completed in itself, embodies incompletedness.

There is one negative characteristic of Kafka's parables that forces itself on our attention. It is the absence of those moral 'lessons', that moral concern, that distinguishes nearly all the parables of the Christian and Jewish tradition. The parables of Jesus speak both about the soul's relationship with God and man's relationship to man; often it is in the latter, in human goodness, love, devotion, self-sacrifice that the former becomes manifest. Kafka's parables are entirely lacking in this mighty theme; they are altogether concerned with the relationship of the alienated individual with the authority that dispenses meaning, significance, to life – or rather, with the authority that fails to fulfil the faith of the individual that it will do so. His dramas arise from the contest of man with God, Jacob with the angel; all else drops away.

I believe that we shall find parallels in Kafka's stories and novels for this general evolution of attitude and for the formal structure of the parables, and it is mainly for this wider purpose that I have tried to consider Kafka's parables. There is of course also a closer connexion between these and the stories. In a number of the parables (if we can call them by that name) there is a marked tendency to an individualisation of both the situation and the characters. This we have noticed in 'The huntsman Gracchus'. They can threaten to turn into stories, that is, to overstep the frontiers which the parabolic symbol requires. No sharp distinctions can be made. But some of the later stories even have animal characters and hence seem to indicate a type of fable or parable, perhaps may be seen as evolving out of the fable. We could hardly discuss these without first having examined Kafka's parable-type.

7 · LAST TALES: THE STORIES WITH HUMAN CHARACTERS

'Last tales' is a dangerous rubric to apply to stories of Kafka, not only because at his death on 2 June 1924 Kafka was not forty-one years of age. From 1920 he was repeatedly and for long periods in tuberculosis sanatoria, often exhausted by severe attacks and always under doctor's orders and forced to attend constantly to his malign enemy. His disease did not cripple his creative powers. During the first nine months of 1922 he wrote the main part of *The castle*, a most strenuous achievement, even if he was to put the work finally on one side in September. We cannot call these last works the products of 'late' Kafka, nor can we detect in them, in any decisive sense, symptoms of disease. Also, there is no sharp distinguishing line between these works and earlier – one must, I think, associate a few of the earlier works, like 'Building the Chinese wall' (1917), 'The village schoolmaster' (1914–15), or 'A report for an academy' (1917) with those of these last years, those written after 1920. One from this last period, 'A hunger artist', has indeed already been discussed as a sign of an alteration of narrative manner.

There are two obvious features that characterise these last pieces. One is the frequent use of first-person narrative. This is not always the case, as we have noted also in relation to the narrative form of the late parables, but it is certainly Kafka's favourite instrument in these last works. The second is the prominence, one might say the dominance, of animal stories. If one compares the later stories about human characters with the animal stories it is immediately evident that of the former only 'A hunger artist' has the aesthetic weight and artistic elaboration that we find in 'A report for an academy', 'Investigations of a dog', 'The burrow' and 'Josephine the singer'. Since these two features, one of form and the other of content, overlap we can conveniently treat first the stories with human characters and last the animal stories, all of which are written in the first person. That the study culminates in the latter (since 'A hunger artist' has been given its significance in a different place), this order corresponds to their relative importance in this last period of Kafka's life.

'First grief' ('Erstes Leid', 1922)

'First grief' is one of the stories included by Kafka in his posthumously published volume *A hunger artist*. It is the only one of those discussed in this chapter that is told by an impersonal narrator, the narrative form of Kafka's earlier tales and novels; as in the latter this impersonal narrator betrays no sign of any privileged knowledge, either of the past of his characters or of their hidden thoughts, and confines himself to those features in their behaviour that an observant and ever-present companion could have noticed.

He describes an incident in the life of a variety artist, in this case a trapeze artist, a brilliant performer highly esteemed by his employers and tenderly nursed by his impresario. He lives entirely for his art, one might say 'literally' since he cannot bear to be separated from his trapeze and spends his nights and days up on his bar; in view of his great skill the management make arrangements for him to satisfy his modest needs without leaving his aery perch. When he moves from one engagement to another his impresario makes arrangements to make the disturbance as slight as possible: the trapeze is sent ahead to be ready for him as soon as he arrives; in the train he travels in the luggage rack above his impresario's head, as close an imitation of his trapeze perch as could be found; and racing automobiles wait at the stations to rush him to his trapeze, if possible at night or in the early hours when there will be no traffic delays. But these moves do mean a disturbance, a shock to his nerves. Without them, the narrator tells us, the trapeze artist might have continued the odd but placid routine of his life; but it was these moves that eventually 'destroyed his nerves'. The incident he then describes shows the emergence of the fatal symptoms.

One day in the train the trapeze artist shyly whispers from his luggage rack to the impresario on the seat opposite that he would henceforth want two facing trapezes instead of one. The impresario fully approves the idea, but the performer seems to ignore his opinion and simply asserts that he will never again swing on a single bar; and when the impresario tries to calm him by agreeing that two trapezes would be far better than one, the artist bursts into tears. Startled, the impresario climbs on the seat to comfort him, stroking him and pressing his cheek against the trapeze artist's, getting drenched in the latter's tears. After some time the artist sobs: 'only this one bar in my hands – how can I go on living!', and bit by bit he quietens under the influence of the impresario's petting and comforting; he promises to telegraph from the next station for a second trapeze and praises the artist for his excellent idea. But as they settle down again the impresario cannot read his book and looks anxiously across at his sleeping companion, asking himself where such tormenting ideas will lead his artist, whether they will not grow still more tense and whether they were not a threat to their livelihood; and he even thinks he can see the first wrinkles in the 'smooth childish forehead' of the sleeping trapeze artist. The title, we now see, applies equally to the trapeze artist and his impresario.

This story is like most of the late parables in that it presents not a completed event but a current situation. There is no conclusive ending, no dramatic outcome, but a continuing situation or process, threatening, ominous perhaps, but not catastrophic. Anxiety may be there but not its realisation. We shall see that it shares this basic characteristic with all the later stories.

The theme is clear enough – the obsessive devotion of an artist to his art, which makes him an outstanding and highly valued performer but also separates him from other people, becomes so extreme that it threatens his whole existence – the term *existenzbedrohend*, that comes into the impresario's mind, means for him their livelihood, but Kafka no doubt wished to suggest also the deeper associations of the word 'existence'.[1] This theme, the obsessive artist, is the same as that of 'A hunger artist'. But its peculiarity lies in its tone. For it is not a tragic or bitter story, but tender, delicate, even amusing. If taken apart from its context 'First grief' would perhaps not attract much attention; it is only in relation to the other later works of Kafka that it acquires a special interest and primarily in relation to this prevailing tone.

There is a good deal of humour in the work, much of it coming from somewhat grotesque exaggerations that we are tempted to call typically Kafkaesque. For instance that strange isolation of the trapeze artist on his lonely bar, waited on by a whole series of assistants who tend to his wants, visited only by an occasional acrobat and greeted from the distance by workmen on the roof or an inspecting fireman, the journeys in the luggage rack (in Austria and Germany it was a net and hence would recall the safety net beneath the trapeze) and those racing cars; the sobbing and embracing in the train. The petting and cajoling of this spoilt child is taken to extreme lengths, by all the theatre managements as well as by his impresario. But it is hardly right to call these exaggerations 'grotesque', for they have nothing of the distortion, harshness, ugliness that often appear in Kafka's comic images, not least in 'A hunger artist'. Here they are good-humoured, pleasant; the kindness of the impresario seems inexhaustible, the lonely life on the trapeze an idyll.

Most of this kindly humour derives from the arrangements made by others for the trapeze-artist's well-being. But some of it lies in the telling, and here we become aware of the participation of the narrator. It is actually this anonymous narrator who describes the life up on the trapeze as an idyll. Explicitly he defends it as 'healthy', as if he were concerned to defend and approve it, as if he wished to stress the healthy and hopeful sides of this obsession. Mostly the narrator serves only as a medium for the opinions of his characters, often using free indirect speech for this purpose, but in this story he here and there betrays a personal interest and view and is on the brink of becoming an identifiable person: sympathetic towards the trapeze artist, aware of his oddities and those he causes, and saddened by the likelihood of misfortunes to come.

Thus, though there is an ominous note throughout the story, there is also a contending note of tenderness and humour, a certain charm in the little story. One reads it, if not with a smile, at any rate with a half-smile.

It is for this reason that one can associate the earlier stories, 'The village schoolmaster' (which Brod entitled 'The giant mole') and 'The neighbour', as well as 'A little woman' (1923) with 'First grief'. These others do not touch on the theme of the artist, but all are studies of an obsession. In these, however, Kafka abandons the impersonal narrator and in each case tells his story through the medium of the victim of the obsession.

'The village schoolmaster' ('Der Dorfschullehrer'),
'The neighbour' ('Der Nachbar'), and
'A little woman' ('Eine kleine Frau')

The story of 'The village schoolmaster' is told by a business man who has been fascinated by the rumour of the appearance of a giant mole,[2] a report on which has been published by a local schoolmaster. He describes how, in the interests of truth, he sets about further investigations, with high-minded indignation deploring the indifference or ridicule of the professional scientists. He tries to make common cause with the schoolmaster but finds his help is repudiated by the latter, who looks on him as a rival and wants to keep all the honour and glory of his discovery to himself; the narrator shows how easily the schoolmaster responds to any promise of publicity or acknowledgment. But, though asserting the purity of his own purpose as contrasted with that of the schoolmaster, the business man shows in numerous ways his own longing for fame, his lack of scientific scruples, his impatience and arrogance. Sensitive to the irrational motivations of another, he is naively unconscious of his own obsession. In neither man is the obsession a fateful or malign neurosis, it is emphatically harmless just as its object is accidental, so that the reader can smile without a bad conscience at the evident self-contradiction and absurd self-importance of the schoolmaster, as the business man describes it, and also at the more subtle self-betrayals of the latter, of which he himself is sublimely unconscious. His display of generosity when he praises the schoolmaster's 'honesty' and 'conviction' always bears the implication that what he lacks is the intellectual ability that the business man can provide. Towards the end his hitherto disguised feeling of superiority towards the schoolmaster breaks out into open and spiteful denigration. The story ends abruptly with the unresolved confrontation of the two. Since the whole is told in the past tense we feel there was more to report and that this is truly an unfinished fragment.

In view of the rather frequent presence, or suggestion, of malign obsessions in Kafka's stories, it is natural to suspect some dire symbolical meaning in the rumoured giant mole. But we hear hardly anything about this creature except that there was a rumour and that the schoolmaster gathered whatever evidence was available from those who thought they had seen its traces. All that is told of it is that it is abnormally large. The interest of the story lies in the attitude of the schoolmaster and the business man, and for both of these the mole only offers an opportunity for them to make a mark in the world; for the narrator, indeed, it is an entirely random opportunity and the animal itself has no rational connexion with him. The significance of the rather charming story lies in the light-hearted treatment of this absurd obsession, in the humour which is enhanced by the fact that the narrator unconsciously betrays his impure motives when he is most sincerely asserting his objectivity and scientific devotion. In 1914–15, when this story was written, this light-heartedness was rarely evident in the work of an author who was fearfully acquainted with his own neurosis. But later there are other examples of Kafka's ability to smile over the formation of obsessions which we can, I believe, recognise as a symptom of his coming to terms, in some degree, with his own tormenting neurosis.

'The neighbour' (1917) is one of these examples. Here again it is a business man who writes the story but this time, since he uses throughout the present tense, we are prepared to accept the unresolved situation as the actual theme of the story.

The narrator describes the two rooms that his business occupies, one for himself and one for his two female assistants. A neighbouring apartment has been taken by another young business man named Harras, who arouses his suspicions. They meet occasionally on the stairs but do not speak; he has heard that Harras's business is similar to his own but though he makes enquiries he cannot find out anything about it. He cannot detect any sounds in Harras's room. So he begins to suspect that Harras is sitting there all day listening in to his telephone conversations, in order to profit by the information and perhaps steal his customers.[3]

The slight sketch presents us with the growth of an obsession. The complacent self-importance with which it opens crumbles as his thoughts become engrossed with the imagined rival, his nerve starts to give way. The grounds of the narrator's obsession are reasonable and logical: it might certainly be possible for a rival to obtain and use his business connexions and secrets. There is only one flaw in his deductions, and that is that there is no evidence at all of Harras behaving as he suspects. This is a true obsession, therefore, for it has all the appearance of good sense and logic but is applied to the particular object without any concrete ground. Yet the reader can feel how, as the narrator gets worked up, he becomes the victim of his own suspicions so that the imagined posture and actions of the rival, Harras, become as real and vivid as any actual experience. It is with the description of his rival listening through the wall and hurrying out to profit by his illicit knowledge that the story closes.

This story is not humorous although our first impression of

the narrator suggests fussy and smug self-importance. It rapidly develops into a painful, near-hysterical obsession for which we can imagine no ending – in this sense the lack of an outcome is a true ending to the story. Why the story can be associated with 'The village schoolmaster' is that in both we are shown the emergence and self-deceit of an obsession, its groundlessness. We can understand that it owes its origin to other factors than those that are mentioned, i.e. than the victim himself is conscious of; that is, we understand that its source is irrational. But the primary, explicit theme is the simpler negative one that the obsession is *not* essentially related to the ostensible cause, that it is superfluous, something that does not deserve our respect. Again one must suspect that there is a biographical significance in this cool attitude to obsession.

'A little woman' is the last of this group of stories. It was written late in 1923 and Kafka himself prepared it for publication in the volume *A hunger artist*. It has several similarities to 'The neighbour' and is written in the same form; the victim of an obsession writes it in the first person and the present tense, as an account of a continuing painful situation that comes to no ending. The profession of the writer is not mentioned, and from various comments it would seem to be one without a practical function; and his obsession with a 'little woman' seems to be even more accidental than that of the business man of 'The neighbour' with his imagined rival. Dora Dymant, who was living at that time with Kafka in Berlin, has said that the story reflects Kafka's relationship with their Berlin landlady, and one can readily accept this suggestion. But if so, the story itself has obliterated this lodger–landlady relationship which can be a fertile source of mutual obsessions; as always, Kafka strips his imagined situations of any social specificity.[4]

The story opens with a description of the 'little woman's' dress and appearance which seems to establish the narrator's sincere intention to give a true and objective picture of her. It is only later that we realise that these details – her tight corsets, tasselled dress, blonde, smooth hair, her way of standing, her curious finger-spread – are superfluous, irrelevant. The narrator then finds several expressions for this woman's dislike for him, her resentment against him, and confesses he can find no rational grounds for it. They are scarcely acquainted and he says she could easily overcome it by looking on him as the complete stranger that he really is; this is what he would wish since, as he insists, his greatest concern is the distress he seems to cause her, a distress he is soon calling 'a torment'. He protests a little too nobly that it is only for her sake that he is worrying himself with their relationship, though he admits that when he once tried to suggest to her how to get rid of the vexation he causes her she got into such a state that he had to give it up. He justifies his feeling of responsibility for her by saying that he has heard reports of her looking ill in the mornings, suffering from poor sleep and headaches, for which he is the only person to know he is responsible.

It is at this point, perhaps, that the reader becomes aware that we are given no proof, no evidence that the narrator does actually cause this trouble in the little woman, and that the whole supposed vexation is a fantasy of his. This suspicion that we are being inveigled by an ostensibly sincere and rational report is aroused or strengthened when the account suddenly takes an unexpected turn that reveals something of the uncontrollable forces in the writer. For he admits that he has a suspicion that the little woman is only pretending to be unwell in order to direct the attention of 'the world' to the man who is its cause, and very quickly this suggestion grows into a great conspiracy she is instigating, a 'plan of war' to organise a public protest against the narrator, to stir up public anger with its 'great instruments of power' to condemn him publicly. We see in this outburst all the signs of a neurosis – an inferiority complex, a persecution mania, whatever one may wish to call it. The unhappy man then proceeds to defend himself against any such public charge and admits it will be difficult for him to defend himself against a 'weak sick woman' in spite of the fact that not everyone thinks he is as 'useless' a person as the woman does – another unconscious admission of his neurotic lack of faith in himself.

The narrator then considers whether he might lessen her irritation with him by behaving in a different manner. But he dismisses this hope by attributing to her an implacable hostility that will not forgo battle; he says her 'outbursts of rage' would be 'boundless' if she were to hear he had committed suicide. By this time the reader takes all these ideas and expressions as betrayals of the man's fixation, not the woman's. It surfaces again in the next paragraph when he justifies his rejection of advice he had received from a friend. The friend had told him, sensibly, it would be best if he would leave the city for a holiday, but the narrator argues that this is the very thing he must not do, since that would give the problem an undue and public importance: he must keep calm and see it for what it is, a purely personal affair. His rather too voluble protestations betray an uneasy consciousness.

The last two pages of the story show the narrator swaying between calm and nervousness. He tells himself he cannot expect a decisive outcome, since there can be no proof of his malign effect upon the little woman and in any case he stands in good repute with the public; and then he starts to imagine the host of her partisans, 'useless loungers and air-breathers', who are eager to interfere and already on the scent, 'their noses full of scent' (*die Nase voll Witterung*), and in an upsurge of pride in his honourable status – he has a diploma of some kind – the violence of his hatred of the little woman breaks out in his boast that 'anyone else but me would have long ago recognised her to be a bindweed and without disturbing the public would have noiselessly stamped her to death under his boots'. He ends by comforting himself that it will be easy for him, in spite of everything, in spite of the 'raging' of the woman, to maintain his customary life for a long time yet.

This is the typical ending of these later stories, and it reminds us of the endings of several of the parables like 'Give it up!' or 'Homecoming'. The situation will continue, it will not end in catastrophe nor will it be resolved. It describes a neurotic fixation that in some respects is clearly absurd and that makes us smile from time to time; still more we smile at the pleading of the story-teller, who tries to persuade us that his accusations against the woman are well-founded, that his only wish is to free her from her alleged obsession, and who shows skill and intelligence in his account; but who also unconsciously betrays the true motivations he suffers from through slight confusions of argument and outrageous expressions that uncover passions in himself he either wishes to hide or is unconscious of. As I have said in respect to 'The neighbour', I believe we see here Kafka coming to terms with his neurosis. I do not mean that he is 'overcoming' it, for in both stories it will continue, nor that he can account for it. But he can talk about it, he can see it, and he can see its irrationality and in some respects its comical results; it will remain but he can survive and go on with his ordinary tasks.

All these three stories have the same form: a character writes about the predicament he is still in. In two of them he describes his situation in the present tense, occasionally using the past tense for specific events in the recent past, and though 'The village schoolmaster' is written predominantly in the past tense, here too the problems remain unresolved and the reader is continually aware of the unresolved present. I have therefore considered each of these stories as first-person narratives in which the narrator is the chief character, who unfolds his inner experience to us.

Hartmut Binder rightly insists on the profound difference between the two main types of first-person story, that in which the narrator is the central character and that in which he, though engaged in the events, stands on the periphery of the action and our attention, and is chiefly a medium for recounting the story of another character. These two types must differ since with regard to the main character the former provides an 'inside view' while the latter is largely limited to the 'outside view' available to acquaintances however intimate.[5] The contrast between the two types is sharp since in the first the authority of the narrator is valid for the character's inner experience, feelings, thoughts, delusions, but questionable in relation to external situations and events including other people, while in the second the narrator may see more sharply than the main character all the externals, all the threads of a situation, but is less reliable regarding inner motivations and responses – actually less reliable than the impersonal narrator of third-person stories, who enjoys a magic authority in this respect. But a definition which rests on purely formal characteristics is shaky. When Binder comes to consider 'A little woman' he groups it with the second type of first-person story, though acknowledging that the narrator's 'fate' is closely bound up with that of the 'main' character, the woman, a conclusion he reaches because 'after all its title is "A little woman"'.[8] Binder does not refer in this context to 'The village schoolmaster' or 'The neighbour', but with them there is the same reason to include them in this category. But such a definition goes right against the reader's experience of these tales, for in each case we get to know very much about the hidden being of the narrator while the ostensible subject of the title remains highly obscure and in many respects almost a fiction of the narrator's making. It seems clear that they are first-person stories of the autobiographical type. And the titles? These present another problem. For often the titles of Kafka stories (the titles *he* gave them) clearly do indicate the chief character, even when the narrator is another fictitious person – for instance 'A hunger artist' or 'Josephine the singer'. But there is no rule about this and there is no ground for not taking these other titles, such as 'A little woman', as ironical, since the only person who believes her (or the neighbour or the village schoolmaster) to be the main character is the narrator himself. Kafka is enjoying a little joke at the expense of his narrator, a further indication of his awareness in these late stories of the humorous aspect of obsessions.

One hesitates over the final evaluation of these late stories. They are all slight in comparison with what we should call the great stories. The obsession involved is not baneful like the father-fixation and family-involvement of *The judgment* and *The metamorphosis* or the more obscure compulsions of *The trial* and *The castle*, it does not direct and absorb all the energies of the character. In these late stories the obsession is more accidental, less malign, less mortal. Their form also is slighter. That they are written in the first person and largely in the present tense seems to put limits on their significance, for while this form gives an impression of authenticity it also seems to disavow a more general validity. That Kafka himself published 'A little woman' suggests that he believed it to have more than a personal bearing, but the narrator, the 'hero', of each of the stories seems rather to be trying to become clear about himself and his situation than to have a message for others.

Apart from the unfinished novel *The castle*, the only major product of these last years of Kafka's life that creates what we may call an objective correlative of the writer's intention is 'A hunger artist', and this story, though mediated through a distorting glass that is ignored by most critics, is nearer the familiar image of the tragic, despairing Kafka than these other late tales. The only late stories that have anything like the weight and intricacy of the earlier ones are the animal stories, and these we must now examine. We shall need not only to enquire whether they bear out the implications of the human stories we have considered but also to ask why Kafka should have turned to animal subjects.

8 · LAST TALES: THE ANIMAL STORIES

Kafka's last animal stories have considerable similarities, the most obvious one being their anthropomorphic treatment of the various animals concerned. All these animals think and speak with the mental powers of human beings, they are all able to describe a situation, reflect upon it, make rational decisions, remember, generalise; they all enjoy an individual self-consciousness. That is, these stories are not 'about' animal life but about human life considered through the transparent fiction of animal masks. In this respect the animals concerned – the ape, the dog, the mouse, the badger – perform the function of the animals of traditional fable. Like them, too, their behaviour and mode of thinking recall in certain ways the animals themselves or at least what their actual appearance and behaviour suggest to watching humans. Much of the charm of these stories derives from such associations: the reflexions of the ape remind us of the restless bright beady eyes of the real animals which seem always to be occupied with unfathomable designs, his sophistication seems the translation of the swing and swagger in his short-legged gait; the dog's philosophising recalls those questioning and expectant eyes (I am thinking now of a Jack Russell terrier of my acquaintance) and bouts of frantic barking that ask we know not what, and those sudden flurries of excited chase that interrupt some routine activity. Each of these stories is stamped with the peculiar character of the animal concerned and we should not let the human implications obliterate our appreciation of the delicacy and often humour with which the character is evoked – no more than we do with Jonathan Swift's account of the Houyhnhnms in part four of *Gulliver's travels*, a book that Kafka highly prized.

The four stories are also similar in that each is told by an animal character. Three of them belong to the autobiographical type, in which the fictional narrator is also the main character:

189

the narrative form adopted by Kafka in several of the other stories and parables of these last years. The exception, 'Josephine the singer or the nation of mice', is narrated by an anonymous reflective member of the mice community, a parallel to the Chinese scholar who tells the story 'Building the Chinese Wall'. But it is not sufficient to lump the other three together. As Hartmut Binder has insisted, in his admirable analysis of these tales and the autobiographical form in general, stories in which the narrator is largely concerned with his past may be very different from those in which he confines himself to the present.[1] In all types the narrator has a double function, to tell the story of events and to describe his inner experiences, and the proportions allotted to these two functions will profoundly affect the character of his narrative. 'The burrow' belongs to one extreme where the narrator – for convenience we may call it a badger though it never gives itself a name – writes only about his present situation, his plans, fears, hopes and he writes in the present tense even about his actions, telling us for instance that he is now in a certain part of his burrow, carrying out a certain task; even his falling asleep and waking up are accompanied by his descriptive words. Only very occasionally is this total immersion in the present interrupted by brief statements about past events. We have met this form already in the parable 'Homecoming'. It is rarely used in narrative literature – there is an early example in Schnitzler's *Leutnant Gustl* (1900) – perhaps because the unchanging attention to the self tends to attribute a pathological obsession to the character. In Kafka's 'The burrow' the reader is indeed immersed in the creature's inner experience and has no means to emerge from it, no more than the creature itself.

At the other extreme would be an autobiographical type that is pure objective event without the evocation of the experiencing subject. But Kafka's 'A report for an academy' and 'Investigations of a dog' are not at this extreme. In both the narrator, the ape or the dog, fulfils both functions as teller of events and describer of experience. Both are indeed rooted in the present and their concern is to show what is the principle of their present life; as a result the dog uses predominantly the present tense while the ape refers constantly to the present situation too. But in both cases their present principles and purposes have taken shape in the past and their aim is to describe how this took place. Therefore both give an account of their past life. But they do not attempt to give a continuous account. Each chooses those moments in the past that have contributed to the awakening and development of that understanding of life by which they now live, and they describe these separated events in order to evoke the experience and its importance in their life-story. So there is a constant alternation in both accounts between evocation of experience and reflexion upon it or, to put it in another way, between imaginative identification with the experiencing animal and withdrawal from it in the interests of objective understanding. The narrator alters his focus, sometimes becoming again the animal he was, sometimes withdrawing to a distance, the distance of age, of the present time; with this change the tense of narration changes from past to present and back again. If I use the word 'objective' I do not mean here the authoritative objectivity that belongs to an impersonal narrator, of course. I mean the objectivity that these characters strive for by summoning up all the powers of their intelligence to sift and judge their experience. What is significant is that they are capable of this effort and are not, like the badger, imprisoned in the immediacy of experience.

These two stories share with 'The burrow' the inconclusive ending, for in all the stories, as also in 'Josephine the singer', we are presented with a continuing situation and the attitude that sustains it, all elements of which may be subject to change. But though no animal can find security, the mood of 'The burrow' differs profoundly from that of the others. And this difference is due more to attitude than to external facts, to the attitude of the animal-narrator. For the badger seems to have no defence against the undefined threats with which his existence is surrounded, for every new escape route he invents only adds fresh dangers; the root of the threats lies however in his incapacity to wrench himself out of the present, to find the mental distance that reflexion can give. All the other animal-narrators can achieve this distance, can reflect and take decisions. Perhaps this characteristic is the primary cause of that serenity, so rare in Kafka, that pervades the narratives of the ape, the dog and the mouse.

It has to be stressed that this serenity is not one of secure achievement, of conquest of danger. In all cases we are given an image of life as it is for the experiencing subject, a fragile present moving constantly towards an indeterminate future, never rounded off, its achievements temporary and its projects doubtful. This also is a narrative form we often meet in late Kafka stories and parables; we might even dare to suggest it is the form of *The castle* which is unfinished not perhaps by accident but in principle.

These animal stories then link up in many ways with other products of the last years of Kafka's short life and are by no means oddities. There are still other aspects of them that confirm their significance as embodying a distinctive trend of his work and thought, but for these a closer examination of the texts is required. We shall therefore adopt our normal method and treat each story separately.

'A report for an academy' ('Ein Bericht für eine Akademie',
1917)

This is the earliest of the animal stories, and Kafka published it both in a periodical (*Der Jude*, 1917) and in the selection of tales he published in 1919 under the title *A country doctor*.[2]

It is a report written by an ape, a chimpanzee, to explain to a learned society his development since he was captured and brought to Europe. He is now a famous star of the variety halls, famous not just as a mimic of human behaviour but also for his ability to read and write, to think rationally, to digest human knowledge; he has acquired what he calls 'the average culture of a European'. The object of his report is to explain how he came to these achievements and how he values them.

The style in which he writes demonstrates the qualities, both positive and negative, of his acquired culture. He knows what sort of material will interest a scientific body and keeps his account brief and to the point. He explains not only his behaviour but also its motivation. He sensibly tells his readers that he cannot speak about his life as an ape, before his capture as a youngster, since the great mass of new experiences have blotted out his memories; the storm that the thought of return once raised in him is now 'only a draught that cools my heels'. He may still occasionally feel an 'itch in his heel' but concludes (with a shrewd home-thrust at the learned fraternity): 'Your apehood, Gentlemen, in so far as you have anything of that kind behind you, cannot be more remote from you than mine from me.' This is admirable good sense neatly, expressively and wittily put. But the ape shows also a certain complacent skill in adopting the clichés of official and 'higher' writing. He uses with gusto the correct deferential expressions in addressing the academy and the usual high-flown rhetoric of academic speeches, with appropriate inversions of sentence order; high-minded resolutions are given in full voice: 'Renunciation of all wilful stubbornness was the most sacred commandment I imposed on myself; I, a free ape, submitted to this yoke.' Later we find him using with some smugness the clichés of officialese, demonstrating thus how much he is at home in human society, and he knows how to speak with the conventional sentimental idealism of the sciences and progress when he comes to describe his own mental growth: 'These advances! This penetration of the rays of knowledge from all sides into the awakening brain!' And often he uses extravagantly spiritual and poetic terms for ordinary affairs, like the bad writers of the newspapers. He speaks of his 'inner conflicts' when he struggles to overcome his distaste for schnaps. The sailor who tries to teach him to drink 'sought to resolve the riddle of my being', and when he performs the gestures of drinking before the ape, the latter calls this the 'theoretical' part of his training. There can be no doubt that a considerable part of the human culture the ape has imbibed is culture of a pretty spurious type.

Because of the superficial character of the culture he absorbs and of the complacency with which he mentions his achievements, many critics have considered the story to be a satire upon a conformist who abandons his true individuality (as an ape) to enjoy the comfort of membership of a trivial society. Emrich makes our chimpanzee into a symbol of the inauthentic man of modern culture, a 'hybrid being' who has lost the consciousness of his essential self and believes culture consists in a certain exterior style of life.[3] Some have taken the ape to be a symbol of the assimilated Jew of Western society who has betrayed his inheritance. In 1934 Politzer applied to him the contemptuous term 'assimilant' which suggests a petitioner who remains an alien, but in *Franz Kafka: parable and paradox* of 1962 he sees the work more in the way Emrich does as presenting an image of dehumanisation and abandonment of selfhood.[4] But these harsh judgments take account of only the negative elements in the ape's style and adaptation. It has been pointed out that Kafka may have found an impulse to his account in a little work of E. T. A. Hoffmann, included in the latter's *Kreisleriana* and entitled 'Nachricht von einem gebildeten jungen Mann'.[5] This tells of just such a trained ape as Kafka describes and consists mainly of a long letter that the ape writes to a young female whom he wants to impress with the account of his acquisition of human culture. But Hoffmann's ape, who like Kafka's writes in a cliché-ridden elevated style, is a foolish and conceited ape, the spoilt darling of a trivial and superficial society, who thinks culture is mere polite behaviour and conversation, and who proudly writes that he 'knows everything' and is completely cultured and immensely superior to the apes. Hoffmann's little work is clearly enough an attack on superficial conceptions of culture and the ape is merely the target of his satire.

But Kafka's work and ape are quite different and cannot be

dismissed as if they were nothing more than Hoffmann's. It is true that his chimpanzee has learned to spit, smoke, and drink like a human being, that he can lounge in a chair and read the newspapers, and that his language is often cliché-ridden. But his attitude towards these acquisitions is not conceited and ostentatious but critical, and a serious theme runs through his account.

He describes how he was wounded and captured and shut in the ship in a narrow crate. He realised that escape would only mean punishment or death by drowning; and yet he was tortured by the fact that there was no way out – for in his earlier life in the wild he had always had available several 'ways out'. He does not like to use the great word 'freedom' though in his early existence he perhaps had 'the great feeling of freedom'; but freedom is a treacherous idea, and he limits himself to the more concrete notion of a way out – the German term *Ausweg* means actually 'evasion' as well as 'way out', and Kafka utilises both meanings. In his crate the ape thought hard and came to realise that captured apes belong to cages; if he was to find a way out he had to cease being an ape – he comments on this 'clear, beautiful chain of logic'. So, when the attendants tried to have some fun with him and teach him to do tricks, the ape did his best to please them; they were coarse and sometimes cruel but now and later he does not complain but generously understands that men and menageries must treat animals so. So he practises, he learns to spit and smoke, and even, after an enormous effort at overcoming his distaste for schnaps, he learns to drink. And one day on deck, when many sailors are about and an officer is 'taking the air' among them, he not only swallows a bottle of schnaps but also, to the universal amazement of the men, cries out 'Hallo' – the first step to speech. And here he pauses in his report and sums up: 'I repeat: it did not attract me to imitate men; I imitated them because I was looking for a way out, and for no other reason.'

The theme is repeated when the ship reaches Germany and the ape is subjected to training. He saw, he explains, that he was faced with two possibilities, either the zoo or the variety stage, and he did not hesitate. For the zoo was 'only another cage', the stage was a 'way out'. It was the arduous choice to make, for he had to learn, to drive himself 'ruthlessly' – in fact he 'wears out' several teachers! And the result of 'unparalleled efforts' is his present achievement. This however he only calls 'the average culture of a European', showing that while he can take pride in his efforts to overcome his apish nature he does not overestimate his achievement in human terms (as distinct from Hoffmann's ape). And Red Peter (that is his name, after a red scar on his cheek from a wound his captors dealt him) adds the weighty words:

In itself this [achievement] would be absolutely nothing, but it is something in so far as it helped me out of the cage and provided this particular way out, the human way out. There is an excellent German idiom, *sich in die Büsche schlagen* ('to take cover') and this I have done. I had no other way, always presupposing that there was no choice of freedom.

It is a modest conclusion. He asks to be judged according to his merits, not as a human being, for he knows his achievements are not great in human terms. He knows that he has not become a human being and admits that after his shows and busy social engagements he enjoys his nights with a female chimpanzee 'after the manner of apes'. He is aware that his public success is due to his *not* being a human being. He mentions one point at which he is at loggerheads with the unnaturalness, the affectation of human conventions in relation to the sexual organs – an echo of the indignation of Swift's Houyhnhnms. He complains that a journalist had jeered at him for letting down his trousers in public when he wished to show a visitor the scar on his thigh, another wound inflicted by his captors. And our ape protests that 'in the interest of truth every great spirit will discard the finest manners'.[6] Generally however Red Peter is not concerned to criticise human beings or human society and though there are several aspects of his treatment that show he does observe human faults such as cruelty and arrogance, he remains throughout true to his intention, as he defines it in the final sentence: 'I only want to extend knowledge, I am only making a report.'

It therefore seems to me that the critics who take the ape as the model of a mere conformist are wrong. They do what he begs his reader not to do, they judge him as if he were a human being; they disregard the circumstances into which he fell, the limited choice that was enforced upon him, just as they disregard the modesty and wisdom of his estimate of himself and his achievement. But I believe there is a still deeper meaning to his constant search for a 'way out'. He knows the difference between 'freedom' and a 'way out' and has abandoned any faith that freedom is accessible to him; in fact he acknowledges that he knows freedom only as a vague feeling connected with his youthful life as an ape. Perhaps we are meant to understand here a repudiation not simply of romantic notions of primitive freedom, which some critics think the ape is meant to embody, but also of those existential concepts of the authentic self, the self that frees itself of social ties and determinants, that inspire some of his critics like Emrich? Perhaps Kafka is using the animal model in order to try out an alternative strategy to the heaven-storming of the hero of *The castle*? Some recent critics do indeed adopt some such view. Klaus-Peter Philippi inverts the older criticism of conformism and takes the essential theme of the story to be the elevation of the ape to a human consciousness, so that the story becomes a model of the function of socialisation (in the sociological not political sense) as the instrument of human evolution.[7] But this Hegelian interpretation not only overlooks the modesty of the claims of the ape and the humour of his depiction of the world of man into which he falls; it also ignores the difference between an organic process of socialisation and one that is imposed by a dominant group on an impotent captive. I do not think either Hegel or Marx would have seen the two as identical.

W. H. Sokel's interpretation of 'A report for an academy' remains much closer to the actual situation of the story than most of the views discussed and is a refreshing change.[8] He takes the ape to be a representative of moral realism who, through his mimicry of man, i.e. through his art, becomes adapted to the alien world in which he finds himself. He thus overcomes his own self, his animal being with all its weaknesses, through a 'process of sublimation', replacing the 'will to pleasure and to death' by the principle of 'survival and self-limitation'. Sokel does not overdo the Freudian element in this theme and does justice not only to the concrete outcome of the ape's successive engagements with the reality of the human world but also to his character, rational, self-possessed, determined, so unusual in Kafka's writing. Most critics are so enmeshed in a fixed concept of what Kafka's works stand for that they cannot free themselves to experience the peculiarity of any particular one, and Sokel shows himself able to do this and to acknowledge that this story, at any rate, does not fit our image of the earlier Kafka since it creates a model of a successful battle with alienation. However Sokel, in inverting the Emrich image of an inauthentic self, overestimates the 'integration' and 'humanisation' of the ape, who himself is modest about his achievement and painfully aware that he is now neither human nor ape. He still feels that 'itch in his heel' and his highest hope is not to attain freedom but simply to acquire or preserve a 'way out', to keep his options open. I think too that Sokel overestimates the significance of art in the ape's 'sublimation process'. Mimicry is his calculated strategy and is total, it is not play but an all-embracing lifestyle, and the ape is no longer free to discard his human characteristics just as he can never return to apehood.

Where Kafka critics frequently fail is that they expect of one story what others provide. They ignore those elements that do not fit a stereotype both in theme and style. Thus Peter Beicken concludes his intelligent review of the interpretations of 'A report for an academy' with a reproof that ought to have been unnecessary – 'The ape Red Peter is not Kafka',[9] to which we can add, the ape is not a disguise of the hero of 'The judgment or 'The metamorphosis' or *The trial*. He is not a human being and his achievement is not to be judged in human terms. But, it will be argued, if the ape is not to be seen in human terms, what meaning can the story have for its readers? It is not a study of animal behaviour! And this protest is justified. But the point is, in what way is the story related to human problems? And one's interpretation must take into account all elements, including that of stylistic tone.

The ape is a creature burdened with an alienation for which he is not responsible and faced with the likelihood of a life in a cage, the only purpose of which is the amusement of human beings. Freedom he recognises is inaccessible, indeed he is not sure what freedom is; an attempt at breaking out of his cage will lead, he knows, either to harsher treatment or death. So he comes to terms with his state, his object being to avoid coming to a dead end, to keep an outlet. The strenuous effort of mimicry and acquiring human capacities itself divorces him more sharply from ape life, and of course does not make him a human being; but it keeps an outlet open, even though he cannot know where this outlet will lead. Every such decision and the capacities he acquires are, he knows, little in themselves, but they are important since they keep a way open. This is the esential theme of this story, and here we can discover the parallel to a human situation. It presents an alienation for which the creature is not responsible and for which he knows no permanent remedy. He rejects the option of heroic rebellion, which would achieve and solve nothing, and that of passive suffering, which would mean despair and disintegration. Instead he follows that course that keeps the future open, even though he has no assurance that the opening will lead to freedom – or rather, even if he does not know that an ultimate escape or goal is possible or imaginable. At least he evades despair and at least finds satisfaction in the efforts and acquisitions he makes.

The affinity of this theme to those of earlier Kafka stories is clear enough, since all start from the basic assumption of alienation, helplessness, and uncertainty. The difference lies in the positive option that the ape chooses. And to evaluate this we have also to concern ourselves with the whole tone of this story. Earlier I suggested that it presents a possible alternative strategy with regard to alienation in the form of an experiment, a 'try out'. Kafka does not give us a dilemma with a conclusion; the ape manages to evade a tragic collision and failure by a series of expedients, each of which is temporary, adapted just to that situation, and never reaching some final solution. The whole is presented by the ape himself and what is most characteristic is the lightness of touch throughout, the evasion of tragedy and pathos; often there is humour, partly arising for the reader out of the ape's unconscious complacency, sometimes humour that the ape himself enjoys. If we can smile at his high-flown style, we can also enjoy with him many of his expressions and images, for their aptness, their shrewdness.

But there is something else too that creates the tone and mood of 'A report for an academy', something that embraces the ape and his doings. It is the tone of fantasy, of playfulness. We know fantasy in the earlier Kafka usually in the form of a distorting exaggeration, often ugly and terrifying, where even ostensibly innocent or indifferent features can become sinister. But in this story the fantasy of the comically sophisticated ape with his astonishing abilities is full of charm, since it remains on the level of a playful hypothesis and does not seek to assert any dogmatic truths. Nor are we to take it as a satire, even though many critics wish us to believe that Kafka intended to show some great fault in this shrewd ape. For Red Peter has the same sort of reality as the animals of fable. We do not think of criticising the fox because he excuses his failure to reach the grapes by his 'sour grapes'; our criticism is reserved for humans who in similar situations behave like this. So here, in Kafka's charming story, we can enjoy the play of fancy; perhaps indeed he chose an animal subject for this very purpose, so that the story might be removed to a serene distance from our unquiet consciousness, until after its close we reflect on its meaning.

It is because of these various features of style that we are enabled to experience this story not as an erratic block in

Kafka's works, as a cancellation of other works, but as another possible attitude in face of the dilemmas of existence. While the K.s of *The trial* and *The castle*, confronted with the evasiveness and uncertainty of their goal – court or castle – cling to their image with self-destructive devotion, the ape presents a possibility rarely found in Kafka's stories. If freedom is vague and inaccessible, can one not cease hankering after it, dispense with it, and make do with reality on the best terms available? If redemption is not to be won perhaps a solution can be found, a *Lösung* in place of *Erlösung*? 'A report for an academy' presents this hypothesis seriously yet playfully, not with the passion of a dogma but as a possibility that is not fully evaluated and judged because its hero is a creature of fantasy and because it is not taken to an end, bitter or otherwise. We are left at the end, as in many of Kafka's late first-person tales and parables, suspended in a process and direction that has no conclusion.

'Investigations of a dog' ('Forschungen eines Hundes', 1922)

Most of the critical discussions of the story to which Max Brod, its first editor, gave the title 'Investigations of a dog' would never suggest to the reader that this is a work of the greatest charm and grace. Most critics give it little importance, like Politzer who says it 'dissolves in imperfection' or Gray writes that 'as an allegory' it needs 'little comment'. Others, like Sokel, detect in it a weighty theme and manifold analogies that crush its delicate fabric and fantasy. Even Beicken's courage deserts him here. A rare exception is Anthony Thorlby's short but thoughtful discussion with its appreciation of the work's 'gentle irony', which he places in the concluding chapter of his survey.[10] Charm and grace do not exclude seriousness, and in this work the seriousness lies within the grace and never separate from it. In an excellent passage defining the grace (*Grazie*) of Kafka's language Günther Anders, who otherwise does not discuss 'Investigations of a dog', makes what seems to be an indirect reference to this story:

Grace emerges when Kafka's language, like a playful dog, romps round the all-powerful world occupying the whole breadth of the street; its lightness is the lightness of one who, in comparison with the weight of the world, is found to be too light; and its gaiety that of something that is not taken seriously, not of something that is not serious.[11]

We can extend this definition to the whole character of Kafka's story, not only the language and style.

Although written five years after 'A report for an academy', 'Investigations of a dog' is closer to the earlier tale than to the later 'The burrow' or 'Josephine the singer'. Both stories present an account by a reflective 'philosophical' animal of his life hitherto as an attempt to come to terms with his encounter with the world; neither reaches a conclusive outcome since both are written in the midst of the continuing encounter. But, if the ape represents one hypothetical posture, the dog embodies a totally contrary one. The ape is a pragmatist, the dog a speculative metaphysician; the ape is sophisticated, self-critical, the dog is naive, a perpetual innocent. Their object in writing is different, too. The ape is giving a report to a learned society, to explain to men, in human terms, his behaviour and motivation, to enlarge their understanding and also to justify himself. The dog – for whom, to whom is he writing? There are phrases that suggest a conversational situation but no partner and it lacks the sharpness and vigour of dialogue. It is a long meditation upon the peculiarity of his character and his quest, entered upon in order to discover self-understanding, to justify himself to himself.

This difference of purpose entails marked differences in style and language. The ape is conscious of his audience, displays the professional rhetorical figures required to convince, conventional poses and clichés alternating with sharp intelligence and telling images; his story is skilfully composed to form a cogent argument. But the dog rambles, interrupts his theme from time to time, contradicts himself, finds it difficult to formulate his position, for instance his relationship to other dogs. He uses many old-fashioned terms and often expresses an old-fashioned attitude, as in his reflexions on thoughtless youth; we imagine a rather dull but sincere plodder, anxious not to upset other dogs, concerned for the old virtues of unselfishness, politeness, respect for age etc. If his temperament as a questioner constantly removes him from the normal society of dogs, he eagerly upholds the laws and rights of the community and asserts his patriotism. The humour of his vocabulary for his fellow dogs, which is of course adapted from human speech, is obvious when he addresses his 'fellow dogs' (*Mithunde*) or speaks of the race as 'dog-kind' (*Hundeschaft, Hundegeschlecht*) or simply 'nation' (*Volk*). But this gentle humour acquires a different flavour in the numerous composites based on *Volk – Volksgenossen, Volksbeschluss*, the adjectival *volklich* and the related *Artgenossen* – for these untranslatable terms were the peculiar invention of extreme nationalist and racist groups in Germany and Austria, the so-called *Völkische*, to replace the democratic terms 'nation', 'state', and 'citizen'. It is clear that Kafka's dog attaches no specific political meaning to these words, but his use of them startlingly emphasises the 'childish nature' the 'old dog' still confesses to. This old-fashioned simplicity and naivety of the dog does not necessarily, or not at all, depreciate his insight or quest, but it gives a peculiar tone to the whole, a certain humour and charm that elicits from the reader a sympathetic smile and matches the unpretentiousness of the dog's claims.

To enable the reader to grasp this tone of the story, its serious humour, its 'grace', I start with a translation of its first paragraph; here and there I have added the original text in brackets where the suggestiveness of the original is lost in translation.

How my life has changed but how at bottom it has not changed! When I now think back and recall the times when I still lived among my kind [*Hundeschaft*], took part in everything that engaged their concern, a dog among dogs, I find on closer inspection that from the beginning something was wrong, a tiny fracture was present, a slight unease would seize me in the middle of the most venerable national [*volklich*] occasions, yes, sometimes in an intimate circle, no not sometimes but very often, the mere sight of a dear fellow dog [*Mithund*], the mere sight seen somehow with fresh eyes would make me embarrassed, shocked, helpless, even reduce me to despair. I would try to soothe [*begütigen*] myself as it were, friends to whom I confessed my condition would help me, calmer times would come again – times in which such surprises were not lacking but were taken with greater equanimity and fitted more calmly into life, that perhaps made me sad and tired but after all did not dispute my right to go on as a somewhat cold, reserved, timid, calculating but still all in all a right and proper [*regelrecht*] dog. Without these intervals of convalescence how could I have reached the age I now rejoice in, how could I have won my way to the calm with which I contemplate the terrors of my youth and bear the terrors of old age, how could I have managed to draw the conclusions from my admittedly unhappy or, to put it more prudently, not very happy temperament and to live almost completely according to it. Withdrawn from society, lonely, busied only with my hopeless but to me indispensable little investigations, thus I live, yet from the distance I have not lost my people [*Volk*] out of sight, news often reaches me and I see that I am heard from here and there. People treat me with respect, they do not understand my style of life but do not resent it and even young dogs whom I see running past here and there in the distance, a new generation of whose childhood I have scarcely a faint memory, do not refuse me a respectful greeting.

The long multiple sentences with their variations of syntax, the lack of firm pauses and emphases (commas instead of semicolons and full stops, questions without question-marks etc.) tell us we are reading a meditation, an inner reckoning, rather than an account, argument, self-defence directed to someone else. The pace is slow and circumspect, stopping at times to correct a phrase, for the narrator is as concerned with the present as with the past and moves freely between the two; yet though the sentences tend to be involved, the movement forward is steady and clear. From time to time the dog uses clichés yet surprises us as he breaks out of them with original observations. When he starts 'When I think back' one expects a normal perhaps nostalgic recollection but meets the account of the 'fracture', his alienation. Often such surprises have an involuntarily comic effect as when 'the age I rejoice in' is followed by 'the terrors of old age'. The dog's vocabulary has repeatedly a touch of humour, not only in the terms he invents for his fellow dogs that are based on human terms for humans. For when he speaks of comforting himself he uses 'soothe', and the German term *begütigen* is quaint here, since it implies how a nurse or mother might soothe a child, not a conscious person himself. To claim to be 'a right and proper dog' using a German word *regelrecht* that suggests that doghood is proven by observing certain rules, is also a comic misuse of language. By such means Kafka gently and lightly reminds us of the distance between the narrator (and his experiences) and mankind and warns us against making crude identifications. More generally this opening paragraph also introduces us to a deeper theme that runs throughout the book, the effort of the dog to assure himself of his membership of the race of dogs, of their respect for him and his for his fellows, while at the same time, with modesty but some pride, he acknowledges his painful but distinguished singularity: he will never give up his hope of squaring this circle. That he can find comfort in the 'respectful greeting' of the young is a sign that his alienation will never grow into a tragic rift. Throughout the paragraph, and indeed the story, there is a charming naivety that creates the serenity of tone.

This naivety of the dog involves him in all sorts of obvious contradictions, some of which seem to disqualify his claim to be a questioner. His object is to understand the life of a dog in terms of a dog's experience and he describes his objective in a manner we might perhaps expect from a human philosopher speaking about man:

Only with the help of the dog-nation did I begin to understand my own questions ... I was concerned only with dogs. For what else is there apart from dogs? Whom else can one invoke in the wide, empty world? All knowledge, the totality of all questions and all answers is contained in dogs etc.[12]

So he eliminates mankind from his considerations as a human philosopher would ignore dogs. But the results of this omission are well nigh disastrous.

He only refers to mankind on one occasion and then only indirectly, as if embarrassed by so unpleasant a topic. It is in the second paragraph, when the dog is explaining that there are many varieties of creatures beside dogs – 'poor, inferior, mute beings, limited to certain calls' – which dogs study and 'seek to help, to educate, to improve and so on'. In a lordly fashion the dog dismisses them: 'In so far as they do not try to disturb me they are indifferent to me, I do not distinguish one from the other, I ignore them.' But then he adds something that seems more specifically to apply to humans:

> But one thing is too striking to have escaped my attention, namely how little, compared with us dogs, they hold together, how they pass one another by in silence, like strangers and with a certain hostility, how only the most vulgar common interest brings them to a meagre external unity and how hatred and conflict arise even from this common interest. We dogs, how different! One might say that we really all live in one single pack, differentiated though we are by the innumerable and profound distinctions that have arisen in the course of the ages.

Perhaps Kafka is allowing his dog to quote Georg Simmel's description of metropolitan man? His contrast with dogs seems to be persuasive and powerful. But immediately, as he continues, he falls into confusions for he does not hide certain 'difficulties', notably the fact that many dogs follow 'professions' that their neighbours cannot understand and obey 'regulations' that are not within dog law and even opposed to it (again the reference to human control and training is oblique). And the dog also has to admit, with grief, that just by considering these problems and asking questions he himself withdraws from the dog community. Later, when he celebrates the great store of wisdom in the dog community (p. 333), he has to bewail the fact that though dogs know everything, they refuse to communicate their wisdom and in all their 'embraces', 'nuzzling', 'howling' they remain taciturn, mute. No wonder the dog has so frequently to assure us that he loves dogs, wants to be faithful to his kind etc., since in his simple sincerity he finds he is repeatedly denying them the virtues he has earlier attributed to them. He defends the refusal of dogs to share their food against the charge of selfishness by saying it is a law, 'a unanimous decision of the people arising out of a victory over selfishness' (pp. 331–2). Such quaint sophistry is accompanied by the confused logic with which he 'proves' that he, the questioner, is not a renegade dog. 'Every dog has the urge to ask questions', he asserts, claiming that he has many *Artgenossen*, fellow questioners; the fact that, as he admits, he can never find one does not lead him to change his conviction (p. 339). Similarly though he professes utter devotion to the traditions and laws of dog-kind, he continually broaches heresies, even to the point of challenging in practice the sacred prohibition of fasting (pp. 349–50).

I stress these confusions in the dog's mind not in order to denigrate his purpose; in fact, while they are amusing they are also attractive and charming since they arise from the sincerity and whole-heartedness of his questioning. But it is necessary to be aware of them for they affect our whole response to the dog's account. Many critics, like Sokel, fail to take into account that all our information about the dogs derives from this narrator and is coloured by his character and interest. Sokel can thus take the questioning dog to be a true representative of dog-kind since 'every dog has the urge to ask questions' and fails to see that the narrator-dog's claim to be truly a normal dog is only the desperate plea of an outsider.[13] As we often find with a Kafka text, the subjective source of much if not all the writing makes the question of its truth a teasing one.

When we come to the account of the actual 'investigations' the dog undertakes, it would seem that Kafka delights in their patent and comic unsoundness. The first decisive experience, that decided the whole direction of his mind, occurred when he was young. The dog had been running a long time through the darkness with a 'presentiment of great things' (he is honest enough to tell us this foreboding could deceive since he 'always' had it) when he came across a lighted space, and suddenly, with a great burst of wondrous music, a group of seven dogs emerged into the light and began to dance, to execute strange and complicated figures in time with the music. He observes that though they bring the music with them they themselves do not open their mouths; and when he barks a greeting to them they do not answer but continue their dances, concentrating anxiously on their evolutions. The music transports, entrances him, though he is appalled to see them disregarding the most sacred law of dogs and walking on hind legs. But then the music stops, the dogs vanish from the light, and he is left with problems – why did the dogs not respond to his call? Why did they walk on their hind legs? And a mystery – what is the meaning of this strange scene and the unearthly music emanating from the strange dogs? The problems he can speculate about, the mystery remains with him for ever as a transcendent vision.[14]

It is clear to the reader that the dog has adventured into a circus and seen a group of performing dogs. Since his principle of ignoring the presence of mankind forces him to look in some other direction for the explanation of the dances and the music he postulates a metaphysical source and creates an insoluble problem; this experience is indeed decisive for him, as he says, because it affirms as he believes a spiritual dimension. From this time he begins to ask questions, to investigate problems of a dog's existence, but not always the scientific questions that can yield answers but metaphysical questions which imply non-material forces and meanings.

He gives an example of his method when he ponders on the term *Lufthunde* – literally 'air dogs' – that he hears used (pp. 336–9). When he first heard the term, he says, he ridiculed the notion, but since he has heard it used frequently, he no longer doubts the existence of these air dogs and shares the amazement of other dogs over their ability to hover in the air. But the question he pursues is not, '*Are* there such dogs?' but '*Why* do these dogs soar, what is the sense of this calling?' The 'mute senselessness of this existence', their parasitic idleness, for 'they toil not neither do they spin' (the dog can quote the New Testament), is the problem they set him, though other dogs do not venture on such a question. As he never meets one he cannot examine them directly, but he imaginatively builds out the speculations of other dogs into a picture of a breed of dogs who spend their time in talking of their observations and reflexions, though he hears also that their contributions to knowledge are in fact 'worthless and irritating'.

Surely there can be no doubt that the reader is here confronted with a rather elaborate joke upon the meaning of the term *Luftmensch* – 'man of air' – a term frequently used in those years of crisis and inflation for men who, apparently without assets, capital, or profession, seemed to enjoy unlimited credit and mysterious resources.[15] The dog takes the image literally, a procedure which is often used in Kafka's writings as a source of satirical, often grotesque fantasy. Here the fantasy is playful and charming rather than grotesque, and the emphasis is on the strange logic of the dog, who accepts without any sufficient proof the existence of these strange creatures, the hovering dogs, in order to hurl himself into the metaphysical question of why they do so; his consequent speculations thus being evidently absurd. But then the dog adds a comment that transforms the knock-about comedy into something else. 'Must I not take these dogs,' he asks, 'so odd, senseless, unfit for life, as the sort I myself belong to?' And if there occurs such an 'air dog' here and there, if they beget offspring, even though externally they (like himself) look like other dogs, 'can I not live in the faith that I am not utterly lost?' He continues:

My fellows must have a special destiny, though I shall never be able to detect their existence, if only because I shall scarcely recognise them. We are those who are oppressed by muteness, who out of hunger for air wish to break the silence, while the others seem to find silence comfortable.

Suddenly we learn that the 'air dogs' are only a metaphor for the dog's own dilemma, a bit of fantastic and good-tempered fun that gracefully introduces us to the true search of the dog-writer, his search for the ground of his own curious existence.

This is the theme of the main part of 'Investigations of a dog', though his enquiries continue to have that absurd, unscientific, illogical character that, combined with the dog's pedantic thoroughness, keeps a smile hovering on the reader's lips. It is however an affectionate, not a jeering or derisive smile, for bit by bit we can see ourselves in him and his 'dog-kind'.

The dog describes how he has applied himself to a central issue of canine life, namely, the problem of nourishment. Where does food come from and what guarantees its arrival? He explains he is not a scientist and is not concerned with the physical nature of food or soil. It is a law of the nation of dogs that, if food is to be assured, dogs must water the soil; and he fully respects the injunction 'Make everything wet.' But he notices that most of their food comes 'from above' and that they catch it before it touches the earth, so that he asks whether the accompanying 'ceremonies' – leaping, dancing, barking (he calls it 'song') – are not as necessary as the cultivation of the soil. Other dogs dismiss such questions with the vigorous pragmatism of 'If you've got the food in your muzzle, you've solved all questions for the time being.' But our dog starts on a long series of investigations, all based on his refusal to recognise the simple but for him humiliating fact that it is their human masters who provide dogs with food and who like throwing it to them for them to catch (pp. 343ff).

He soon observes that the food that comes 'from above' sometimes falls straight down, sometimes in an arc, and he tries various methods of behaviour at feeding time to see whether the omission of part of the ritual, or a different form, will affect the arrival of food. Unfortunately he finds that his uncontrollable greed frustrates his experiments so that he decides to make an extreme test. He withdraws into a desert, where he will be far from all sounds and smells of food, to undergo a complete fast in order to see whether, in the absence of the ritual ceremonies, food will come or not.

Knowing that any interruption of his fast will make any result inconclusive, the dog heroically resists all temptations and grows weaker and weaker until, lying in his own vomited blood, he realises he will not be able to recover. And at this point his isolation is shattered by a stranger, a 'hunter dog', who tells him that he is trespassing on his territory and must leave. There is then a charming dialogue between the two dogs in which our hero explains he cannot move and asks why it is necessary for him to leave while the other, normal dog simply reiterates he 'must'. But a miraculous change occurs. The neighbourhood of the strange dog, his voice and scent, bring new life into our 'hero', and as they talk he begins to hear a wondrous music emanating from the stranger, a music that does not come from his mouth and is inaudible to any other creature. He suddenly has the strength to leap joyously away pursued by the mighty melody, and in a few words he tells how he returns to his friends and soon recovers from his starvation.

In the last paragraph the dog tells how he has now turned to the study of the music of dogs, that magic music he had first heard with the dancing dogs and that now he believes belongs mysteriously to all dogs. He seems to have forgotten his setback with the inconsequence of a dog, but he at least now knows that his investigations will not pass 'the slightest scientific test'. He confesses that he has no scientific capacity but 'with a certain happiness', for this incapacity arises from an 'instinct'. And in a rather cryptic ending he brings his story to a close:

It was instinct that, perhaps on behalf of science – but of a different science than is practised today, an ultimate science – led me to value freedom higher than anything else. Freedom! It is true, the freedom possible today is a meagre growth. But still it is freedom, still something one can possess.

We might have expected, and could understand, a conclusion that would justify a concern for matters not subject to scientific examination, that would even ridicule the objectives and methods of science. But the sudden introduction of the topic of freedom is rather baffling. Throughout the dog has been at pains to claim his normalcy, his allegiance to the 'dog-kind' and respect for its laws. We have seen him continually veering away from the normal in his questioning search, his fanatic readiness to starve and even to die, yet he himself has never as it were championed this rebellion as a principle. Has he now acknowledged that the spirit of his investigations was indeed an assertion of his own peculiar nature, his 'peculiar instinct'? Clearly there can be no other meaning for 'freedom' in this context, it can have no political or social content. Yet it would therefore have an unexpectedly anarchic ring for which the reader is hardly prepared. Sometimes indeed I have felt a parodistic note in this final appeal to freedom such as would be appropriate to a creature unable to understand its own motives and goal.

It is not surprising that at the end of 'Investigations of a dog' we are left with uncertainties. For it is the narrative of a dog, an eccentric and gullible seeker, and we know no more than he knows and can communicate; and though he writes about the past and can reflect upon the meaning of his experiences, he has not reached a point of conclusive understanding, but once more is setting out hopefully upon a hopeless quest. So his conclusion hangs in the air, sufficient to justify his further search but not to clarify and settle matters. Critics have compared the dog with the searchers of *The trial* or *The castle*, Sokel even draws a parallel between the dog and the 'countryman' of the parable 'Before the law'. But he lacks the persistent fierce passions of humans, the sharp spur of the sense of guilt as well as its paralysing anguish, the insatiable craving for justification. He has that blessed gift of dogs to be able to break off suddenly from a fruitless occupation and start with fresh zeal on another. He is not a tragic character; like Kafka's ape he is a survivor, one not daunted by failure.

What should we mean here by 'failure'? The dog's object is to distinguish in his life those experiences which remain significant for him, which give him the sense of living, and to try to formulate their 'meaning'. Their meaning is shown usually to be due to a delusion he is subject to, to an error of observation or thought, perhaps to the delirium of illness. But his mistakes do not mean that the raptures of experience, the feeling of wonderful insight, were false or non-existent; they occurred and remain with him for ever, constituting the essential reality of his being. His error seems rather to lie in the effort to formulate what escapes words, he is trying to find explanations for experiences which cannot be clearly stated, about which the Wittgenstein of the *Tractatus* said one should be silent. They are like those religious tenets, beliefs and proofs that Nietzsche ridiculed and rejected but which he admitted had made man 'subtle, delicate and inventive', and that encouraged Nietzsche to replace them not with scepticism but with other, better, more life-giving illusions. But as soon as one looks for human parallels to the dog's endeavour one finds the identity of Kafka's story disintegrating. For there is little that is positive in the dog's endeavour and achievement, he has no universal objectives, no prophetic fire, no rhetoric; he desires to clarify his experiences modestly, with diffidence. The story does not offer a great message but remains tentative and retains its humorous, self-depreciating character to the end. The work's gentle seriousness never forbids and often invites a smile, but it always keeps the sublime, the tragic and the terrible at arm's length. That bloody vomit in which the helpless, apparently doomed, dog lies, that recalls appalling incidents in Kafka's own fatal illness, is in 'Investigations of a dog' joyously forgotten as the dog regains health and hope.

These qualities contribute to the charm of Kafka's story, but when one compares it with the earlier stories they also reduce its relative weight of import. The terrifying elements of the major tales are absent – the deathly rivalry of father and son, the unremitting self-accusations that culminate in suicide or transformation into a loathsome insect, the fascination of cruelty and torture in 'In the penal colony', of self-laceration in *The trial* with its rooms of secrets and horrors, the despair of the K. of the two novels in his ceaseless struggle with an implacable authority, and that black humour in which repeatedly human figures lose their human nature and become grimacing and hostile automata. These are not elements that can be removed, for these belong not just to Kafka's imaginative world but to the world of men, our world, as we only too grievously know. They are not totally eliminated from the animal tales but their presence is less pervasive and powerful and the ape and dog show how they survive the threats and thus in effect diminish their significance. It is for this reason that I take these animal stories to constitute a sort of hypothesis or experiment demonstrating how a creature might find a sense in existence, not a symbol of existence in the full sense, like the earlier tales. And perhaps this is the secret of the use of the non-human figures, for any such hypothesis or experiment must operate with a reduced model of human life.

When we consider these two animal stories against the background of the great tradition of animal tale and fable, we cannot fail to be struck, as when considering Kafka's parables, by the lack of something else too, namely the lack of the simple moral and social categories. Some of the famous animal stories must have been in Kafka's mind, Aesop and Apuleius' *The golden ass*, probably Cervantes' dialogue between the two dogs in the Resurrection hospital, *Dialogue between Scipio and Berganza*, and certainly Swift's account of the horse civilisation in *Gulliver's travels*, as well as the Hoffmann pieces that he demonstrably used. All these, like their late offspring Orwell's *Animal farm*, are consistently and profoundly concerned to offer a criticism or satire of human behaviour and morals, whether the animals they invent act as direct reporters on the humans among whom they live, as in Cervantes and Hoffmann, or whether, as in Swift and Orwell, the animals provide a comment on human society through their own social attitudes and relationships. Hartmut Binder, who acknowledges the traditional predominance of moral concern, 'the criticism of the human world from outside it', does not believe this criticism is lacking in Kafka's dog-story but that it is 'merely transformed' in the sense that while there is no explicit comment on human behaviour the dog-world is 'itself an image of the human'.[16] This statement is true in so far as the relation of the metaphysical questioner to his fellow dogs is concerned, since the position in the human world of the Kafka-type is reflected in that of the questioner to other dogs, who grow impatient with his search for 'why', perhaps intolerant, and to the community which through its 'law' tends to be indifferent or hostile to questioning. But what we miss in Kafka's community of dogs, as so often in his human characters and world, is a concern for those personal and social relationships that involve such moral qualities as selflessness, devotion to others, love, kindness, honesty that not only affect interpersonal relationships but also determine the legitimacy of authority and the individual's relationship to society as a whole. These do not figure in the dog-world, or rather, do not deeply occupy the narrator-dog's consciousness, since if he transgresses canine tradition or law he evades trouble by affirming his loyalty and if he observes objectionable behaviour, selfishness over food for instance, he whitewashes it by saying such behaviour is decreed by the community and therefore not selfish. The lack of a moral–social dimension is a feature that in my view seriously diminishes the stature of Kafka in the perspective of the world's great literature.

I have sometimes thought of Kafka's dog as a Don Quixote of the dog-world, since Cervantes' hero also perceives or seeks another reality behind actual appearances, a reality that in many instances is simply an illusion, giants where there are windmills, the stratagems and spells of enchanters where mere accident prevails, a great devotion to a beloved and to rescuing the unfortunate which leads to absurd self-deception and error. Both are ready to risk their lives for their beliefs. Yet with both heroes we think their illusions and longing are finer, nobler than the crude pragmatism of their fellows, that their questioning, even if it often provokes delusions, is more than a mere evasion of an unpleasant reality or of necessity and the only hope of deeper understanding and a better reality. Just as we can see in the Don's reflexions and constructions, however crazy, a mental dimension beyond Sancho's earthly commonsense, so Kafka's dog reveals even in baseless speculations about musical dogs or 'air dogs' a power of imagination and logic beyond that of his community. In the conversation with the 'hunter dog' at the end Kafka's dog shows true elevation of character when, on the other's insistence that, since he himself must hunt, the sick dog must leave, the latter remonstrates: 'I must leave, you must hunt, sheer musts. Do you understand why we must?' And when the other answers: 'There's nothing here to understand, they are self-evident, natural matters', Kafka's dog says: 'Not at all. You are sorry you have to chase me away and yet you do it' (pp. 351–2). Here we see the wisdom that comes from reflexion, and here the dog's questioning does really acquire a moral dimension.

But it is extremely rarely that moral issues are raised in this story, and this is where the comparison with Don Quixote fails. For continually the Knight's imaginations and objectives are sustained by moral feeling and principle, a moral instinct indeed which remains remarkably true to itself even when it leads him into absurd actions – I think of his sympathy for the suffering, which leads him to free the criminals on their way to the galleys, or his defence of ladies whose virtue he wrongly believes to be threatened, or his ideal of selfless love. But most clearly this wider concern for human relationships speaks in the instructions he gives Sancho when he is to take over his governorship, for these evoke not only the admiration of Sancho but also that of the reader. It is this element that is lacking in Kafka's dog and in his work altogether.

In another way, however, the comparison of the two works leads to a surprising result. Don Quixote before dying renounces his imaginings and dies in peace with his estate and church as a country squire. But Kafka's dog never renounces or gives up but, 'old dog' that he is, starts again on his never-ending pursuit. The story is one of endless hope even if realisation of the hopes is always remote; despondency and despair never assail the questing dog. It is an unusual mood and spirit for a Kafka story and character and it is for this reason that I have called 'Investigations of a dog', like 'A report for an academy', a hypothesis, a try-out of a possibility. And perhaps because of this it links up with a brief reflexion on *Don Quixote* that Kafka wrote in 1917 and to which Max Brod gave the title 'Die Wahrheit über Sancho Pansa' ('The truth about Sancho Pansa'):

Sancho Pansa, who incidentally never boasted about this, succeeded in the course of years, by putting together in his evening and night hours a mass of romances about knights and robbers, succeeded in so diverting from himself his devil, to whom he later gave the name of Don Quixote, that the latter got out of control and carried out the craziest exploits which, however, for lack of any prescribed object, which should have been Sancho Pansa himself, did no harm to anyone. Sancho Pansa, a free man, imperturbably followed Don Quixote upon his exploits, perhaps out of a certain feeling of responsibility, and had from it all, till his death, great and useful entertainment.[17]

The fragment is cryptic, not easy to interpret, but I understand it thus: Sancho, the crude pragmatist, was able to conquer the dangers of the imagination by projecting them into an image. In this form his imagination could riot without doing harm and he had both 'great and useful entertainment' from faithfully attending his creature. The fragment might perhaps have been entitled 'The truth about Don Quixote', for it tells us how such seekers and rebels arise out of the very need of the practical world, how they contribute to the survival of humanity. These late animal stories that Kafka wrote seem to have been projections of a similar character, investigations into the techniques of survival.

'Josephine the singer, or the nation of mice' ('Josefine die Sängerin, oder das Volk der Mäuse', 1924)

This was the last story Kafka completed, and he himself published it in the Prager Presse and prepared it for inclusion in the posthumous volume entitled *A hunger artist*.

It is even less of a story than the other late animal pieces. Like them it presents the reflexions of an animal round one central theme, an animal which has the language and power of

thought of the animals of fable. It differs from the others in that
the animal-narrator, in this case a mouse, is not himself the
object of his reflexions, and because of this it lacks the autobiographical element that contributes to whatever narrative,
story-pattern, the other tales show. This mouse writes about a
remarkable fellow citizen, a female bard, a unique phenomenon
for the community to which they belong, and his essential concern, as the secondary title suggests, is the relationship between
this striking individual, Josephine, and the mice community.
The narrator–mouse is an observer and philosopher, not unlike
Kafka's ape and dog but more akin to the scholarly narrator of
'Building the Chinese wall', curious, well-informed, prudent
and scrupulous, capable of quite bold thoughts but also preserv-
ing a cautious detachment. He does not recount a particular
event or series of linked events but follows a philosophical
enquiry that arises from the characteristic impacts that
Josephine's calling makes upon the community, for this purpose
recalling scenes that illustrate the different facets of his theme.
The whole is told in the present tense since it is essentially the
unfolding of an argument, not a life. There is no element of
historical development in the material the narrator surveys,
sifts and ponders; the story ends not with an event but the final
conclusions of the enquiry. Not even the death of Josephine
could affect these conclusions and we are even told at the end
that though she must one day die she will never grow old and
her voice will never alter.

Yet we do not read 'Josephine the singer' as if it were a
treatise or a parody of a treatise. Not only are the characters
emphatically fictional, the anthropomorphic animals of fable,
whose behaviour and thought amusingly recalls that of human
beings. But also its theme is as much the ways by which the
narrator reaches his conclusions as these conclusions themselves.
Though his account is purposeful, it is not systematic and
abstract; it is not dominated by his final conclusion, to which
he comes only gradually, building on this or that experience,
venturing occasional generalisations which he must then

modify, referring to memories from Josephine's life and to the life of the mouse community in order to sustain or correct a formulation. We see the narrator struggling for an exact word, a precise judgment; and his scruples and effort are not abstract, but derive from his own mousehood. The problems that Josephine's existence creates for the community are his problems too and the procedure of his thought, his enquiry, crystallises the instinctive behaviour of the community towards the bard and discovers its rationale.

In this respect we might say that the quiet, pertinacious construction of this awareness is the 'story' of Josephine the singer'. Perhaps because of this the narrator lacks a power that normally would be considered to be an essential quality of a Kafka narrator, namely, the power of insight into the main character, the power of identifying with the character. Even the ape, dog, and badger of Kafka's animal tales have this power, since they tell their own story. But for the narrator of this last story, Josephine is as much outside his consciousness, as accessible and inaccessible, as any real person is to any other. He does not even enjoy the intimacy and 'inside' knowledge that the anonymous narrator of 'A hunger artist' boasts of. Like any other mouse he can observe Josephine's behaviour, watch and hear her concerts, describe the response and the attitude of the other mice; but he can never tell us of the hidden thoughts of Josephine. This narrator is not a privileged fiction, and he reminds the reader of this frequently by qualifying much of his information, as well as the thoughts he builds on it, by the prudent addition of a 'perhaps' or 'this is how one might understand the implications'. Instead of claiming the licence of the traditional narrator of a fiction, this narrator–mouse only claims the sort of veracity that a real person might aspire to. This sort of veracity might not be sufficient to serve a story the centre of which is the personality of Josephine; but its limitations turn into its strength when, as here, the objective is to show how the community comes to terms with the strange phenomenon of the bard.

The choice of such a narrator has a peculiar and important stylistic effect. The reader will very soon observe that this story lacks the linguistic oddities of 'A report for an academy' and 'Investigations of a dog'. The flamboyance, sophistication, the occasional officialese of the ape, the quaint vocabulary and logic of the dog, have no parallel here. We follow the exposition and descriptions with sympathy and respect, scarcely ever smiling at the mouse though often smiling with him. When he refers to the generality of mice he uses the word *Volk*, folk or people, sometimes such a word as 'the crowd' (*Menge*) or 'audience', words which are as appropriate as possible (*Volk* is often poorly translated as nation, a term that suggests an organised political entity and might raise a smile in this context). The narrator allows himself a little joke when he writes that Josephine's audience becomes 'as still as a mouse' (*mäuschenstill*), and his descriptions of Josephine's tantrums similarly show his own sense of humour. But only very rarely is he the unconscious source of amusement, as when in contrasting the attitude of the whole mouse community to that of a single individual he once uses for the latter the designation 'a man'. It is clear that this avoidance of humorous oddities in thought or speech is deliberate and I think we can define Kafka's intention. In the case of the ape and the dog – as indeed of the anonymous narrator of 'A hunger artist' – the colourful style is intended to characterise the narrator and hence to interpret the temperament of the character who writes; for this temperament is the central object of the story in each case. But in the case of 'Josephine the singer' the sole function of the narrator is to be the medium through which the bard herself and the people to which she belongs become tangible and understandable, a medium that must be transparent and utterly reliable, hence without characteristic quirks.

It is time to leave these general statements and give them concreteness by an analysis of the work. Any analysis requires a summary of the ideas of the narrator and is therefore necessarily more systematic than the mouse's own lively and attractive account; in particular it will not do justice to the to and fro of the mouse's thoughts between the community and Josephine.

The narrator's opening words make his theme and claim to veracity plain and frank:

Our singer is called Josephine. If you have not heard her you do not know the power of song. There is no one who is not carried away by her song, and this is all the more significant since on the whole our race does not love music.

Here the two main elements of the enquiry are defined – the song and singer on one side and on the other the community of mice – and a bold generalisation links them. In the next paragraph the narrator sharpens the statement 'does not love music' to 'After all we are utterly unmusical' and the reader might think he is offered here a figure of style rather frequently met in Kafka's work, a confident and comforting generalisation rapidly disintegrating under the impact of a series of conscious or unconscious qualifications. This occurs after the badger, for instance, praises the stillness of his burrow only to demonstrate how 'deceptive' this stillness is ('The burrow', p. 361[18]) or at the beginning of 'A hunger artist' after the narrator has lauded the universal popularity of the hunger artist only to betray, a few lines further on, that most adults came to view him only as a joke or to be in the swim ('A hunger artist', pp. 163–4). This unconscious self-contradiction is normally humorous, since it shows the self-betrayal of the narrator just when he hopes to be most impressive. But with the mouse the effect is different. The qualifications are here made consciously, are indeed taken into account before the generalisation is made, since what he is saying is that even this unmusical race is carried away by Josephine's song, and this fact greatly enhances its power and makes its investigation all the more worthwhile.

Throughout the piece the mice community is always referred to as an undifferentiated totality, without any social organisation or stratification, and this in itself warns us against looking for precise allegorical parallels to human society, such as are invited by Swift's account of his horse society or Orwell's *Animal farm*. All mice share equally in their much-endangered life in which every day 'brings surprises, worries, hopes and terrors'. Each individual is so weak that he needs the protection, the 'warm proximity' of the crowd; he could not bear the burden of life without the support of the others, and the image of this 'folk' that we are given is always of a tangible presence of warm bodies busily scurrying across each other's paths and at moments of danger flocking together in great 'assemblies'. The pressure of the struggle for existence is so great, the perils so numerous and incalculable, that 'peace is for us the most precious music', and their chief and most valued quality is a certain 'practical slyness' which makes them suspicious of higher ideals of happiness. Their most effective means of defending themselves against the perils of existence is their fertility, the generations succeeding one another so swiftly that before one has got used to the new generation another brood has already taken its place. Yet there is scarcely any differentiation even between young and mature. There are no schools and as soon as the children can run they have to fend for themselves. Thus the mice 'do not know youth' nor do they enjoy a true childhood, the age of carefree play; as a compensation, or punishment, they retain a sort of childishness throughout their lives and at any moment, despite their prudence and cunning, may suddenly 'act foolishly in the way children do, senselessly, extravagantly, frivolously, and all this often just for a bit of fun'.

Such a people, needing to be perpetually busy in order to cope with the needs of life, lacks the leisure and the temperament for art. They are all 'prematurely old': 'a broad streak of weariness and hopelessness traverses the nature of our people in spite of their being in general so tough and strong in hope'. The only artistic gift they possess is their cheeping,[19] but the narrator immediately qualifies his claim and says it is 'not an art at all but a characteristic expression of our life':

We all cheep, but actually no one thinks of calling it an art, we cheep without taking any notice of it, yes, without being aware of it and there even are many of us who do not know that cheeping is one of our peculiarities.

They cheep when things are going well with them, thoughtlessly, as a mere habit. Perhaps, the narrator says, our people once knew what music was and was musically gifted. Our legends tell us so and some songs are preserved from ancient times, though no one nowadays can sing them. But 'we are too old for music, too heavy and weary for its ecstasies'. We are content with this meagre piping, this cheeping, which if it can be called music is music 'reduced to the utmost nullity'.

But in this uniform people there is one exception, Josephine. The narrator does not wonder so much at her uniqueness, but at the strange fact that she is revered by so pragmatic and unmusical a people. She loves music, composes and sings songs; this cannot be explained. But what the narrator's enquiry shows is that she builds her popular success precisely on the circumstances that would seem to forbid it.

The first question asked concerning Josephine's music is, 'Well, is it truly song? Is it perhaps only cheeping?' And the narrator has to admit that it is nothing more than cheeping, indeed cheeping 'scarcely above the normal level', of poorer level than the thoughtless cheeping of any manual labourer. But this qualification only deepens the mystery of her great influence. If you were merely to listen to her, the narrator goes on, you would only hear cheeping. But she does not merely produce sounds. What she does is something customary and normal, but in abnormal circumstances. The narrator compares the performance with cracking a nut. We all crack nuts in the same way, he says, and pay no attention to the method but only to the result; an artistic nut-cracker would aim at winning our attention for method, 'the essence of nut-cracking'. 'Perhaps it is the same situation with Josephine's singing' he adds, and refers to an occasion when a bystander had once, tactfully and modestly, drawn Josephine's attention to the cheeping of mice.

Josephine had responded with 'an insolent arrogant smile' and had violently denied any connexion between her art and cheeping, and the narrator, who can see the 'vulgar touchiness' in this response, is yet forced to agree since 'When one sits in front of her, one knows: what is being cheeped here is no cheeping.' That is, divorced from the normal circumstances of cheeping, and from the normal function of cheeping, something new comes into being, song. So that the wise narrator knows that the question 'Is it song or is it cheeping' is a very complex one and he can even widen it, when he comes to discuss the great concerts that Josephine gives to an entranced audience: 'Is it her song that delights us, or is it not rather the solemn stillness by which her frail little voice is surrounded?' The fact that she does not properly sing but can only cheep turns in the end into a great advantage, since the mice would not bother to listen to anything so far from their own form of self-expression as song.

In the same way Josephine turns the adverse conditions of mouse existence into a means of success. The narrator has explained that the constant threats to peace and security make mice extremely sober and pragmatic and indisposed to and incapable of art. But he also tells us that Josephine recognises perils and scares as her opportunity. When the first signs of danger appear she prepares to sing, takes up a posture 'head leaning back, half-open mouth, eyes turned upwards'. She spares no efforts to attract attention, throwing even shameless tantrums. If a crowd does not quickly collect she becomes furious, cursing, even biting. We are forced to do everything to bring the masses along till she can be prevailed upon, after much *prima donna* touchiness, to sing, and then we stand rapt: 'we plunge into the feeling of the crowd, listening, warm body by body, scarcely breathing'. We spare no trouble to provide the audience, to overcome her resistance.

'Why should our people take so much trouble for her?' asks the narrator, and he answers that the question is no simpler than that about her cheeping song. It is not that we are uncon-

ditionally devoted to her or to art. We are too practical and
shrewd for that, he says, and he describes how, when Josephine
has asked to be freed from the labour of ordinary life as a
tribute to her art the people quietly refuse her any such distinction, to her bitter resentment. But still 'the people are devoted
to her, though not utterly'. No one would, for instance, ever
laugh at her, however weird her gestures and feeble her voice.
Sometimes, the narrator says, he has the impression that the
people feels that this frail, vulnerable creature has been
'entrusted' to them and they must take care of her, protect her.
And this they can do in a way that no individual guardian
could since all they need to do is 'to draw their ward into the
warm proximity of the crowd' and she is protected enough. It
is true, he says, that Josephine rejects any suggestion that she
needs protection (again with a little joke when she uses the
German idiom 'I pipe at your protection' in the sense 'a fig for
your protection'). But our clever mouse knows her indignation
only confirms her need, for it is 'the rebellion of a child', the
sort of 'gratefulness', he ironically comments, a child expresses
to her parents.

Josephine herself is of the opposite opinion, it is not the
people that protects her but she who protects the people. For
allegedly, in 'evil political or economic situations', her song
rescues us. And that is a fact, the narrator admits, even if her
song does not dispel the threatening disaster, since 'at least it
gives us the strength to bear it'. She herself does not say this
explicitly, but if she finds we disregard her signals, are tossed
to and fro by rumours and do not grow still, she will stretch her
long neck and 'gaze over her herd like a shepherd before a
thunderstorm'. Our narrator is not gullible, and even at this
juncture he remarks that it is easy to 'play the saviour' of this
people, which is used to disaster and suffering, does not spare
itself, is acquainted with death and though apparently timid is
also capable of bold decisions; 'it has always somehow or other
managed to survive, even with great losses'. But he answers his
own question:

But still, it is true that it is just when we are in desperate straits that we listen better than at other times to Josephine's voice. The threats that encompass us make us quieter, more modest, more pliant to Josephine's leadership. We are glad to assemble, glad to press close to one another, particularly because the cause is something quite apart from the main source of our anxiety; it is as if we quickly – yes, speed is necessary, Josephine only too often forgets this – drank together one last cup of peace before the conflict. It is not so much a concert as a public assembly, and in fact an assembly in which except for that weak little cheeping before us there is utter silence; the hour is much too serious to be passed in chatter.

The portrait of Josephine's person and behaviour that the narrator draws is anything but impressive. She has all the conceit and absurdity of a spoilt *prima donna*. If she is praised she is scornful and indignant, confident that she is not appreciated for the right reasons; if she is slighted she is bitter and revengeful, using all sorts of tricks to show her resentment. If a great audience does not swiftly collect to hear her, she throws tantrums; when at last a crowd is collected and waits in reverent expectancy, she will refuse to sing, alleging she has been unpardonably insulted, or that she is ill, or has hurt a leg etc., inviting the most abject and servile requests before she will accede. She will even threaten to leave the community, indeed at one time it was said she had done so, though at this point the narrator points out that she is going too far and risking her whole existence, as after all the 'folk' may just let her go and simply forget her for ever, for as he says 'the folk can only give gifts and never receive them', and if she departs it will merely continue on its way.

But this showmanship of Josephine's is not taken seriously by the people. As she stands before them, stretching her neck absurdly, making clumsy grand gestures, curling her lips, puffing out the air between her little front teeth, 'expiring in admiration over the notes she herself produces and using this exhaustion in order to animate herself to new and even more incomprehensible heights of achievement' – and all the time merely producing that feeble cheeping – it is only the young

who are interested in the singer herself and 'gaze in astonishment' at her performance. But the great assembly of mice
listening to her song does not notice all this to-do. It has, the
narrator tells us 'withdrawn into itself', and now he ventures
on his boldest explanation of the power of Josephine's song:

Here in the meagre pauses between their struggles the people dream, it
is as though the limbs of each one of us were loosened, as though the
restless for once is permitted to relax and stretch out according to his
sweet will in the great warm bed of the people. And into these dreams
there rings here and there the cheeping of Josephine; she calls it 'pearl-
ing', we call it staccato, but in either case it is here in its rightful place as
nowhere else, as music scarcely ever does find the moment that is waiting
for it. Something of our poor brief childhood is in it, something of lost,
never to be recovered happiness, but also something of the active life of
the day, of its slight, incomprehensible cheerfulness that lasts in spite of
all and is inextinguishable. And all this, truly, is not spoken in resound-
ing tones but softly, in a whisper, confidentially, sometimes a little
hoarsely. Naturally it is cheeping. How could it not be? Cheeping is the
language of our people, only many cheep their whole lives through and
do not know it, but here cheeping is liberated from the fetters of daily
life and liberates us too for a short while. Certainly we would not wish
to miss these concerts.

This passage is unparalleled in Kafka's work. It is a hymn
to art, and significantly it is at the same time a hymn to the
harmony of artist and audience, of artist and society. It celebrates that peculiar exaltation that art evokes, its power to
liberate us from the daily round, from pressing needs, business,
and fears; its power to allow us to become conscious of our
existence, that coenaesthesis of which music is the supreme
agent. But while it speaks to each one of us of our self, it does
not speak of the peculiar self but the common selfhood we enjoy
as members of a community and race, so that this heightened
selfconsciousness is at the same time a merging in the community, in its totality, its vital activity, its joys that, however
meagre, are immortal (here as elsewhere in 'Josephine the
singer' the 'warmth' of the herd is lauded, without open or
hidden irony, as if Kafka would challenge Nietzschean elitist

arrogance). And Josephine's music achieves these profound effects not with grand and sublime tones and words, but through the medium of a feeble voice and through sounds that are the least solid and tangible of all forms of artistic expression. It achieves its purpose through the instrument we ourselves use in daily practical life, through that monotonous 'cheep, cheep' that automatically accompanies the mouse's everyday activity, to which we attribute no special meaning or merit until suddenly and mysteriously it is dissociated from its normal context and function and becomes a purpose to itself. Thus we become aware of the 'might of song', its power to reach us 'almost as a message from the people as a whole to each one of us'. It is as if, the narrator continues, 'the thin cheeping of Josephine in the midst of arduous dilemmas is almost like the frail existence of our people within the tumult of the hostile world'. True to his mouse nature our narrator also does not indulge in grandiose words and his last sentence, 'we would not wish to miss these concerts', are characteristically prudent and sober.

Finally, after this celebration of the meaning of Josephine's music for her people, the narrator considers what it means for her; and here again we may be surprised by the positive evaluation:

Josephine's path can only go downhill. The time will soon come when her last cheep will sound and fall dumb. She is a small episode in the eternal history of our people and the people will get over the loss. It will not be easy for us; how can the assemblies be held in complete muteness? But after all, were they not mute with Josephine? Was her actual cheeping noticeably louder and livelier than the memory of it will be? Was it after all during her lifetime anything more than a mere memory? Is it not the case that, in its wisdom, the people has valued Josephine's song so highly precisely because in this way it could not be lost?

Perhaps therefore we shall not be deprived of very much, but Josephine, redeemed of her earthly tribulations, which in her opinion is only the lot of the elect, will cheerfully lose herself in the innumerable throng of the heroes of our folk and soon, since we do not make history, will in heightened redemption be forgotten like all her brothers.

It is Heinz Politzer who uses 'heightened redemption' as the translation of the strange term *gesteigerte Erlösung*, but he understands it in a very limited sense. 'Redemption' he takes to mean only release from the tribulations of life, from suffering, giving the word only the negative value of an end to misfortune. And 'heightened' he understands as the 'national' aspect of this personal end, and therefore as meaning that Josephine also 'dies to her nation' and enters that 'mausoleum of oblivion' in which she joins the other forgotten heroes of this 'people without history'. Thus Josephine's life and death are reduced to nullity.[20] But Politzer's interpretation in no sense does justice to the word 'redemption' nor to the meaning of the ending. *Erlösung*, that I have called a 'key-word' of the literature of Kafka's period, has many meanings in this period, from the banal 'end to suffering' to the mystic transcendence of a spiritual being that replaces man's earthly integument. But in all serious contexts it has more than the meaning of a mere release, it has the positive suggestion of the triumphant survival of a spiritual being, be it as a personal immortality or a more sophisticated sort of spiritual affirmation.[21] This is so even when, as with the many adherents of Schopenhauer, it means redemption from that individuation that is man's curse and re-absorption in that mystic whole that is our source. So 'redemption' is used by Kafka as a term that implies a spiritual fulfilment as well as a release from 'earthly tribulations', and that strange term 'heightened', the Goethean *gesteigert*, which Politzer rightly says applies here to the national aspect of Josephine's death, means at the same time 'raised to a higher level' in a spiritual sense too. So we are meant to understand that she lives on in her people, not as a person or an individual memory, for this people of mice has no historical memory, but absorbed into the being, the nature and habits, of this people; personally forgotten but immortal in her contribution to the survival of her folk.

In this positive evaluation of Josephine's fate, in life as in death, I seem to be more completely perhaps than ever at variance with the commonly accepted interpretations.[22] Some of these are of the arbitrary type which Kafka texts seem to provoke. For instance Max Brod, and following him several other commentators, have seen in the mice nation an allegory of the suffering and constantly endangered Jewish people, in spite of the fact that the absence of historical memory in the former, either of events or the national heroes, is so startlingly different from the Jews, who, above all people, dwell in the ever-renewed memory of their past heroes, blessings and disasters. Politzer, who rejects Brod's suggestion, himself adduces an entry in Kafka's diary for 1911 (!) on the significance of a national literature for small, weak nations as a clue to the meaning of the work. Sokel, searching in his usual thorough manner throughout Kafka's works for similar images and themes, finds in a letter from Kafka of 1917 to his friend Felix Weltsch an account of a 'terrible experience', a night disturbed by the ceaseless noises of mice, gnawing, scuttling here and there, cheeping etc., and relates this to the 'fearful, horrifying nature' of the mice in 'Josephine the singer'. Sokel makes even a larger leap across the years by relating the 'inexorable power' of the mice community over the individual Josephine to that of the fathers over the sons in the early tales 'The judgment' and 'The metamorphosis'.[23] But Kafka's story, in which it is true the ultimate authority is ascribed to the community, in no sense presents this as a terrifying enemy, nor are its habits of ceaseless scurrying activity described with anything but sympathy, and its relationship with Josephine herself is, as Sokel rather surprisingly adds, of a 'utopian' harmony as far as the main issue, her singing, is concerned.

All these authors often show insight and wide scholarship to which every student of Kafka is indebted, and occasional aberrations (if, as I believe, they may be called) are readily understandable in view of the many riddles that Kafka propounds. It is a rather more serious matter with a widespread opinion, of which Politzer may be taken to be the spokesman, that this story, which indisputedly describes the relationship of an artist to the community to which she belongs, presents this relationship as a disastrous and tragic one, under which the artist

Josephine suffers in her life from disdain and neglect and in her death from utter oblivion. It is true that the narrator repeatedly stresses the inadequacies of Josephine, her poor delivery and feeble voice which indeed is not a voice but the same cheeping that any mouse emits, her absurd pretensions, her claims for distinctions and privileges that are always ignored by the mice; it is stated emphatically that the community can dispense with Josephine and will not even miss her when she dies, while she depends entirely on the community. And the narrator frankly asserts that this people of mice is 'utterly unmusical' and cannot, in view of its hard and endangered life, 'soar to such remote things as music'. So that Josephine is ranked with the so-called artist of 'A hunger artist' as typical examples of the alienation and tragic fate of the modern artist.

Such a view seems to misread 'Josephine the singer' in favour of a preconceived theory. It confuses what is said in the story about the person of Josephine and her art, even though we are explicitly told at the beginning that the 'power of her song' is all the more astonishing since the mice as a rule are unmusical, and by 'power of her song' the narrator clearly means its power over the community of mice. He differentiates sharply between the person of Josephine, her self-esteem, her conception of her own significance and rights, even her conception of the dignity of her art, and her art itself. And the art is made all the more venerable because the mice, including the narrator, perceive clearly the contradiction between her performance and behaviour on the one hand and on the other the profound import of that feeble song. In times of danger the mice need her song, and all the more because it is not related to the immediate circumstances, it does not explain their situation or instruct them on safety methods; it recalls them to themselves, their identity as individuals and their common being as a community, transporting them from their actual cares and dangers and filling their existence with an exalted dignity as if, the narrator tells us, through this weak voice 'the whole people' were speaking to each one of them. Josephine herself has the conceit and ambition of many an artist, and the people has little sympathy with or understanding for this; but her art is revered without reserve as the great resource in times of need. Can there be a higher acknowledgment of the value and necessity of art? And to this is added that last paragraph in which it is stated that when Josephine dies she will scarcely be missed and will be forgotten like all the other 'heroes of our people'. I have already explained that this 'heightened redemption' she now will enjoy, into which she enters, we are told, 'cheerfully', is the truest immortality, since though as an individual she will be forgotten, she will be for ever embodied in the life of her people. This is no tragic story of the misunderstood artist but the very contrary, the story of the triumph of art.

EPILOGUE

EDITORS' NOTE

Here we print two incomplete sections of Roy Pascal's type-script. The first passage continues the analysis of 'Josephine', beginning immediately after the concluding sentence of chapter 8. Roy Pascal clearly intended to qualify – but not to undermine – the generalisation with which the chapter ends.

But I can hear a friendly reproving voice saying to me: 'Come come! you are over-stating your case. One could think you were defining the occasion when, in dark hours of national danger, Winston Churchill closed a sombre yet inspiring speech with the lines of Arthur Hugh Clough "Say not the struggle naught availeth." But Kafka's story is about mice and a quaint mouse-bard and in addition there's not a memorable exhilarating phrase in it.' Of course the reproving voice is right, and I have to qualify my generalisation – following a practice we have observed in Kafka, though I hope not bound to pare the bold generalisation down to a splinter.

First on the language of 'Josephine the singer': I have pointed out at the beginning of this section that the narrator's language lacks the 'oddities', the characteristic touches, that we find in the style of Kafka's ape and dog, and that it is rather colourless, inviting neither to satire nor to strong sympathy. The narrator speaks of the great issues of his people, dangers, terrors, death and of the wondrous power of Josephine's song over a rapt audience, yet his language is always undistinguished, ordinary, rather banal, very sober, inclining to the cliché. Its course is broken by hesitations, modifications, that prevent any great movement of thought or feeling, even at its highest moment when the meaning of Josephine's singing for the people is described (pp. 180 1) and which concludes with so flat a statement as 'we would not wish to miss these concerts'. Yet, as

Dentan has said in an incomparably precise and perceptive appreciation of the style of this work, the undistinguished style of the narrator, like the feeble cheeping of Josephine herself, contains a 'secret beauty'.[1] After demonstrating how the rather random advance of the story enhances the uncovering of its true origin and purpose, how the somewhat uncertain and varying terms used for the mouse people and for Josephine's cheeping kindles in the reader's imagination rich associations and analogies in human society and art without making undue and limiting claims, so that in these respects the 'insufficiency' of the style becomes its power, its incoherency suggests a coherency, a truth, that cannot be translated into precise words but is all the more significant for resisting definition. Among the ambiguities in which 'Josephine the singer' is so rich, that of the relationship of the gravity of tone to the often slightness of content is constantly present. There is very little in the style that is unambiguously comic or humorous (Dentan's chief concern is Kafka's humour), but this interplay of gravity, even pedantry, of tone and the quaint world of mice, between the gravity of issues too and the language in which they are delineated, is for Dentan a supreme example of that play element in Kafka's work that is so often overlooked by critics.

It is in this context that Dentan speaks more particularly about the language of 'Josephine the singer':

Kafka's game consists in discreetly unveiling the insufficiency of the language but in such a way that by its very insufficiency it is orientated towards what surpasses it. One never quite forgets that the story unfolds at the level of a world of mice, even though the language applies to an order of human concerns. From time to time Kafka exploits this contrast but in an almost imperceptible manner. For example he says that Josephine's audience is 'as still as a mouse'; he speaks of 'trouble with the lighting'; the word 'concert' also has something comic about it if you think of an audience of mice. But this is only a secondary aspect. In a more general fashion all the language is slyly compromised by its application to the little world of mice. The questions at issue are constantly grave problems and elevated subjects: the needs of the soul, the nostalgia for happiness, the miseries of life, the problem of art and its spiritual contribution, the status of the artist in society, the goal and the possibilities of life, the problem of childhood etc. These themes are evoked in a very general manner and by the means of a conventional vocabulary and even clichés, as we have seen. This is also what produces their ambiguity: their generalness, their conventional character exposes them and reveals their insufficiency; but this very generality, their abstractness and vagueness or, if you like, the fact that their meaning will not limit itself to the insignificance of the subject to which they apply, confers upon them an indeterminate power, a sort of multi-disposability for a more complex and richer reality. For example we have seen above the insufficiency of the vocabulary of the phrase 'Our life is very agitated, every day brings surprises, worries, hopes, and terrors, and no individual could bear all this if he had not, day and night, the support of his fellows' [Raabe, pp. 174–5]. Still more derisory is the pathos in the description of Josephine's song: 'There she stands already, the frail creature, palpitating just beneath her breast in an alarming fashion' [Raabe, p. 175]. The words seem so poor in the first phrase or on the contrary so comically excessive in the second only because of their disproportion to the subject to which they apply; there remains in them something further disposable for one knows not what subject. It is both too much and too little: too much for the concerns of the mice and the song of Josephine, too little for what they suggest beyond the immediate subjects.

Dentan detects this playful element in several of the late Kafka texts also, for instance in 'First grief' or 'A report for an academy'; he rightly says that sometimes it goes so far as to leave the reader baffled as to its function both in the structure of the work concerned and in the possible symbolic applications. Though he contrasts the works in which it predominates with those in which the main character perishes, reduced to despair and nullity by a hostile, implacable and incomprehensible world, Dentan sees these other works, with their uncertain endings and the gaiety of their sometimes extravagant fantasy and with their deliberate 'insufficiency' of language as complementary to the tragic works, that is, as a confession of the impossibility of finding any authentic language for a less disastrous view of this world.[2] This opinion, which must command respect, fails in my opinion to do full justice to these late stories of Kafka.

Dentan's fine analysis exaggerates, I believe, both the

inadequacy of the style of 'Josephine the singer' and the indeterminacy of the relationship of this animal story (and by implication of the other animal stories) to the human situation and human possibilities. Because the teller of the tale in each case is an animal, and one of a specific character and temperament, we are able to adjust what are perhaps inadequate linguistic means to our own mental habit and read into their insufficiences the meanings their situation deserves – much as we do with human beings, children or inarticulate or inhibited speakers and writers. The insufficiency of the animals may make us smile but does not lessen the truth and seriousness of their concerns.

EDITORS' NOTE

Roy Pascal's death prevented the completion of this analysis. Here are some jottings he made for his conclusion:

The search for authenticity. The search for the appropriate narrative perspective, and for a story without definite contours, without fulfilment, endings, conclusions. An ongoing situation, not a plot; the present tense, not the past; immersion in the now, not retrospective understanding and judgment. At the same time a means of facing the riddle and threat of existence without terror, of exorcising the terrors. The meaning of the animal stories, fantasy as 'hypothesis'. The *Werden* ['growth'] of Kafka...

NOTES

INTRODUCTION: NARRATOR AND STORY

1. E. M. Forster, *Aspects of the novel*, London 1927. Graham Greene is one of the few serious modern novelists to acknowledge without embarrassment the responsibility of composing an entertaining story.

2. W. B. Gallie, *Philosophy and the historical understanding*, New York 1964. For the function of narrative as a means of understanding, see also H. R. Jauss, *Literaturgeschichte als Provokation*, Frankfurt am Main 1970. I have considered some of the issues involved in 'Narrative fictions and reality', *Novel*, XI, 1 (Fall 1977).

3. Miguel Cervantes, *Don Quixote*, 1605–15. See in particular part 1, the opening of chapter 1, book 2; and part 2, chapters 2 and 3 of book 1.

4. P. Lubbock, *The craft of fiction*, London 1921; F. K. Stanzel, *Die typischen Erzählsituationen im Roman*, Vienna 1955 (trans. as *Narrative situations in the novel* by J. P. Pusack, Indiana 1971).

5. Schnitzler could not escape this danger in his notable first-person, present-tense stories, presented throughout as interior monologues, *Leutnant Gustel* and *Fräulein Else*.

6. Roy Pascal, *The dual voice: Free indirect speech and its functioning in the nineteenth-century novel*, Manchester 1977.

7. M. M. Bachtin, *Problèmes de la poétique de Dostoïevski*, Lausanne 1970. This is a translation of the revised text (1963) of a work that first appeared, in Russian, in 1929. An English translation was published in 1973.

8. The most notable definitions of the structure of novelistic narrative before Lubbock's *Craft of fiction* are the various prefaces that Henry James wrote for the collected edition of his works in the first decade of this century, and the doctoral thesis of Käte Friedländer, *Die Rolle des Erzählers in der Epik*, Berlin 1910 (reprint Darmstadt 1965).

9. J. P. Sartre, *Qu'est-ce que la littérature? (What is literature?)*, published in *Situations 2*, Paris 1948.

10. Though all these tenses are used in English, French and German, there are deep differences in their meaning. English uses the preterite much more freely than the other two, while its composite past ('I have visited my aunt') is strikingly different in implication from the comparable French or German form, which, much used in the colloquial idiom, strongly evokes the presence of the speaker. The English translation of Camus's *L'Etranger* renders the composite past in which this story is told by the preterite and thus muffles or distorts a very important element in the story.

11. Theodor Adorno's essay, 'Standort des Erzählers im zeitgenössischen Roman', 1954, is reprinted in his *Noten zur Literatur*, I, Frankfurt 1965. I have discussed Adorno's views in relation to Thomas Mann's

The magic mountain in '*The magic mountain* and Adorno's critique of the traditional novel', *Culture and society in the Weimar Republic* (ed.) K. Bullivant, Manchester 1977.

12. Frank Kermode, *The sense of an ending*, Oxford and New York 1967, in which is sketched a valuable theory of structural narrative fictions that I have discussed in my essay in *Novel* (1977) (see note 2 above).

13. Hartmut Binder, *Motiv und Gestaltung bei Franz Kafka*, Bonn 1966, pp. 188–264, and particularly pp. 253–9.

1 THE KAFKA STORY: STRUCTURE AND MEANING

1. See Kafka's comment on his 'unashamed imitation' of *David Copperfield* in *Tagebücher 1910–1923* (ed.) M. Brod, New York 1951 pp. 535–6.

2. *Franz Kafka, Sämtliche Erzählungen* (ed.) Paul Raabe, Frankfurt 1970. All page references in the present study to the text of Kafka's stories are to this excellent and convenient edition.

3. *Ibid.*, p. 393, 'Erzählungen und Texte'.

4. Heinz Hillmann, *Franz Kafka. Dichtungstheorie und Dichtungsgestalt*, Bonn 1964, pp. 161–94, defines five different types of story in Kafka: *Betrachtung, Parabel, Geschichte, Roman, Bericht*. From my remarks it will be clear why I have ignored two of these groups, 'observation' and 'report', except where particular examples have a strong story element.

5. 'Das Ganze erscheint zwar sinnlos, aber in seiner Art abgeschlossen', p. 139.

6. Friedrich Beissner, *Der Erzähler Franz Kafka*, Stuttgart 1952 and *Franz Kafka der Dichter*, Stuttgart 1958 (the latter is translated in *Kafka. A Collection of critical essays* (ed.) R. Gray, New Jersey 1962. Beissner's view of the submergence of the narrator in the character was challenged by Martin Walser (*Beschreibung einer Form*, Munich 1961), who would only allow a 'convergence' of the two. Ingeborg C. Henel has indicated more precisely the meaning of this distinction for interpretation in 'Die Deutbarkeit von Kafkas Werken', *Zeitschrift für deutsche Philologie*, LXXXVI (1967), 250–66. These and most subsequent studies of Kafka's narrative perspective are devoted to the novels *The trial* and *The castle*, as is Beissner's first essay. Among the most valuable are Winfried Kudszus, 'Erzählperspective und Erzählgeschehen in Kafka's *Prozess*', *Deutsche Vierteljahrsschrift für Literaturwissenschaft und Geistesgeschichte*, XLIV, 2 (1970) and his 'Changing perspectives: Trial/Castle' in the collection of miscellaneous pieces edited by Angel Flores, *The Kafka debate*, New York 1977; and two studies of R. W. Sheppard, *On Kafka's Castle*, London 1973, and 'Trial/Castle: an analytical comparison' in the above-mentioned miscellany edited by Angel Flores. The most comprehensive and pentrating of all such studies is Hartmut Binder's *Motiv*.

7. Heinz Politzer, *Franz Kafka: parable and paradox*, Ithaca and New York 1962.

8. Politzer gives a useful sketch of the history of Kafka criticism in the 'Einleitung' to the edition he has made of selected critical texts entitled *Franz Kafka*, Darmstadt 1973. Throughout this present investigation I have been repeatedly indebted to the valuable critical summary of studies of Kafka, particularly of the separate stories, by Peter U. Beicken, *Franz Kafka. Eine kritische Einführung in die Forschung*, Frankfurt 1974. Two other handbooks have been of great use – Hartmut Binder, *Kafka: Kommentar zu sämtlichen Erzählungen*, Munich 1975; and Chris Bezzel, *Kafka Chronik. Daten zu Leben und Werk*, Munich and Vienna 1975.

2 THE IMPERSONAL NARRATOR OF THE EARLY TALES

1. In Raabe's edition *Das Urteil* occupies pp. 23–32 and *Die Verwandlung*, pp. 56–99.
2. On the earlier use of free indirect speech see my study *The dual voice*. I there explain why I prefer this term to *erlebte Rede*.
3. Professor John Ellis, whose excellent essay on '*Das Urteil*' (in his *Narration in the German Novelle*, Cambridge 1974) I shall often refer to, believes this conversation reveals a remarkably sudden change of mind in Georg and hence indicates his instability of character (p. 198). But Ellis fails to notice that the report of the exchange between Georg and Frieda is introduced by 'Oft sprach er mit seiner Braut über diesen Freund...', so that the report is a bold form of reported speech, a reduction of many discussions during which Georg came gradually to change his mind. My reading is anticipated in Binder's excellent *Motiv*, p. 270.
4. Binder, *Motiv*, pp. 244–347.
5. Friedrich Beissner, *Kafka der Dichter*.
6. Ellis, '*Das Urteil*', pp. 191–3 and W. H. Sokel, *Franz Kafka. Tragik und Ironie*, Vienna 1964, p. 45. In Sokel's volume *Das Urteil* is discussed pp. 44–76.
7. Ellis, '*Das Urteil*', pp. 202–7.
8. *Ibid.*, pp. 208–10.
9. *Ibid.*, pp. 207–8.
10. H. Politzer, *Franz Kafka der Künstler*, Gütersloh 1965, p. 102.
11. Ellis, '*Das Urteil*', p. 188.
12. Thus my formal examination supports those interpreters (including Edmund Wilson, Günther Anders, F. D. Luke and W. H. Sokel) who see the guilt feelings of Gregor Samsa as the source of his transformation into a bug. Professor Sokel discusses the more important interpretations of 'The metamorphosis' in 'Kafkas Verwandlung: Auflehnung und Bestrafung', published in English in *Monatshefte*, XLVIII, 4 (1956) and in German in *Franz Kafka* (ed.) H. Politzer. Sokel's article contains a useful bibliography of studies of 'The metamorphosis'.
13. In his long investigation of the narrative structure of *The metamorphosis* Hartmut Binder has clearly shown the narratorial implications of the

several examples of 'Zeitraffung', the reduction of time, in this story. Binder assumes however a distinct difference between this function of the narrator and that involved in the description of situation (as opposed to event), which he believes to be presented always from the point of view of the main character, Gregor. He overlooks the examples I have given (Binder, *Motiv*, pp. 265–98). These interventions of the impersonal narrator have the effect of bearing objective witness to the 'truth' of Gregor's metamorphosis and thus prevent the reader from reading the story as a mere illusion of the fictitious character.

14. Kafka, diary entry for 19 January 1914 in *Tagebücher 1910–1923*, p. 351; and letter to Felice Braun, 6/7 December 1912.
15. Kafka, *Ein Landarzt*, 'Die Sorge des Hausvaters' (*Sämtliche Erzählungen* (ed.) Paul Raabe, p. 139).
16. M. Dentan, *Humour et création littéraire dans l'oeuvre de Kafka*, Geneva and Paris 1961, p. 171.
17. *Ibid.*, p. 109.
18. Roy Pascal, *From naturalism to expressionism*, London 1973, pp. 220–55, where the titles of the many works will be found upon which my brief résumé is based.

3 OFFICER VERSUS TRAVELLER: 'IN THE PENAL COLONY'

1. There is a helpful review of the immense literature on *In the penal colony* in Beicken's *Franz Kafka. Eine kritische Einführung in die Forschung*. After sketching the religious interpretation offered by Austin Warren in *The Kafka problem* (ed.) Angel Flores, New York 1946, Beicken adds: 'Mit persönlichen Varianten folgen die meisten Deuter diesem religiösen oder metaphysisch-existentiell verbrämten Schema Warrens' (p. 288). Beicken's own intelligent and critical résumé of this tradition has scarcely checked its flow. In *The Kafka debate*, a memorial volume of selected essays again edited by Angel Flores, the contribution of Malcolm Pasley, 'In the penal colony', still moves in the framework of these traditional assumptions. Though Ronald Gray in *Franz Kafka*, Cambridge 1973, has qualified some of the views expressed in his earlier study, *Kafka's castle*, Cambridge 1956, and points out some of the difficulties dogging the interpretation of 'In the penal colony' as a religious allegory, he still holds the work to belong within that 'region of meaning'.
2. Gray, *Franz Kafka*, pp. 99–102 and R. Thieberger, 'The botched ending of *In the penal colony*' in *The Kafka debate* (ed.) Angel Flores, pp. 308–10. Wilhelm Emrich, *Franz Kafka*, Bonn and Frankfurt 1958, offers a different view. Emrich does not question the validity of Kafka's ending, nor does he see the tale as a religious allegory. But like so many other critics he disregards the whole question of the narrative structure and discusses the officer's statements and pleas as if they were the direct expressions of the views of an objective authority. As a consequence

he does not attribute any significance to the traveller, treating him as a mere onlooker of a contest between the old and new commandant.

3. Page references in brackets are from Raabe's edition.

4. W. H. Sokel has also seen that the reader sees this story through the medium of the traveller and that there is therefore a double focus. But he insists that 'the officer is the hero of the story' he finds that the ending ruptures the 'unity of mood'. If he had grasped its dialectical structure he would have been able to dispense with the idea of a hero and to grasp the true unity of the work and the significance of the traveller as the perspectival focus – 'Das Verhältnis der Erzählperspektive zu Erzählgeschehen', *Zeitschrift für deutsche Philologie*, LXXXVI (1967), 267–300.

5. Hartmut Binder, in his comprehensive examination of 'als ob' clauses in Kafka's novels and stories, comes to the same conclusion viz. that, where there is no explicit indication of a person in whose mind such hypothetical inferences are made, this form presents 'the psychic constitution of the other figures in the simplest way possible – as an interpretation offered by the character who conditions our perspective' – the latter being in 'In the penal colony' the traveller. The same conclusion would apply to statements governed by *es schien* or introduced by the impersonal *man sah* of which there are several examples in this story.

Binder notes that the gestures of the traveller are not accompanied by such hypothetical explanations and suggests the reason to be that guesses are not required since the gestures 'unambiguously reflect the mental background' of the traveller. This is not very satisfactory since we are in fact told very much more about the mental processes in the traveller than in the officer. Surely the explanation for the lack of guesses about the traveller's thoughts lies in the narrative perspective, which places us within the traveller's mind and renders guessing normally unnecessary? (*Kafka in neuer Sicht*, Stuttgart 1976, pp. 230–1).

In *Motiv* Binder's observations on Kafka's style and narrative perspective in 'In the penal colony' are as elsewhere more precise than those of other critics. Here, while acknowledging that the traveller provides the narrative perspective, he notes that certain statements, such as those I here refer to, do not 'formally' fit this perspective though they may still be understood as the traveller's observations. But Binder gets into a difficulty because of his scrupulousness. He recognises that usually in Kafka's stories the character that provides the narrator's perspective is the 'main character', the 'hero', but like Sokel and others he considers the officer to fill that role in 'In the penal colony'. He can with impunity call it an exception, but he also tries to find an analogy in a Kafka story-type in which the narrator is not the central character but one on the 'periphery' of the action, as for instance in 'Building the Chinese wall' or 'Josephine the singer'. But these are first-person stories, and 'In the penal colony' still remains an exception. Further it is Binder's contention that in this type of story we are given not an 'inside view' of the characters but an 'outside view' and this again does not fit 'In the penal colony' since, while the officer is seen from outside, there is abundant 'inside' information on the traveller. These difficulties are I believe all cleared up if we see the story as belonging formally to the normal Kafka type of third-person narrative, i.e. if we assume that the traveller is intended to be the 'main character', Binder, *Motiv*, pp. 330–4, 395.

6. This double reference is a familiar feature of free indirect speech – see my *The dual voice*.

7. Both Gray, *Kafka* and Thieberger 'Botched ending' discuss these alternative endings.

8. Malcolm Pasley, 'In the penal colony', *The Kafka Debate* (ed.) Angel Flores, pp. 302–3. There are other occasions in this brief essay where the author adopts similar interpretations.

9. In V. S. Pritchett's *Midnight oil* (London 1971), p. 169, in a passage describing the author's 'unease' as a foreign correspondent in the colonial states of North Africa, there is an explicit formulation of the traveller's dilemma: 'Also in Algeria I felt the guilt of being a tourist who is passing through and who is a mere voyeur.'

10. A brief account of the tempestuous response of German intellectuals to the outbreak of the First World War is given in my *From naturalism to expressionism*, pp. 105–23.

11. Franz Kafka, *Tagebücher 1910–1923*, pp. 419–21, 437. Though 'In the penal colony', was written in October 1914, it was not published till 1919. The only appreciative review was that by Kurt Tucholsky in the *Weltbühne*, who sees its theme as the internal collapse of a power-system. Klaus Wagenbach, who includes a fragment from Tucholsky's review and relevant passages from Kafka's 1914 diary in his excellent edition of *In der Strafkolonie* (Berlin 1975), shares Tucholsky's interpretation of the story as an image of corrupt power. Neither examines the narrative structure and though I find their view more convincing than many, I believe they fail to appreciate that the story does not present the final conclusion of an objective observer, but a painful dilemma from which neither the traveller nor the author is released.

4 THE BREAKDOWN OF THE IMPERSONAL NARRATOR: 'BLUMFELD, AN ELDERLY BACHELOR'

1. In his *Kafka: Kommentar*, pp. 190–2, Hartmut Binder, adducing many references from Kafka's diary of this time to his incapacity for marriage and the loneliness of his bachelor existence, calls 'Blumfeld' the 'precipitation' of Kafka's internal debates and indeed insists that the story should be read as an autobiographical contribution. But this evidence and argument leaves out of account the transference of such experiences to an imaginary person who though a bachelor is totally different from Kafka in character and profession. The serious personal concern turns, through the invented person and story, into a grotesque caricature, a

comic extravaganza that releases the author at least temporarily from his anxieties.

2. Roy Pascal, *The dual voice*, pp. 79–80.

3. *Ibid.*, pp. 145–6.

4. Binder (*Kafka: Kommentar*), notes the replacement of the past by the present tense, but makes no comment upon it and does not distinguish between its use in reported speech and that in normal narrative. Though at other times, e.g. in his comments on 'Investigations of a dog', Binder makes interesting comments on the style of the story, it is regrettable that he overlooks here stylistic and structural factors. As is often apparent in studies of Kafka's style, the mere registration of a grammatical feature is pointless unless its functioning is discussed. Another common error of criticism occurs when Binder, referring to the two dancing balls, states that this pair 'corresponds' to other pairs in Kafka's work, such as the pair of 'assistants' in *The castle*. But while there is a striking likeness between such pairs (or trios) of subordinate characters, it is an empty formalism to compare the balls with human figures. For the effect of such figures is bound up with the comic or sinister identity of figures that being human, are independent and separate, as I have suggested p. 45 above, while balls are manufactured articles, made to be identical, and contain no such eery problem.

5. Figures in brackets refer to Raabe's edition in which 'Blumfeld, ein älterer Junggeselle' occupies pp. 264–84.

5 THE IDENTIFIABLE NARRATOR OF 'A HUNGER ARTIST'

1. For a résumé of critical studies on 'A hunger artist' see Beicken, *Franz Kafka. Eine kritische Einführung in die Forschung*, pp. 319–24 and Eberhard Frey (see below, note 4). Brigitte Flach writes (*Kafkas Erzählungen: Strukturanalyse und Interpretation*, Bonn 1967, pp. 147–8): 'The story consists of the recollections of an anonymous figure who reports the decline of a hunger artist. On the whole the report betrays a certain sympathy with the fate of the hunger artist... More specifically, it consists of objective constatation of facts, of sympathetic reflections, of commentary that entreats our understanding.' In the following outline of the story there is no further reference to this narrator, no consideration of his function or role, and the summary concludes with a dogmatic statement of the 'meaning' of the story: 'The intellectual content of the tale concerns the conflict which derives from the fact that on the one hand the artist lives exclusively for his art because nothing else appeals to him, while on the other hand the artist and his art are dependent on a public and on the interest of this public.' Thus the individuality of the story is reduced to a trite generalisation. Many critics fail to mention a narrator at all, and those who do recognise his presence fail, like Brigitte Flach, to detect any significance in this

medium of the story, e.g. H. M. Waidson, 'The starvation artist and the leopard', *Germanic Review*, xxxv (1960). Herbert Deinert calls the narrator: 'a sober, dispassionate reporter' and adds 'nowhere does he allow himself to pass judgment' ('Franz Kafka. "Ein Hungerkünstler"', *Wirkendes Wort*, xiii (1963)). Benno von Wiese uses similar terms (*Die deutsche Novelle von Goethe bis Kafka*, Düsseldorf 1956). [Roy Pascal seems to have been unaware of Richard Sheppard's article, 'Kafka's "Ein Hungerkünstler"', *German Quarterly*, xxxxvi (1973), 219–33, which also concentrates on the narration. Eds.]

2. The text referred to is that in Raabe's edition.

3. Gray, *Franz Kafka*, pp. 179–82.

4. Eberhard Frey, *Franz Kafkas Erzählstil*, 2nd edn, Bern and Frankfurt 1974. References in my text to 'Frey', with page numbers, apply to this volume, which also contains (pp. 294–314) a useful résumé of critical interpretations of 'A hunger artist'. Frey's analysis of this work, that fills pp. 143–292 of his book, is only part of a wider theoretical stylistic investigation, the aim of which is to establish firmer and more objective grounds for literary evaluation. With a similar objective Brigitte Flach bases her analysis of 'A hunger artist' on what she believes is a valid general theory of story-structure. But in neither case do these theoretical scruples and systematic methods shield against naive pre-judgments and textual insensitivity.

5. Meno Spann quotes an English handbill of 1950 advertising a German 'Hungerkünstler', on which with some linguistic sensitivity the performer is called a 'Starvation artist', not a 'Hunger artist' ('Franz Kafka's Leopard', *Germanic Review*, xxxiv (1959)). The French translation used by Michael Dentan, 'champion de jeûne', has a still more sobering effect (*Humour et création littéraire dans l'oeuvre de Kafka*, Geneva and Paris 1961). This excellent, discriminating study unfortunately, like others, lumps the hunger artist with the trapeze artist of 'First grief' and the bard of 'Josephine the singer' as undifferentiated symbols of 'the' artist (p. 143).

6. In a final comment on the clumsy officialese of the story, in the course of a comparison of its style with that of Thomas Mann's *Das Wunderkind*, Frey writes (p. 290): 'The most striking feature of Kafka's style in the "Hunger Artist" is, of course, the officialese. It occurs almost eight times more frequently in Kafka than in Thomas Mann, and thereby the narrative acquires a dry impersonal atmosphere.' The observation of the fact is correct, but the estimate of its effect is the essential fault in Frey's reading; yet Frey is less wide of the mark than Deinert or von Wiese or many others who call the style *sachlich* ('factual').

7. This characteristic of chapter headings and marginal glosses I have discussed in my 'Tense and novel', *Modern Language Review*, lvii, 1 (January 1962).

8. Among the relevant passages from Kafka's diary and letters that Hartmut Binder collects for his commentary on 'Ein Hungerkünstler' (*Kafka:*

Kommentar, pp. 257–61) is an entry in his diary, just about the time of the composition of the story, in which Kafka speaks of his own 'Hauptnahrung' ('staple food') in a spiritual as opposed to its normal material sense (29 January 1922). Binder is right to remind us of these references, that include a statement from a letter to Felice Bauer that though he himself cannot abide meat or beer or coffee he likes to see other people enjoying these things. One remembers how his hunger artist enjoys seeing his 'guards' tucking into a hearty breakfast. But all Binder's references are of this type, that is, they all direct the reader to look on the hunger artist as an image of Kafka himself; and the critic disregards all those features of the story which distance the character from the author. Interesting as his commentary is, because of this biographical fixation it becomes a hindrance to the text.

9. Felix Weltsch, 'Religiöser Humor bei Franz Kafka' – appendix to Max Brod, *Franz Kafkas Glauben und Lehre*, Winterthur 1948, p. 128.

10. This is the main reason why I cannot accept Herbert Tauber's interpretation of the hunger artist as a charlatan nor his argument that since he starves out of necessity (lack of appetite) he cannot be an artist (Herbert Tauber, *Franz Kafka. Eine Deutung seiner Werke*, Zürich and New York 1941, pp. 181–3). Benno von Wiese makes a similar criticism of Tauber's interpretation in *Die deutsche Novelle von Goethe bis Kafka*, p. 333. But even von Wiese, whose other *Novelle* interpretations are sensitive and illuminating, fails to detect the character of the style of 'A hunger artist', and hence never comes to grips with the text and quality of Kafka's story.

11. Goethe, *Aphorismen und Pragmente*, Gedenkausgabe, Zürich 1952, vol. 17, p. 705. The whole statement is: 'Das ist die wahre Symbolik, wo das Besondere das Allgemeiner repräsentiert, nicht als Traum und Schatten, sondern als lebendig-augenblickliche Offenbarung des Unerforschlichen.'

12. The most emphatic advocacy of this view is to be found in Harry Steinhauer's *Die deutsche Novelle 1880–1950*, New York 1958.

6 THIRD-PERSON AND FIRST-PERSON FABLES AND PARABLES

1. A brief account of this theme in German literature is given in my *From naturalism to expressionism*, chapter 7.

2. For Kafka's use of Jewish stories see chapter 4, 'Jüdische Erzählstoffe', of Hartmut Binder's *Motiv*. Kafka knew Martin Buber personally and possessed in his library a volume of Jewish legends and myths – see Klaus Wagenbach, *Franz Kafka*, Bern 1958, p. 256.

3. Heinz Politzer, *Franz Kafka: parable and paradox*, p. 17.

4. Ingeborg C. Henel 'Die Deutbarkeit von Kafkas Werken', *Zeitschrift für deutsche Philologie*, LXXXVI (1967) 250–66.

5. 'Kleine Fabel' is found in P. Raabe's edition of the *Sämtliche Erzählungen*, p. 320. 'Vor dem Gesetz' is published by Raabe, pp. 131–2, in

the form in which Kafka published it in *Ein Landarzt*, 1919. It occurs in *The trial* in the chapter entitled 'In the cathedral'.

6. G. Lukács, *Versuch einer Typologie der Romanform*, reprinted in his *Die Theorie des Romans*, Berlin 1920, p. 95: 'That the world has been abandoned by God reveals itself in the disproportion that exists between the soul and practical activity, between inwardness and adventure: in the lack of any transcendental underwriting of human effort.'

7. Politzer also sees the chaplain as a further obstacle between the seeker and the law. Although Politzer's explanations of the traditional Jewish elements in this parable are of great value, I believe he errs in taking the term 'man from the country' to mean a boor or barbarian. He is surely one of those simpletons of whom it was said 'theirs is the kingdom of heaven'. H. Politzer, *Franz Kafka: parable and paradox*, pp. 173–82.

8. Binder, *Motiv*, pp. 171–85. 'Der Jäger Gracchus' is in Raabe's edition, pp. 285–8.

9. 'Gibs Auf!', Raabe, p. 358.

10. 'Fürsprecher', Raabe, pp. 322–3.

11. See J. P. Stern, 'The law of the trial' in *Kafka. Semi-centenary perspectives* (ed.) F. Kuna, London 1976.

12. 'Fürsprecher' and 'Gemeinschaft' were first published posthumously by Max Brod and both titles were invented by him. 'Gemeinschaft' is in Raabe, pp. 308–9.

13. The unfinished 'Beim Bau der Chinesischen Mauer' was first published by Max Brod and fills pp. 289–99 of Raabe's edition. But Kafka himself published the 'legend' 'The emperor's message', both in a Prague periodical and in the collection *A country doctor*, 1919. In his edition of the tales Raabe also gives the separate version of this parable with the other pieces from *A country doctor*.

14. 'Heimkehr' received its title from Max Brod who was its first publisher. Raabe includes it pp. 320–1.

15. Hartmut Binder, *Kafka: Kommentar*, pp. 239–41.

16. J.-P. Sartre in an interview with Benn Levy, translated in *The Observer*, 20 April 1980.

17. W. H. Sokel, 'Das Verhältnis der Erzählperspektive zu Erzählgeschehen'. Professor Sokel explains that this article supplements and corrects earlier views of his in 'Kafka als Expressionist', *Forum*, x (1963) and his book *Franz Kafka. Tragik und Ironie*.

7 LAST TALES: THE STORIES WITH HUMAN CHARACTERS

1. 'Erstes Leid', Raabe, p. 157.

2. In Raabe's edition 'Der Dorfschullehrer' occupies pp. 252–64. 'The village schoolmaster' was first published by Max Brod who gave it the title 'Der Riesenmaulwurf' ('The giant mole').

3. 'Der Nachbar' is found in Raabe's edition, pp. 310–11. It also was first published by Max Brod who gave the untitled story this title ('The neighbour').
4. In Raabe's edition 'Eine kleine Frau' occupies pp. 157–63. For the reference to Dora Dymant see Binder, *Kafka: Kommentar*, pp. 300–1.
5. Binder, *Motiv*, pp. 299ff.
6. *Ibid.*, p. 331.

8 LAST TALES: THE ANIMAL STORIES

1. Binder *Motiv*, pp. 299–346.
2. 'Ein Bericht für eine Akademie' is found in Raabe's edition, pp. 147–55.
3. W. Emrich, *Franz Kafka*, Bonn and Frankfurt, 1958, pp. 127–9.
4. Heinz Politzer in *Vor dem Gesetz*, edited by Heinz Politzer, Berlin, 1934, p. 78 and Politzer, *Franz Kafka: parable and paradox*, pp. 91–2
5. We owe the recognition of the Hoffmann source to Binder, *Motiv*, pp. 147–66. In relation both to the 'Report for an academy' and the 'Investigations of a dog' Binder has traced numerous threads of connexion with Hoffman's animal tales, but this does not prevent him from recognising the individual and peculiar use Kafka made of these instigations.
6. The scar that the ape uncovers has been thought to mean castration. But there is no other or direct suggestion of castration, and to suppose it means this (the ape's account here is not precise) destroys the main purpose of the passage which is to highlight the natural *animal* attitude to those organs which human beings, by contrast, call pudenda.
7. K.-P. Philippi, *Das Schloss: Reflexion and Wirklichkeit*, Tübingen, 1966, pp. 116–47.
8. W. H. Sokel, *Franz Kafka: Tragik und Ironie*, pp. 330–55. I find that Professor Sokel over-interprets in several ways, most seriously when he writes of the ape's loss of his 'old self', his apehood, of his 'integrated' personality, and of his having become 'a member of a different type and species'. I also think it false to take the ape as a direct model of a human being, which leads the critic to overlook much of the sly humour and irony of the ape's account.
9. Beicken, *Franz Kafka: Einführung*, p. 311.
10. *Ibid.*, p. 327; Politzer, *Franz Kafka: parable and paradox*, p. 319; Gray, *Franz Kafka*, p. 184. Of the philosophical interpretations that of Emrich (*Kafka*) is the most consistent reading of the story as criticism of positivism from the existential position. A. K. Thorlby's concrete and discriminating interpretation is contained in *A student's guide to Kafka*, London 1972, pp. 84–94. I shall have occasion later to refer to the illuminating account of Kafka's sources and the skilful comments in Hartmut Binder's *Motiv*, pp. 147–70.
11. Günther Anders, *Kafka Pro und Contra*, Munich 1951, p. 69.
12. In Raabe's edition 'Josephine' occupies pp. 172–85.
13. Sokel, *Franz Kafka: Tragik und Ironie*, pp. 227–8.

14. Hartmut Binder (*Motiv*, pp. 151–61) has unearthed an important source of this scene in E. T. A. Hoffmann's 'continuation' of Cervantes' *Dialogue between Scipio and Berganza, the dogs of the Hospital of the Resurrection* from the *Novelas Ejemplares* of 1613. In the *Nachricht von den neuesten Schicksalen des Hundes Berganza*, published in Hoffman's *Fantasie- und Nachtstücke*, are to be found many motifs and items that Kafka adopted (though usually subjecting them to a great transformation). These seven dancing dogs are prefigured in Hoffman's tale by seven witches, gigantic, shrieking, half-naked, dancing round a kettle.

15. It is strange that few German critics have recognised a typical Kafka literal joke on the term *Luftmensch*, a play on the literal meaning of a figurative expression. Binder (*Motiv*, p. 156) suggests its source in the *Sagen der Juden*, one of the books in Kafka's library. Here there is a brief reference to the beings who dwell 'in the space between Heaven and earth' – 'human beings, some pure, kind, and full of grace, some impure, agents of destruction and torture' who 'fly around in the air'. This image has scarcely any reference to Kafka's 'air dogs'. Perhaps Binder overestimates the book sources for Kafka, and overlooks the pressures of the social environment, for in those years of inflation, of sudden fortunes and bankruptcies, everywhere the news and talk was of *Luftmenschen*. The verbal connexion of 'inflation' and 'men of air' might well have amused Kafka.

16. Binder, *Motiv*, pp. 157–8.

17. *Die Wahrheit über Sancho Pansa*, first published by Brod in 1931.

18. Figures in brackets refer to Raabe's edition, where 'Josephine' is found on pp. 172–85.

19. Kafka uses throughout *pfeifen*, distinguished from squeak (*piepsen*). As 'piping' is not appropriate in all situations, I have adopted 'cheep', which is close to the noise we hear from mice, and is also the noise of chipmunks (which have incorporated this sound). *Pfeifen* is differentiated from *zischen*, *piepsen* – 'hissing' and 'squeaking'.

20. Politzer, *Fraz Kafka: parable and paradox*, p. 318.

21. Roy Pascal, *From naturalism to expressionism*, pp. 194–7.

22. A reliable summary of the different types of interpretation is given by Hartmut Binder, *Kafka Handbuch*, 2 vols, Stuttgart 1979 vol. 2, pp. 38ff.

23. Sokel, *Franz Kafka: Tragik und Ironie*, pp. 567–8.

EPILOGUE

1. Michel Dentan, *Humour et création littéraire dans l'oeuvre de Kafka*, Geneva and Paris 1961, pp. 161–4.

2. *Ibid.*, especially pp. 167–8.

INDEX